Copy Chart of Centra as soon as possible.

Show Shire as including Hundred, latter to include $\left\{\begin{array}{l}\text{Township}\\\text{Manor}\end{array}\right\}$ with Borough as a separate unit, included, but not joined to the others.

THE MAKING

OF THE

ENGLISH CONSTITUTION

449–1485

BY

ALBERT BEEBE WHITE

PROFESSOR OF HISTORY IN THE UNIVERSITY OF MINNESOTA

———

G. P. PUTNAM'S SONS
NEW YORK AND LONDON
The Knickerbocker Press
1908

The Knickerbocker Press, New York

PREFACE

A TEXT in English constitutional history which is neither antiquated nor obscure has long been needed. It has been the author's ambition to meet this need. In preparing the present book, he has made three main assumptions: that a college text in history should be brief, and designed for the accompaniment of much collateral reading; that it is impossible in the medieval period, with which this volume is concerned, to combine the narrative of English history and an account of the making of the constitution; and that to follow rigidly either the chronological or topical arrangement in a constitutional history of England does violence to the nature of the subject. It has been taken for granted that the student will use some good text to acquaint himself thoroughly with the general history of a period before attempting to study its institutions; and, in the matter of arrangement, it has been the aim to show the general evolution of the English government as a whole, without, at the same time, artificially dividing the great topics into reigns or other time units. A constant compromise between the demands of chronology and the desire for continuity in the treatment of the theme in hand has been found necessary.

The emphasis throughout has been upon evolution rather than upon description. The purpose has been to furnish a logically satisfying account of the genesis of each institution as far as present knowledge permits —to show exactly how it has become what it is. This has made it necessary to hold steadfastly to a given line of argument and to shun many alluring, and perhaps profitable, bypaths; while, on the other hand, it has sometimes entailed an apparent interruption of the theme in order to develop a line of thought needed for logical completeness. More time has been spent upon origins than upon descriptions of finished products or upon definitions, in the belief that students should obtain much from detailed and special works which would clog a general account of institutional development.

On the basis of his experience as a teacher, the author has brought out a college text upon the English constitution which closes at 1485. At that date, the distinctively creative period, the period when the constitution was in the making, ended. In studying this period, it is possible and, indeed, essential to separate sharply between the work on the narrative and that on the institutions. Moreover, upon the English middle ages, the scholarship of the last generation has been especially active; but its work is at present in a complex and unformulated state, and the average student should not be directed immediately to the mass of monographs and detailed works of reference; he needs an intermediary and guide. The modern period, on the other hand, has not been primarily a period of creation; in it, the newly made constitution has been tested and developed, and institutional concerns have borne a very intimate relation to the events and conditions prominent in a general narrative; it lacks the long sequences of institutional evolution which characterise the middle ages. In studying it, the narrative and the constitution must be handled almost simultaneously, and its literature is much better prepared for the immediate use of the undergraduate. A text-book dealing with the constitution after 1485 should be a superfluity.

While it is the office of this book to present to students the results of scholarship and serve as an introduction to the writings of the leading authorities, the author is ready to claim that its general conception and construction are largely his own. There has been no attempt to make an ideal allotment of space to the several divisions of the subject. Here the author has been influenced by what he has regarded as *desiderata* in other texts and by the present state of knowledge. He has felt, for instance, that the judiciary has been slighted, while Maitland's work has made possible a treatment of it which cannot be accorded some other topics which have traditionally received more attention. Moreover, classes in English constitutional history ought to contain a good number of prospective lawyers. It seems hardly necessary to seek to justify the copious quotations from Maitland. If nothing further were accomplished than to properly introduce the student to this scholar's writings, the author would feel quite content. In general, there has been more of quotation than is customary; but it is believed that when an important or difficult point has been stated superlatively well, it is justifiable to use such statement in a work of this sort, especially if it originally appeared where it would not be likely to be widely read by undergraduates.

The present volume has not undertaken the complete analysis or exposition of documents or provided any substitute for the first-hand study of documents in class. In the case of any given document, only its most salient feature, as bearing upon the matter under consideration, has been pointed out. The lists of suggested reading are only designed to indicate a moderate amount of reading that is scholarly, stimulating, and to the point. Their chief virtue, perhaps, is their freedom from the trammels of traditional authorities. The bibliography, it is hoped, contains most of the material likely to be of real service to undergraduates. The author here takes pleasure in acknowledging a debt, in the matter of bibliographical data, to Professor Gross's *Sources and Literature of English History*. The indebtedness to the works of Maitland, Stubbs, and Medley is apparent throughout, while, in particular parts, the obligation to other well-known authorities has been equally great. The author wishes to make an especial acknowledgment of what he owes Professor George B. Adams. It was Professor Adams who introduced him to the study of the English constitution, and whose influence determined him to make history his life-work; and, in the preparation of this book, he has received encouragement and invaluable suggestions from the same source. The author is also under obligation to Professors West

and Anderson of the University of Minnesota for much
kindly encouragement and counsel.

A. B. W.

THE UNIVERSITY OF MINNESOTA,
August 12, 1908.

CONTENTS

PAGE

BIBLIOGRAPHY xiii

SUGGESTIONS FOR COLLATERAL READING . . xxv

PART I. THE ANGLO-SAXON PERIOD. 449–1066

SECTION

I. THE ANGLO-SAXON CONQUEST AND ITS PRO-
BLEMS 3

II. THE LOCAL GOVERNMENT 16
  1. The Classes of Men 16
  2. The Hundred and Shire and their Courts . 17
  3. Origin and Early History of Boroughs . 31
  4. Anglo-Saxon Feudalism 37

III. THE CENTRAL GOVERNMENT . . . 50
  1. The King 50
  2. The Witan 57

IV. THE ANGLO-SAXON CHURCH 63

PART II. THE NORMAN CONQUEST—ITS MORE IMMEDIATE RESULTS. 1066–1100

I. NORMAN INSTITUTIONS AND IDEAS AT THE TIME
OF THE CONQUEST 73

II. NORMAN AND ANGLO-SAXON INSTITUTIONS
COME TOGETHER 78
  1. The Classes of Men and the Introduction
of Feudalism 79

ix

SECTION   PAGE

2. The Local Courts, Communal and Private .   90

3. The Boroughs   96

4. The Central Government—King and Curia
   Regis   99

5. Taxation.   104

6. The Church.   109

PART III.   THE PERIOD OF CONSTITUTION
            MAKING.   1100–1485

I. THE MAKING OF THE JUDICIARY .   .   .   123

   1. Origin and Early Development of the
      Three Central, Common-law Courts and
      the Circuit Court System .   .   .   124

   2. The Displacement of the Old Local Courts
      by a New Local System of Royal Courts   167

   3. The Later Judicial History of the Curia
      Regis, Especially the Origin and Early
      History of the Court of Chancery .   200

   4. The Common Law   220

   5. Relations of the State Courts and the
      Church Courts   238

II. THE EXECUTIVE   253

    1. The Genesis of Limited Monarchy .   .   253

    2. The Council   285

III. THE MAKING OF PARLIAMENT .   .   .   298

     1. Origin of the House of Lords .   .   .   298

     2. Why there was a Middle Class in England.
        Origin of Popular Election and its Con-
        nection with Representation .   .   .   306

     3. Origin of County Representation in a Cen-
        tral Assembly   317

Contents

PAGE

4. Condition of the Boroughs in the Thirteenth
   Century, and the Origin of their Representation in a Central Assembly . . 322

5. Form and Composition of Parliament from
   1265 to the Middle of the Fourteenth
   Century 326

6. The Electors, the Elected, and the Election
   in County and Borough during the First
   Two Centuries of Parliament . . 341

7. Origin of the Chief Powers of Parliament.
   Control over Taxation; Legislation; a
   Share in Administration . . . 354

8. Parliament in the Fifteenth Century. The
   Lancastrian Constitution . . . 378

INDEX 403

BIBLIOGRAPHY

ADAMS, G. B. "Anglo-Saxon Feudalism." *American Historical Review* vii., 11–35. New York, 1901.

> Emphasises the fact that all the fundamental ideas of institutional feudalism were brought to England from the continent through the Norman Conquest.

—— "The Critical Period of English Constitutional History." *American Historical Review* v., 643–658. New York, 1900.

> A valuable discussion of the fundamental principles of Magna Carta.

—— "The Origin of the English Constitution," I. and II. *American Historical Review*, xiii., 229–245; 713–730. New York, 1908.

> The author finds the germ of constitutional monarchy in the contract element in feudalism.

—— and STEPHENS, H. M. *Select Documents of English Constitutional History.* New York, 1901. Reprinted, 1902, 1904, 1906.

> The best collection of translated documents for the study of the constitution.

ANDREWS, C. M. *The Old English Manor.* Baltimore, 1892.

> A useful account of the life and internal relations of the manor.

ANSON, W. R. *The Law and Custom of the Constitution.* Oxford, 1886. 2nd edition, 1892. Vol. ii., pt. i., 3rd edition, 1907.

> The book aims "to state the law relating to existing institutions, with so much of history as is necessary to explain how they have come to be what they are." The historical explanations, briefly connecting the past with the present, are very enlightening to the student.

ASHLEY, W. J. *An Introduction to English Economic History and Theory.* 2 vols. London, 1888–1893. 3rd edition of vol. i., 1894.

> Vol. i. is very useful to the student of history; ch. i. contains an excellent account of the manor.

—— *Surveys, Historic and Economic.* London, 1900.

> Contains valuable reviews and summaries of important books and articles on medieval agrarian and urban history.

BAILDON, W. P. (editor). "Select Cases in Chancery." *Publications of the Selden Society* x. Introduction, pp. xi.–xlv. London, 1896.

BALDWIN, J. F. "Beginnings of the King's Council." *Transactions of the Royal Historical Society*, vol. xix. London, 1905. "Early Records of the King's Council." *American Historical Review* xi., 1–15. New York, 1905. "Antiquities of the King's Council." *English Historical Review* xxi., 1–20. London, 1906. "The Privy Council of the Time of Richard II." *American Historical Review* xii., 1–14. New York, 1906. "The King's Council from Edward I. to Edward III." *English Historical Review* xxiii., 1–14. London, 1908.

> These studies are excellently supplementing Dicey's brief work.

—— *The Scutage and Knight Service in England.* Chicago, 1897.

BATESON, MARY (editor). "Borough Customs." *Publications of the Selden Society*, xxi. Introduction, pp. xv.–clix. London, 1906.

> "The chief purpose of this Introduction must be to explain how the borough customs differed from the law of the land, why they differed, and in what way they were brought ultimately into such harmony that borough custom has ceased to be a matter of much practical interest."

BEARD, C. A. *The Office of Justice of the Peace in England, in its Origin and Development.* New York, 1904.

BÉMONT, C. *Chartes des Libertés Anglaises* (1100–1305), *publiées avec une Introduction et des Notes.*

> The most useful text of Magna Carta and its early confirmations. The Introduction and biographical notes are of much value.

BIGELOW, M. M. *History of Procedure in England* (1066–1204). London, 1880.

BÖHMER, H. *Kirche und Staat in England und in der Normandie im XI. und XII. Jahrhundert.* Leipzig, 1899.

> The best account of the constitutional effects of the Conquest upon the church, and a valuable introduction to the relations of church and state until the Reformation.

BRUNNER, H. *Die Entstehung der Schwurgerichte.* Berlin, 1871.

> This work proved that the jury was of continental origin.

CHADWICK, H. M. *Studies on Anglo-Saxon Institutions.* Cambridge, 1905.

—— *The Origin of the English Nation.* Cambridge, 1907.

> This and the preceding throw new light upon several Anglo-Saxon institutions, especially upon the origin of kingship.

CHEYNEY, E. P. "The Disappearance of English Serfdom." *English Historical Review* xv., 20–37. London, 1900.

DICEY, A. V. *The Privy Council.* Oxford, 1860. Reprinted, London, 1887.

> An excellent brief work. There is no detailed history of the Privy Council.

DOWELL, STEPHEN. *A History of Taxation and Taxes in England.* 4 vols. London, 1884. 2nd edition, 1888.

> The best work on taxation, but not entirely satisfactory for the middle ages.

Essays in Anglo-Saxon Law. Boston, 1876. "Courts of Law." By HENRY ADAMS. "Land Law." By H. C. LODGE. "Family Law." By E. YOUNG. "Legal Procedure." By J. L. LAUGHLIN.

FORTESCUE, SIR JOHN. *Governance of England.* Edited by Charles Plummer. Oxford, 1885.

FREEMAN, E. A. *History of the Norman Conquest.* 6 vols. Oxford, 1867–1879. 2nd edition of vols. i.–iv., 1870–1876. 3rd edition of vols. i., ii., 1877.

> The principal work upon the subject. With a long introduction upon the Anglo-Saxon period, it covers to the end of Stephen's reign and concludes with a supplementary sketch to 1272. Freeman's generalisations must be accepted with great caution. Many of them have been corrected through the work of Round and other recent writers.

FUSTEL DE COULANGES, N. D. *The Origin of Property in Land.* (Translated by Margaret Ashley.) London, 1891. 2nd edition, 1892.

> The author contends that primitive ownership of land was individualistic and aristocratic. There is a valuable Introduction by W. J. Ashley.

GARDINER, S. R. *A School Atlas of English History.* London, 1891.

> Though supplemented in some respects by Reich's more recent work, this remains the most useful atlas of English history for students.

GEE, H., and HARDY, W. J. *Documents Illustrative of English Church History.* London, 1896.

> The documents selected cover from the earliest times to the end of the 17th century and are translated and edited in a very scholarly manner.

GNEIST, R. *Englische Verfassungsgeschichte.* Berlin, 1882. Translated by P. A. Ashworth: *The History of the English Constitution.* 2 vols. London, 1886. 2nd edition, 1889. A one-volume edition, 1891.

> The best of the constitutional histories of England by foreigners and one of the standard general works upon the subject.

GREEN, J. R. *History of the English People.* 4 vols. London, 1877–1880. Reprinted, 8 vols., 1895–1896.

> "The most important general history of England, devoting much attention to the social condition of the people."—GROSS.

————— *The Conquest of England* (829–1071). London, 1883. Reprinted, 2 vols., 1899.

> The most valuable study of the Danish invasions and conquest.

————— *The Making of England* (449–829). London, 1881. Reprinted, 2 vols., 1897.

> Makes valuable use of the topographical features of ancient England in studying the invasions and settlements of the Anglo-Saxons.

GREEN, MRS. J. R. *Town Life in the Fifteenth Century.* 2 vols. London, 1894.

> Covers the period from the Norman Conquest to the end of the middle ages.

GROSS, CHARLES (editor). "Select Cases from the Coroners' Rolls." *Publications of the Selden Society* ix. Introduction, pp. xiii.–xliv. London, 1896.

> The Introduction contains the best account of the origin of the coroner and throws light upon the early history of the jury.

————— *The Gild Merchant: A Contribution to British Municipal History.* 2 vols. Oxford, 1890.

> The best work on the subject.

————— *The Sources and Literature of English History from the Earliest Times to about 1485.* London, 1900.

> The first important bibliography of English history, and a work of great completeness and authority for the period it covers. Indispensable to the student of English history.

HASKINS, C. H. "Knight Service in Normandy in the Eleventh Century." *English Historical Review* xxii., 636–649. London, 1907.

HOLMES, O. W. *The Common Law.* Boston, 1881. London, 1882.

HUNT, WILLIAM, and POOLE, R. L. (editors). *The Political History of England.* 12 vols. London, 1905–1908. i., *From Earliest Times to 1066.* By THOMAS HODGKIN. ii., *1066–1216.* By G. B. ADAMS. iii., *1216–1377.* By T. F. TOUT. iv., *1377–1485.* By C. OMAN. v., *1485–1547.* By H. A. L. FISHER. vi., *1547–1603.* By A. F. POLLARD. vii., *1603–1660.* By F. C. MONTAGUE. viii.,

1660–1702. By RICHARD LODGE. ix., *1702–1760.* By I. S.
LEADAM. x., *1760–1801.* By WILLIAM HUNT. xi., *1801–1837.*
By J. C. BRODRICK and J. K. FOTHERINGHAM. xii., *1837–1901.*
By S. J. Low and L. C. SANDARS.

> A detailed work of collaboration, containing the results of recent scholar-
ship.

JENKS, EDWARD. *Edward Plantaganet (Edward I.), the English
Justinian or the Maker of the Common Law.* London, 1902.

> Contains a valuable discussion of Edward's legislation.

—— *Law and Politics in the Middle Ages.* London, 1898.

> A brilliant and concise discussion of the origin of various governmental
institutions and principles.

—— "The Myth of Magna Carta." *The Independent Review*
iv., 260–273.

> Contends somewhat violently for the aristocratic nature of the movement
resulting in Magna Carta and the constitutional futility of the document itself.

KERLEY, D. M. *An Historical Sketch of the Equitable Jurisdiction
of the Court of Chancery.* Cambridge, 1890.

LAPPENBERG, J. M., and PAULI, R. *Geschichte von England (to
1509).* 5 vols. Hamburg, 1834–1858.

> Vols. iii.–v. still remain the most valuable detailed account of large por-
tions of the period from 1154 to 1509.

LARSON, L. M. *The King's Household in England before the
Norman Conquest.* Madison, 1904.

LEA, H. C. *Superstition and Force: Essays on the Wager of Law,
the Wager of Battle, the Ordeal, and the Torture.* Philadelphia,
1886. 4th edition, 1892.

> The best account of the kinds of trial which antedated the jury.

LEADAM, I. S. (editor). "Select Cases in the Star Chamber,
1477–1509." *Publications of the Selden Society* xvi. Introduction, pp. ix.–cliv. London, 1903.

> Part i. of the Introduction contains an exhaustive discussion of the pro-
cedure, composition, and jurisdiction of the Court of Star Chamber for the
period under consideration.

—— "The Security of Copyholders in the Fifteenth and
Sixteenth Centuries." *English Historical Review* viii., 684–696.
London, 1893.

McKechnie, W. S. *Magna Carta: a Commentary on the Great Charter of King John, with an Historical Introduction.* Glasgow, 1905.

> The best commentary upon the individual articles of the Charter. The introduction is valuable.

Maitland, F. W. *Domesday Book and Beyond: Three Essays in the Early History of England.* Cambridge, 1897. Reprinted, 1907.

> The most brilliant recent work on Anglo-Saxon institutions.

—— *English Law and the Renaissance.* Cambridge, 1901.

> An illuminating discussion of the distinguishing characteristics and constitutional importance of the common law.

—— *Justice and Police.* London, 1885.

> This brief work shows admirably the historical relation between the present theory and practice in justice and police and the medieval.

—— (editor). *Pleas of the Crown for the County of Gloucester.* Introduction, pp. vii.–l. London, 1884.

> The Introduction contains an excellent account of the procedure in the itinerant justice court in the early thirteenth century.

—— (editor). "Records of the Parliament at Westminster. in 1305." [Half-title: Memoranda de Parliamento.] *Rolls Series* Introduction, pp. ix.–cxxi. London, 1893.

> The Introduction contains valuable comment upon the primitive Parliament and Council.

—— *Roman Canon Law in the Church of England.* London, 1898.

> Consists of six essays reprinted from the *English Historical Review*, and the *Law Quarterly Review*. Essay iv. contains the best discussion of the matters at stake between Henry II. and Becket.

—— (editor). "Select Pleas in Manorial and other Seignorial Courts." *Publications of the Selden Society* ii. Introduction, pp. xi.–lxxvii. London, 1889.

> The Introduction gives the best account of private jurisdictions in the thirteenth century and of the origin of the sheriff's *tourn*.

—— (editor). "Select Pleas of the Crown." *Publications of the Selden Society* i. Introduction, pp. vii.–xxviii. London, 1888.

> In the Introduction is an important discussion of the origin and early history of the Courts of King's Bench and Common Pleas.

—— *The Constitutional History of England.* London, 1908.

> A course of lectures delivered at the University of Cambridge.

MAITLAND, F. W. "The History of a Cambridgeshire Manor." *English Historical Review* ix., 417–439. London, 1894.

> Traces the history of an individual manor from the thirteenth to the fifteenth century.

—— "The Origin of the Borough." *English Historical Review* xi., 13–19. London, 1896.

> The author emphasises the importance, in municipal beginnings, of the group of midland boroughs having a military origin; he finds in the *burh-peace* the germ of the borough court and, through it, of the borough government as a whole. See also pp. 172–219 in his *Domesday Book and Beyond*. For a criticism of Maitland's theory, see James Tait in *English Historical Review* xii., 772–777.

—— "The Suitors of the County Court." *English Historical Review* iii., 417–421. London, 1888.

> He argues that the duty of attending the shire court had become territorialised, only those freemen attending whose holdings owed suit of court.

—— *Township and Borough*. Cambridge, 1898.

> Deals primarily with the change of a rural community into an urban community, showing the persistence of many rural features and their later influence.

MAKOWER, F. *Verfassung der Kirche von England*. Berlin, 1894. Translation: *The Constitutional History and Constitution of the Church of England*. London, 1895.

> The best general work on the subject.

MEDLEY, D. J. *A Student's Manual of English Constitutional History*. Oxford, 1894. 4th edition, 1908.

> A condensed but comprehensive presentation in topical form, based upon the best authorities.

NORGATE, KATE. *England under the Angevin Kings*. 2 vols. London, 1887.

> One of the best narratives of the last half of the twelfth century.

—— *John Lackland*. London, 1902.

> A continuation of the author's *England under the Angevin Kings*, but a work of greater scientific value.

OMAN, C. W. C. (editor). *A History of England*. (From the earliest times down to the year 1815.) London, 1904, etc. i., *From the Beginning to 1066*. By C. W. C. OMAN. ii., *1066–1272*. By H. W. C. DAVIS. iii., *1272–1485*. By OWEN EDWARDS. iv., *1485–1603*. By A. D. INNES. v., *1603–1714*. By G. M. TREVELYAN. vi., *1714–1815*. By C. G. ROBERTSON.

PAGE, T. W. *The End of Villainage in England.* New York, 1900.

PEARSON, C. H. *Historical Maps of England during the First Thirteen Centuries.* London, 1869. 2nd edition, 1870.

> The maps are: Brittania Romana, Brittania Cambrica, Saxon England, Norman England, Monastic England. They bear the stamp of their author's originality and are accompanied by a valuable text.

PIKE, L. O. *A Constitutional History of the House of Lords.* London, 1894.

> A work of very great value; throws light upon related institutions and constitutes a history of the English nobility.

—— *A History of Crime in England.* 2 vols. London, 1873–1876.

POLLOCK, FREDERICK. *The Land Laws.* London, 1883. 3rd edition, 1896.

> Especially useful in explaining the changes subsequent to Edward I.'s time.

—— and MAITLAND, F. W. *The History of English Law before the Time of Edward I.* 2 vols. Cambridge, 1895. 2nd edition, 1898.

> Has superseded all previous works on English law for the period which it covers, and, in its lavish comprehensiveness, goes far to supplement and correct the older constitutional histories.

POOLE, R. L. (editor). *Historical Atlas of Modern Europe, from the Decline of the Roman Empire.* Oxford, 1902.

> The best historical atlas. It contains about one hundred maps with explanatory text. Of these, seventeen relate to the British Isles.

RAMSAY, J. H. *Lancaster and York (1399–1485).* 2 vols. Oxford, 1892.

> The most detailed narrative of the fifteenth century.

—— *The Angevin Empire, or the three Reigns of Henry II., Richard I., and John (1154–1216).* London, 1903.

—— *The Foundations of England, or Twelve Centuries of British History (B. C. 55–A. D. 1154).* 2 vols. London, 1898.

> This, with the preceding, constitutes the best general narrative of English history to 1216.

REEVES, JOHN. *A History of the English Law (to 1509).* 2 vols. London, 1784. 2nd edition (*to 1558*), 4 vols., 1787. 3rd edition, 1814. Vol. v., *Reign of Elizabeth*, 1829. New edition in 3 vols., by W. F. FINLASON, 1869.

> For the period before Edward I., this has been superseded by the work of Pollock and Maitland.

REICH, EMIL. *A New Student's Atlas of English History.* London, 1903.

RIESS, L. "Der Ursprung des englischen Unterhauses." *Historische Zeitschrift* xxiv. (neue Folge), 1–33. Munich, 1888.

> Riess believes that the early representatives to Parliament were summoned primarily to inform the king of the condition of the local administration.

—— *Geschichte des Wahlrechts zum englischen Parlament im Mittelalter.* Leipsic, 1885.

> A brilliant monograph. For a review of this and the same author's *Der Ursprung des englischen Unterhauses*, see *English Historical Review* v., 146–156.

ROUND, J. H. *Feudal England: Historical Studies of the 11th and 12th Centuries.* London, 1895.

> Especially valuable for the essay on the introduction of knight service, upon which subject and the early effects of the Conquest in general Round is the leading authority.

—— *Geoffrey de Mandeville: A Study of the Anarchy.* London, 1892.

> The life of Geoffrey is presented as "the most perfect and typical presentment of the feudal and anarchic spirit that stamps the reign of Stephen." For a somewhat different estimate of the degree of anarchy prevailing, see H. W. C. Davis in *English Historical Review* xviii., 630–641. Various matters of constitutional interest are dealt with.

—— *The Commune of London and Other Studies.* Westminster, 1899.

> These studies are mainly on the twelfth century. In *English Historical Review* xix., 702–706, G. B. Adams contends that London was a *commune* in the technical, continental sense during a part of the reigns of Richard I. and John.

SEEBOHM, FREDERICK. *The English Village Community: An Essay on Economic History.* London, 1883. 4th edition, 1890. Reprinted, 1896 and 1905.

> A work which contained much new information upon classes and tenures in the primitive settlements and precipitated a long contest over the question of the freedom or servility of these settlements. In his later writing, Seebohm has modified his theory of the Roman origin of the English village community while holding to its essentially servile character.

—— *Tribal Customs in Anglo-Saxon Law.* London, 1902.

> Starting with the conclusions reached in his *Tribal System in Wales*, London, 1895, 2nd edition, 1904, the author shows that tribal custom was one important element in shaping Anglo-Saxon institutions.

SHIRLEY, W. W. (editor). "Royal and other Historical Letters Illustrative of the Reign of Henry III." *Rolls Series.* 2 vols. Preface (to Vol. ii.), pp. vii.–xxvi. London, 1862–1866.

> This preface contains a good brief account of the beginning of representation in Parliament.

STEPHEN, J. F. *A History of the Criminal Law of England.* 3 vols. London, 1883.

> This and Pike's *A History of Crime in England* are the most detailed works on the subject.

STUBBS, WILLIAM. *Historical Introductions to the Rolls Series.* Edited by A. Hassall. London, 1902.

> This publication in one volume of the "historical portions of the late Bishop Stubbs's Introductions to certain volumes of the Rolls Series" contains invaluable material upon the reigns of Henry II., Richard I., John, Edward I., and Edward II. "No better judge of the value of Henry II.'s work ever lived; no historian has ever given us a truer and more forcible picture of King John."

—— *Lectures on Early English History.* Edited by A. Hassall. London, 1906.

—— *Select Charters and other Illustrations of English Constitutional History from the Earliest Times to the Reign of Edward the First.* Oxford, 1870. 8th edition, 1895.

> The best collection of constitutional documents for the use of students. The Latin documents are not translated.

—— *The Constitutional History of England in its Origin and Development.* 3 vols. Oxford, 1874–1883. 6th edition of vol. i., 1897; 4th edition of vol. ii., 1896; 5th edition of vol. iii., 1895.

> The best constitutional history of England. It covers only to 1485. The work of Gneist has long stood near that of Stubbs both in scope and authority. As a foreigner, Gneist was impressed with the local origin of much in England's administrative system and the importance of the gentry, especially in the local government; these aspects of the constitution are emphasised in his books. During the last generation, the work of Stubbs and Gneist has been supplemented by a great deal of valuable monographic writing, and Pollock and Maitland's great treatise on the history of English law touches many phases of constitutional history.

—— *The Early Plantagenets (1135–1327).* London, 1876. 5th edition, 1886.

> An excellent short narrative of the period, containing much of value to the student of the constitution.

TASWELL-LANGMEAD, T. P. *English Constitutional History.* London, 1875. 6th edition, by P. A. Ashworth, 1905.

> Especially valuable after the thirteenth century.

THAYER, J. B. *A Preliminary Treatise on Evidence at the Common Law.* Part i., "Development of Trial by Jury." Boston, 1896. Reprinted with part ii., 1898.

> The best general work on the jury; especially valuable for the institution's later history.

TRAILL, H. D. (editor). *Social England: A Record of the Progress of the People in Religion, Laws, Learning, Arts, Industry, Commerce, Science, Literature, and Manners, from the Earliest Times to the Present Day.* By various writers. 6 vols. London, 1894–1897. Vol. i., 2nd edition, 1894. A new edition (illustrated), TRAILL, H. D., and MANN, J. S. (editors), 1901–1904.

> Maitland's contributions to the first two volumes are of especial value to the student of the English constitution.

VINOGRADOFF, P. "Folkland." *English Historical Review* viii., 1–17. London, 1893.

> This article established the nature and significance of the long misunderstood *folkland*.

—— *The Growth of the Manor.* London, 1905.

> Argues for the communal organisation of the primitive English township and its late manorialisation.

—— *Villainage in England: Essays in English Medieval History.*

> These essays deal mainly with the twelfth and thirteenth centuries, and constitute the best work on the medieval peasantry before the forces leading to the end of serfdom became dominant.

ZINKEISEN, FRANK. "The Anglo-Saxon Courts of Law." *Political Science Quarterly* x., 132–144. Boston, 1895.

> A good brief correction of some of the older misconceptions.

ABBREVIATIONS

ADAMS, G. B., and STEPHENS, H. M. *Select Documents of English Constitutional History,* referred to as A. and S.

POLLOCK, F., and MAITLAND, F. W. *The History of English Law before the Time of Edward I.,* referred as to P. and M.

SUGGESTIONS FOR COLLATERAL READING

PART I. THE ANGLO-SAXON PERIOD. 449-1066.

§ i. THE ANGLO-SAXON CONQUEST AND ITS PROBLEMS.

CHADWICK, *Origin of the English Nation*, chs. iii., iv.; ASHLEY, *Surveys*, "Medieval Agrarian"; MEDLEY, *Constitutional History*, § 2; MAITLAND, *Domesday Book*, pp. 220-226.

§ ii. THE LOCAL GOVERNMENT.

MAITLAND, *Domesday Book*, essays i., ii.; STUBBS, *Constitutional History*, §§ 45-50; P. and M., vol. i., bk. i., ch. ii.; vol. ii., 598-603 ; CHADWICK, *Origin of English Nation*, chs. vii., xi.; *Studies*, pp. 239-248; MEDLEY, §§ 3, 47, 57; HODGKIN, *History of England (to 1066)*, ch. vi.; *Essays in Anglo-Saxon Law;* ADAMS, *Courts of Law;* LAUGHLIN, *Legal Procedure;* ZINKEISEN, *Anglo-Saxon Courts of Law;* LEA, *Superstition and Force*, i., The "Wager of Law," ii., "The Ordeal"; THAYER, *Evidence*, ch. i.; VINAGRADOFF, *Folkland; Growth of the Manor*, bk. ii.; ADAMS, *Anglo-Saxon Feudalism;* FUSTEL DE COULANGES, *Property in Land*, especially Ashley's Introduction; LIEBERMANN, *Ueber die Leges Edwardi Confessoris.*

§ iii. THE CENTRAL GOVERNMENT.

STUBBS, *Constitutional History*, §§ 51-62; CHADWICK, *English Nation*, chs. vi., xii.; *Studies*, pp. 357-366, ch. ix., and Excursus iv.; MEDLEY, §§ 72, 73, *passim;* PIKE, *House of Lords*, ch. i.; P. and M., i., 18-21; TASWELL-LANGMEAD, *English Constitutional History*, pp. 22-28; LARSON, *The King's Household.*

§ iv. THE ANGLO-SAXON CHURCH.

STUBBS, *Constitutional History*, ch. viii.; GNEIST, *English Constitution*, ch. v.; MEDLEY, §§ 82-84, *passim;* MAKOWER, *Constitutional History of the Church of England*, §§ 1-3; BÖHMER, *Kirche und Staat in England*, pp. 42-79.

PART II. THE NORMAN CONQUEST—ITS MORE IMME-
DIATE RESULTS. 1066–1100.

§ i. Norman Institutions and Ideas at the Time of the
Conquest.

P. and M., vol. i., bk. i., ch. iii.; Haskins, *Knight Service in
Normandy;* Adams, *Civilisation during the Middle Ages,* ch. ix.;
Emerton, *Medieval Europe,* ch. xiv.; Seignobos, *The Feudal
Régime.*

§ ii. Norman and Anglo-Saxon Institutions Come Together.

P. and M., vol. i., bk. ii., ch. i., §§ 1, 3, 5, 12; ch. ii., §§ 1, 2, 3;
Stubbs, *Constitutional History,* ch. ix.; Gneist, *English Constitution,* ch. viii.; Medley, §§ 4, 5, 61, 75; Vinogradoff, *Manor,*
bk. iii.; *Villainage in England, passim;* Ashley, *Economic History,*
vol. i., ch. i.; Round, *Feudal England,* pp. 225–314; Baldwin,
Scutage and Knight Service; Maitland, *Suitors of the County Courts;*
Pike, *House of Lords,* chs. ii., iii.; Adams, *History of England* (1066–
1216), pp. 10–23, 38–50; Makower, §§ 4, 5; Böhmer, pp. 79–162.

PART III. THE PERIOD OF CONSTITUTION MAKING.
1100–1485.

§ i. The Making of the Judiciary.

P. and M., vol. i., bk. i., chs. iv., vi., vii., and pp. 439–457; bk.
ii., ch. iii.; vol. ii., pp. 558–573, 617–661; Maitland, *Pleas of the
Crown for Gloucester,* pp. xvii.–xliv.; *Select Pleas of the Crown,*
pp. xi.–xxiii.; *Select Pleas in Manorial Courts,* pp. xv.–lxxiii.;
Year Books of Edward II., i., ix.–xx.; *English Law and the Renais-
sance; Roman Canon Law,* essay iv.; Bigelow, *Procedure,* ch. iii.;
Traill, *Social England,* i., 274–298, 408–410; ii., 32–38, 476–489;
Medley, §§ 48–56, 58; 84, 85, *passim;* Thayer, *Evidence,* chs. ii.–
iv.; Adams, *Henry I.'s Writ* and *Descendants of Curia Regis* in
American Hist. Review, viii., 487–490; xiii., 11–15; Round, *Com-
mune of London,* ch. iv.; Gross, *Coroners' Rolls,* pp. xiv.–xxxv.;
Beard, *Justice of the Peace;* Cheyney, *English Serfdom;* Page,
Villainage; Pike, *House of Lords,* chs. x., xi.; Pollock, *Land Laws,*
ch. iv.; Stubbs, § 179, *passim;* Jenks, *Law and Politics,* pp. 32–45;
Edward Plantagenet, ch. ix.; Adams, *History of England,* ch. xiii.;
chs. xiv., xv., *passim.*

§ ii. THE EXECUTIVE.

ADAMS, *Critical Period of English Constitutional History; Origin of the English Constitution; History of England*, ch. xxi.; MEDLEY, §§ 8–15, *passim;* McKECHNIE, *Magna Carta,* pp. 215–561, *passim;* BÉMONT, *Chartes des Libertés,* Introduction; JENKS, *Myth of Magna Carta;* DICEY, *Privy Council,* pts. i., ii.; BALDWIN, *Beginnings of the Council; Early Records; Antiquities; Council of Time of Richard II.; Council from Edward I. to Edward III.;* STUBBS, § 367; MAITLAND, *Memoranda de Parliamento,* pp. xxxiv.–xlvii.

§ iii. THE MAKING OF PARLIAMENT.

STUBBS, *Constitutional History,* §§ 200–218; chs. xvii., xx.; PIKE, *House of Lords,* chs. iv.–ix.; xv., pt. i.; GNEIST, *English Constitution,* chs. xxiv., xxv.; MEDLEY, §§ 18–26, 76 77; 28–31, 33–39, *passim;* TASWELL-LANGMEAD, chs. viii., ix.; RIESS, *Wahlrecht zum englischen Parlament; Ursprung des englischen Unterhauses;* MAITLAND, *Memoranda,* pp. xxxiv.–lxxxix.; SHIRLEY, *Royal Letters,* ii., pp. xiv.–xxiii.; DAVIS and TURNER, *The St. Albans Council of 1213,* in English Historical Review, xx., 289, 290; xxi., 297–299.

PART I

The Anglo-Saxon Period

449–1066

SECTION I

THE ANGLO-SAXON CONQUEST AND ITS PROBLEMS

TO study the constitutional history of England means to study the origin and growth of those institutions which have to do with the government of the English people. It is true that nearly everything in a people's life has at least an indirect bearing upon the making of its government; but in the study of this subject it is a practical necessity to fix the attention especially upon certain phases of the people's activity. Probably no two scholars would agree as to just where the domain of constitutional history ends and that of such subjects as legal or economic history or sociology begins. Such agreement is neither possible nor necessary; there will always be debatable ground, always some overlapping. But one cannot go far upon the wrong road, if he keep his eye fixed constantly upon the sole purpose of his study—an understanding of how the present English government has come to be what it is.

The broad, fundamental divisions of English history are the following[1]:

[1] Strictly speaking, of course, there was no English history in the island of Britain until the arrival of the Anglo-Saxons.

3

a. Britain before the Roman occupation began, namely, before 55 B. C. This is practically prehistoric Britain.

b. Roman Britain, 55 B. C.–407 A. D.

c. England from the Anglo-Saxon conquest to the Norman Conquest, 449–1066.

d. England from the Norman Conquest to the end of the middle ages, the period when the English constitution was in the making, 1066–1485.

e. The modern period, when the constitution was tested and developed.

Constitutional history has nothing to do with the first division, and very little to do with the second, from which latter period little or nothing that is found in the later English government came. Our institutional story has its beginning in the third division, the Anglo-Saxon period. It is exceedingly important to notice, however, that this is distinctly an introductory period. In its fullest sense, English constitutional history did not begin until the Norman Conquest, because, until that time, there were not present in England all the materials out of which the constitution was to grow. The Norman people, with the institutions it had developed in Normandy, was lacking. The most important period in our study is the great creative period following the Norman Conquest. This book deals with the introductory, or Anglo-Saxon period, and with the creative period, which latter, speaking broadly, ends with the middle ages.

The Anglo-Saxon period is filled with problems. Maitland states an important truth about all early institutions in the following words concerning primitive law:

The grown man will find it easier to think the thoughts of the school-boy than to think the thoughts of the baby,

And yet the doctrine that our remote forefathers being simple folk had simple law, dies hard. Too often we allow ourselves to suppose that, could we but get back to the beginning, we should find that all was intelligible and should then be able to watch the process whereby simple ideas were smothered under subtleties and technicalities. But it is not so. Simplicity is the outcome of technical subtlety; it is the goal not the starting point. As we go backwards the familiar outlines become blurred, the ideas become fluid, and instead of the simple we find the indefinite.[1]

Some specific reasons for the difficulty which all scholars find in understanding Anglo-Saxon, especially early Anglo-Saxon, institutions may be stated. There was an actual complexity of custom, pettiness of detail, and infinite local variation. The people of those times neither thought clearly nor spoke with precision respecting their own institutions; they were incapable of broad generalisation or exact definition, and never thought of the possibility of saving labour and doubt by striving for greater uniformity and simplicity. Men were interested in the practical problems of a particular time and locality. These characteristics render any records, which they have left, exceedingly difficult to interpret. And these records, as we now have them, are very fragmentary and incomplete.

A prominent feature of the Anglo-Saxon government, alike in the separate kingdoms and in England as a whole after the approximate union of these kingdoms, was a great lack of co-ordination between the central and local institutions. A great gap existed between them, which many Anglo-Saxon kings strove

[1] Maitland, *Domesday Book and Beyond*, p. 9.

sturdily, but for the most part unsuccessfully, to
bridge. At the centre, were the king and the *witan*,
strengthened in later times by the king's local officials,
the sheriffs; in the localities, were those institutions
and customs in hundred and shire, by virtue of which
the people lived in some degree of peace and administered a rude justice. The local government was more
important than the central; that is, most of the real
governing was done by local means. To local institutions and customs, then, especial study must be given,
not because they involve the solution of interesting
puzzles, but because their subject-matter lies at the
very root of the history of the English constitution. [1]

In order to understand how the early Englishmen
governed themselves in their localities, we must be
able to answer such fundamental questions as these:
Were the majority of the men freemen or serfs? Was
there a nobility? How was the land held? Did the
people live together in villages or were they scattered?
How were their local assemblies made up? Were there
varying grades of assemblies, and, if so, how were they
related? How were their laws made and how were
they enforced? Though they might be multiplied
indefinitely, these inquiries serve to indicate the nature
of the subject-matter and the important lines of investigation in the early Anglo-Saxon period. [2]

We are now to deal with the institutions of a country

---

[1] It will become apparent that England is not alone concerned
here, but that we are looking into some of the basic matters of the
constitutional history of all Germanic peoples.

[2] It should be said in advance that our knowledge of all Anglo-
Saxon local institutions is still very incomplete, and that on many
important matters scholars are far from being in agreement. This
work can attempt nothing more than to reflect the present stage of

after a great invasion and conquest have taken place.
An invading people has more or less completely displaced the former inhabitants.   We must know at this
point, at least in a summary fashion, something of the
condition of the people in Britain just before the conquest, something of the conquerors and the manner of
their invasion, and the more obvious and immediate
results of the contact of the two peoples.   These three
lines of consideration will be briefly discussed in the
order mentioned.

We cannot here consider at any length the extent
to which the native Britons had become Romanised
during the four centuries in which Britain was a Roman
province, or how much Roman law and custom survived the withdrawal of the legions.[1]   Britain was
the last of Rome's provinces to be gained and the first
to be abandoned.   Rome's famous capacity for assimi-
lation declined rapidly not long after Agricola had
finished his work; and, moreover, there were reasons
why no great efforts were made towards a complete
colonisation of the island: Britain was the most
northern of the provinces, and its peculiarly dense
forests and well-nigh impassable marshes required long-
continued and persistent effort before subdual.   This
was the very thing that the Romans were not capable
of at that time, and, as they have left on record their

scholarship on these questions.   If the problems themselves can
be so stated as to be clearly understood, much has been accomplished; and enough is now known so that an intelligible story of
institutional development can be told.

[1] These questions have been long and hotly debated and the
contest is not yet over.   There can be no doubt, however, as to
which side scholarly opinion is more and more favouring.   The
older, and, as it may be called, orthodox view seems likely to be
substantiated.   It is essentially that given in the text.

abhorrence of the cold and rainy climate, we may feel
sure that disinclination was added to inability. And
so the Romanisation of Britain did not go much below
the surface. This is not to deny that many striking
things were accomplished. Many military stations
were founded, some of which early grew into considerable cities; magnificent roads were built; colonists
settled in favourable places, established villas on a
large scale, and lived in great state; mines were worked
as never before; Bath became a fashionable resort, and
London a commercial centre. But all this was done
without touching the mass of the population. A superficial observer of the time, visiting London and York,
might have come to the conclusion that the same thing
had happened in Britain that had happened in Gaul
and Spain. But outside the city walls and the few
Roman villas was the old wild, tribal, druidical
Britain; and the material remains of Rome's occupation
which one sees in England to-day are out of all pro-
portion to the effect which that occupation had upon
the Britons themselves. A satisfactory refutation of
the theory of a continuance of Roman law and custom
is that, in the later England, there is almost nothing
Roman whose origin cannot be traced to some later
importation. When, in the early years of the fifth
century, Stilicho recalled the legions from Britain,
the Roman inhabitants of the island were left unpro-
tected from the wild native tribes; these Romans of
necessity followed the legions, and the native Britons
were left to work out their own salvation in the troublous times that followed. Only about a generation
intervened between this and the conquest of the country
by German tribes from the continent. There were

thus in Britain, just before the Anglo-Saxon conquest, barbarous and disunited Celtic tribes, a small city population with some veneering of Roman civilisation, and, doubtless, some survival of the characteristic Roman agricultural community, the villa. But this last could have existed only in very limited portions of the island.

Of the Angles and Saxons in their native land, little is known.[1] There is evidence that, before the conquest of Britain, the Angles had kings and a well-defined military class, and that this nation played the leading part in the undertaking. Probably other surrounding peoples besides the Saxons contributed to the movement; but only in the case of the Angles was there anything in the nature of a national migration.[2] It is a trite observation, but so important that it will bear repetition, that the insular character of Britain has been one of the most important influencing factors in the history of her people. The fact that the Anglo-Saxons had to come over-sea made the Germanic invasion of Britain different from that of any other part of the Roman empire. The boats were small and the sea tempestuous, and, however purposeful the movement may have been upon the part of the fighting class, the number of invaders could never have been overwhelmingly large at any one time. Families,

[1] See Chadwick, *The Origin of the English Nation*, for valuable investigations concerning the original location of the Angles and Saxons and the primitive civilisation of the Angles.

[2] Chadwick conjectures that the invaders of southern Britain were termed Saxons by the natives because of one or more reigning families there of Saxon extraction, and that, in general, Angles and Saxons were mingled in the invasion, the Angles probably constituting the nobility. Kent, the Isle of Wight, and part of Hampshire were settled by Jutes.—*Ibid., passim.*

cattle, and household goods were probably left behind at first. It was only very gradually and after much fighting that, precisely after the fashion of the Danes, four centuries later, the invaders became colonists and brought over what they would permanently need. We may well suppose that the invaders were, for the most part, freemen, although the non-noble freemen probably did not come in great numbers until the fighters had gained a hold upon the soil. There would be small use in bringing slaves when plenty could be had from among the conquered Britons, and without doubt many wives were provided from the same source. It is also warrantable to suppose that, whatever minor class distinctions may have existed in the fatherland, the leaving all the old associations, going a long sea voyage in small boats, and settling a new country, where land was plenty but had to be fought for, had a levelling and democratising effect. The actual coming in of the Anglo-Saxons lasted over a century, and it was two centuries before the conquest of the island approached completion. That the invasion of Britain was extremely slow should be carefully noted here, for it helps account for the conditions which prevailed in the succeeding period.

Of the immediate results of the contact between Britons and Teutons, perhaps the most striking and important was that the Britons were exterminated or displaced with comparative completeness in the extreme east and south-east, and that as the invasion extended towards the west, larger and larger numbers remained alive and on their land.[1] The ground was not con-

[1] It may be useful here to point out some important methods of investigating early Anglo-Saxon history. The most obvious method

tested with the same desperation by the natives when they had much territory to withdraw to as when they found that territory growing dangerously limited. This is not to deny, however, a very sturdy resistance at all times. On the other hand, the invasion spent its force in the east, where the first comers settled down and occupied the land. The more remote regions were taken up more gradually by smaller bands that represented later and more straggling arrivals from the continent, or, as was often the case, colonies that left the older and more thickly settled portions near the shore. Long contact had also tempered the race animosity that seems to have been bitter at first. The conquerors were learning that the Britons might be made very useful, and the latter were coming to choose a life of greater or less servility in preference to death. At the conclusion of the conquest, then, England presented by no means a uniform appearance,

---

of studying any period is, of course, to collect all the written records, public and private, of that period, organise them, study them critically, and draw conclusions. But, as has been before stated, written documents relating to the period in question are so scanty and unsatisfactory that could they not be supplemented by something else we could hardly hope to reach many trustworthy conclusions. Two other methods of research have produced encouraging results and seem by no means exhausted. The first is the study of the land itself, the physical geography and general topography of England. In the matter of the Anglo-Saxon conquest, much has been learned by the study of rivers and mountains, the location of ancient forests and marshes. It can be learned in this way what routes the various bands of invaders must have taken, where their way was barred, and where the enemy was able to make a particularly stubborn resistance. Many obscure passages in the scanty records have thus been supplemented and explained. This study also gives valuable hints of the manner of life after the conquest, which is the vital question. Nothing fades out so slowly as the impress made upon the appearance of a country by its early

and this broad distinction between the east and the west, not to mention many minor ones, has to be constantly taken into account.

A typical settlement in the east of England in the early Anglo-Saxon period would consist of a group of families, most of them connected by blood, living together in a quite compact village. Each of the houses had its separate garden plot. Lying back of the houses, on all sides of the village, was the arable land, in which each freeman had his portion. This portion, however, did not lie all in one place, but consisted of small oblong strips scattered about very confusedly in different parts of the arable fields. This strange scattering of the individual holdings may possibly have arisen from extreme care to have all the holdings equal in value:

settlers—the way they grouped their houses, laid out their fields, and ploughed them. Such an impress is in the nature of the case so hard to change that many parts of it will outlast by hundreds of years the state of society which produced it. It may be added, however, that no kind of evidence is more likely to remain unappreciated, or is more difficult to handle judiciously when once its real worth has become recognised. The second method of research is that of working backward from a period about which considerable is known to the period anterior about which little is known. If we get a cross-sectional view of institutions during a length of time sufficient to note accurately their directions, correlations, and the forces acting on them, it enables us to conclude with great certainty the roads they have been travelling back in the shadowy region behind. Taken by itself, this method of study would obviously carry us but short distances, but when it can be checked and verified by even a very little evidence of a different sort, then its value becomes great, and the results are illuminating beyond expectation. It is not so much in the mass as in the variety of evidence, the being able to bring one kind to bear upon another, that trustworthy conclusions are attained in the study of history. Green's *Making of England* contains good examples of the first of these methods of study, while Maitland's *Domesday Book and Beyond* is a strikingly brilliant success in the second.

the quality of the land varying from place to place, it was proposed that each member of the settlement should have some of every kind.   The parcels of land being small were necessarily oblong on account of the exigencies of ploughing, it being economy of time and labour to turn the awkward eight-ox team as seldom as possible.   Outside the arable land, lay meadow, pasture, woodland, and waste, in which all the house-holders had their prescribed rights.   These lands were in no way marked off into separate holdings.   Owing to the fact that many individuals did not have a com-plete outfit of the rude agricultural implements of the time nor a sufficient number of oxen, it was the custom of the villagers to cultivate their land by some system of mutual assistance.   Such settlements as these were, doubtless, a reproduction on British soil of something very similar which the Anglo-Saxons had known in their ancient home.   Some slaves there may have been in all of them, furnished from the Britons or as the result of strife among the Teutonic peoples themselves; but in these eastern settlements, the number must always have been small.[1]

In the west, the prevailing type of settlement was quite different and seems to have been determined largely by previous Celtic arrangements, into which the conquerors fitted themselves, as was so generally done by the Germanic conquerors of Gaul.   Instead of compact villages, there were scattered hamlets or isolated holdings, and the number of slaves was large.[2]

[1] For an admirable visualising of such a village community, see map 15b in Putzger, *Historischer Schul-Atlas*.

[2] See the charts, illustrating the two types of settlement and their persistence to the present time, in Maitland, *Domesday Book and Beyond*, between pp. 16 and 17.

The Angles and Saxons seized upon the characteristic small settlements or single farms of the Celts, and, without making important changes, appropriated them, and kept the former holders to labour as slaves; whereas in the east, the traces of the older agrarian system were quite obliterated in the course of the long conflict (after a hundred years, the invasion had advanced but a surprisingly little way inland), and when the newcomers settled down to cultivate the land, they had no ready-made system to adopt.

Between these two types of settlement, there was doubtless a great number of variations. There may also have been places where the Roman villa, that great estate, owned by one lord and worked by slaves and *coloni*, was taken possession of by the conqueror, who now became the lord, and, as far as he was able, continued this Roman agrarian unit without change. The evidence in favour of any survival of the villa system is not positive; and, as the system could never have been widespread in Britain, it may be believed that the extent to which it survived the Roman evacuation, was continued by the Britons, and finally adopted by the Anglo-Saxons, must have been very slight.

Not only was there lack of uniformity in the first Anglo-Saxon settlements in Britain, but in the years following there was constant opportunity for innovation. Colonies were continually being formed in the newer districts, and men were adopting that mode of life which seemed to suit best the particular time and locality; there was little accumulated property, things were in no sense stable, and wars, famines, or pestilences easily broke up existing conditions and gave rise to new ones. "Agrarian history becomes more catastrophic as we trace it backwards,"[1] and we must regard early Anglo-Saxon society and institutions as extremely subject to change. Although, taking the country as a whole, the number of Celts that survived was large, yet, owing to their subordinate condition, they contributed almost nothing in language or institutions to the period that followed. Thus, as very little that was Roman survived the period of Roman occupation, so very little that was either Roman or Celtic survived the centuries of Anglo-Saxon conquest and colonisation. The slowness of the invasion and the resulting bitterness of the conflict[2] precluded the adoption by the conquerors of the manners and customs of the conquered, while it gave every opportunity for change and innovation in the conquerors' own institutions.

[1] Maitland, *Domesday Book and Beyond*, p. 365.

[2] Continental history at this time teaches that sudden and overwhelming invasion often resulted in little bloodshed or displacement of existing populations.

SECTION II

THE LOCAL GOVERNMENT[1]

1. **The Classes of Men.**—Perhaps there is no subject in early English history in which one's modern notions are so likely to lead him astray as in this matter of the classes of men. We have here one of the best examples of the general distinction between the clear-cut and definable ideas of modern times and the vague and fluid ideas of the past.[2] This is especially the case in dealing with the difference between the freeman and the slave. Slavery and freedom in modern times are usually so broadly and clearly separated that a possibility of confusing them seems absurd. But in Anglo-Saxon times, conditions were very different. To be sure, many were slaves because born so, but the class was constantly being recruited in other ways: foes taken in battle, men in every way the equals of the conquerors, and of Teutonic as well as Celtic blood, became slaves; members of a community who may have long lived respected by their neighbours might, owing to a variety of misfortunes, be obliged to bow their heads in the evil time and part more or

[1] In this section, the author is under constant and special obligation to the work of Maitland, especially the *Domesday Book and Beyond*.

[2] See above, pp. 4, 5.

16

less completely with their freedom. It was impossible
with the loose ways of thinking that then obtained to
allow the legal status of a man to be entirely uninfluenced by his personality. " We may well doubt
whether this principle—' The slave is a thing, not a
person'—can be fully understood by a grossly barbarous
age. It implies the idea of a person, and in the world
of sense we find not persons, but men." [1] With this
caution in mind, the Anglo-Saxon population may be
divided as follows: at the bottom of society were the
slaves or serfs, men lacking freedom, but not necessarily
devoid of all rights; next in order came the non-noble
freemen, the *ceorls;* and above them were the nobles,
the *eorls.* This last class constituted a blood nobility
and the term eorl bore no official signification. From
the earliest times are found traces of a nobility by
service, and, with the development of the kingdoms,
such a nobility gained in importance.[2]

2. **The Hundred and Shire and their Courts.**—The names
and sizes of the territorial divisions next larger than
the township [3] were very various in early Anglo-Saxon
times. There were *wapentakes* in the north, *lathes* and
rapes in Kent and Sussex, *shires* in Cornwall, and *hundreds* in many parts of southern and central England, especially in Wessex. Generally, the southern divisions
were much smaller than the northern, as would naturally

[1] Maitland, *Domesday Book and Beyond*, p. 27.
[2] Chadwick, *Studies on Anglo-Saxon Institutions*, furnishes detailed discussions of the early official classes. See the same author's
The Origin of the English Nation, pp. 296, 297, for a theory as to
why there were no freedmen among the Anglo-Saxons.
[3] Township is perhaps the most accurate and convenient term
to apply to the individual settlement or village. The township, while
usually having some economic unity, was not a political division.

2

be the case owing to the greater density of population in the south. In Wessex, the name hundred was quite uniformly used, and there local organisation attained some efficiency earlier than elsewhere. A tradition survives which ascribes to Alfred the division of England into hundreds. When the Danelaw was gradually won back by Alfred and his descendants, and all southern and central England were feeling the unifying influence of the strong West-Saxon kings, many things were made over new, and it is quite probable that a more complete local organisation and the use of the term hundred spread outward from Wessex at that time. *Wapentake*, however, still remained the name used for the corresponding division in the north. The hundred was the smallest governmental division of Anglo-Saxon times, and, serving chiefly a judicial purpose, is often spoken of as the judicial unit.[1]

The origin of the shire, the territorial division next

[1] The name hundred was possibly not indigenous to Wessex itself, and may have been borrowed from the continent, taking the place of an earlier and varied terminology. For further information on the primitive English hundred and, especially, its relation to the continental hundred see Stubbs, *Constitutional History of England*, § 45, and *Select Charters*, pp. 68, 69. The source material following the latter reference could be studied here with much profit. See also Chadwick, *Studies on Anglo-Saxon Institutions*, pp. 239–248. "All Teutonic countries know a unit, which, under the name of *hundert, hærath, hundred, huntari*, comprises a number of villages, and is, at the time when Teutonic history begins, the primary judicial unit. The etymology of the name points irresistibly to the conclusion that it was also, at one time, a military unit. But this is not to say that it had not an older character, and, it may be, an older name. Dr. Meitzen has shown strong reasons for supposing that it is a relic of the pre-agricultural stage, in which the members of a clan fed their flocks and pitched their tents on a patch of territory which afterwards, as agriculture developed,

larger than the hundred, is much better understood.
Some shires, as Kent and Sussex, are coterminous with
the ancient kingdoms bearing those names. These
kingdoms, when they passed under West Saxon control,
gradually became mere local divisions of a united
England and were classed as shires, a name which,
contrary to its earlier use, was being applied to large
instead of small divisions.[1] Other shires, as Dorset
and Somerset in Wessex, and Norfolk and Suffolk in
East Anglia, stand for primitive tribal divisions. Thus
these two classes of shires perpetuate boundaries as
ancient as the Anglo-Saxon conquest. In the midland
districts, the shires are much less ancient and of essentially different origin. When the descendants of
Alfred won back these districts from the Danes, they
divided them into shires for military and administrative purposes, and, in doing so, probably took little
account of ancient boundaries. Here the shire and its
principal town have frequently the same name, the
town often lying near the shire's centre. This probably
indicates that the towns are older than the shires, the
former having been used as fortresses by the West
Saxon kings or perhaps created for that purpose.
Worcester, Northampton, and Bedford are examples
of this midland group of shires. The northern shires,
representing pieces of the ancient Northumberland and

---

became divided into villages. . . . the extraordinary differences
in the sizes and contents of the hundreds seem to show that they
could hardly have been in origin military institutions, . . . A
police institution they do, undoubtedly, become; but this is later."
—Jenks, *Law and Politics in the Middle Ages*, pp. 164, 165.

[1] Many ancient local names that contain the word shire indicate
that in the earliest times it was commonly used for very small
divisions, but with little regularity or definiteness of meaning.

Strathclyde, have, for the most part, originated since the Norman Conquest.[1]   In connection with both hundreds and shires, mention has been made of the unifying and organising activities of the West Saxon kings, and it was undoubtedly owing to the work of these kings in the ninth and tenth centuries that there came to be two quite regular grades of local division with the name hundred applied to the smaller and shire to the larger.

In both hundred and shire, popular assemblies were regularly convened.   That of the hundred, the hundred court, as it is usually called, was concerned with judicial matters only.   From the tenth century, it met normally every four weeks.[2]   It was competent to deal with cases of all sorts, and a case once decided in it could not be carried to any higher court.   In fact there was no such thing as appeal, in the modern technical sense, in the Anglo-Saxon judicial system. The hundred court, however, might, and often did, refuse to entertain a case[3] or fail to reach a decision in one.   Such cases might then be taken to the shire court, and, if not decided there, to the king; and occasionally cases were carried directly from the hundred

[1] See Stubbs, *Constitutional History of England,* § 48.

[2] There seems no doubt that there were local popular courts in districts including a number of townships long before there was any regular division of the country into hundreds and shires.   The use of a small territorial division for police purposes, perhaps in part its creation to that end, appears to have been one of the very earliest of governmental efforts among Germanic peoples.

[3] Perhaps because of its importance; but more often because of some malice or disability under which the party to the suit was labouring, or the unrighteous exercise of power on the part of some local lord, the case was thus refused.

to the king.[1] Taking cases to the king was, however, discouraged. The hundred court was convened by a hundred-man or hundred's-ealdor and was presided over by a reeve, representing, very possibly, the king's interest. Probably most of the free landholders of the hundred attended either in person or by deputy, and this body of freemen exercised the judging function, as far as any true element of judgment entered into their procedure. There was nothing in the nature of a professional body of judges or lawyers in England until long after the Norman Conquest.

The shire court was convened twice a year by the sheriff, and he, together with the *ealdorman* and bishop, was present at the sessions. The ealdorman, originally having an official character, was, towards the end of the tenth century, fast becoming the independent local noble with control over vast territories, and his attendance at shire courts must have been increasingly irregular. Whether he or the sheriff was regarded as the presiding or constituting officer of the court, it is impossible to tell. The bishop was there to declare the law of the church and look after the interests of the clergy, inasmuch as the court dealt both with ecclesiastical cases and ecclesiastical persons. All men of importance in the shire seem to have attended the shire court as a matter of course; but it is hard to make any accurate statement regarding the others who attended. It is conjectured that in very early times this was a thoroughly popular assembly, and, in those shires which perpetuated the boundaries of early independent tribes or petty kingdoms, may have been a lineal descendant of a tribal assembly attended

[1] See Stubbs, *Select Charters*, pp. 71, 73.

by the armed body of freemen.   But it had become a burdensome thing to attend the now regularly summoned and peaceful shire court.   Travelling even a short distance was a difficult matter in those days, and the time consumed by the sessions and the journey might seriously interrupt the rural economy.   At the time we get our first certain knowledge of the make-up of the court, there was no complete attendance of the freemen, and, very possibly, the territorialising process, by which, after the Norman Conquest, the burden of suit of court became attached to certain holdings of land, had begun.[1]   But, notwithstanding this, it may be said of the shire court, as of the hundred court, that it was, and always remained, an essentially popular assembly.

In these courts, a body of unwritten customary law was being administered by the people from whom it had sprung, and in whose hands it was undergoing a natural development.   It was, however, a very primitive law, dealing largely with criminal matters, but without making any conscious distinction between what was criminal and what was civil.   Deeds of violence were very common, manslaughter, wounding, and cattle-stealing being the most numerous.   The Anglo-Saxon period strikingly illustrates the transition from the primitive state of society, in which men right their own wrongs, to the time when something which

[1] It was a tendency characteristic of the middle ages to territorialise public duties.   To exact such duties of large bodies of men by dealing with them personally overtaxed the very slight executive powers of the time.   A piece of land was a stable thing, always to be found, and could stand for a fixed amount of public service to be enforced against its holder or holders, without reference to changing numbers or personnel.

may be roughly called the state steps in between the wrong-doer and the wronged and does the righting. The individual or the kin still had a good deal to do about it, but there were public courts which prescribed just how it should be done and themselves took a large share in the procedure.[1]

The procedure began with the summoning of the defendant to the court. This was done, not by an officer, but by the plaintiff himself, who had to be very careful, however, to do it in the prescribed manner and at a certain length of time before the meeting of the court. Such summons was often ineffective, and the courts had a great deal of trouble in making their authority felt, especially in getting criminals before them. The imposition of fines, which was the principal means of compulsion, would, in many cases, amount to little, and, as a last resort, the man who could be dealt with in no other way was outlawed: that is, he was put outside the protection of the law, so that he might be killed at sight like a wild beast. But supposing both parties to the suit to be in court, the next step was the taking of the fore-oath by the plaintiff. In this, he stated his case according to a set form of words. The fore-oath was followed by the equally formal oath in rebuttal by the defendant. But it might happen that he could not take it; the oath was a solemn matter, and, if guilty, he might hesitate to stand before his assembled neighbours and make the assertion which carried with it a damning guilt. On the other hand, plaintiff or defendant might trip in repeating their

[1] For a valuable account of the important parts of this procedure, see P. and M. ii., 598–603; also Maitland in Traill's *Social England* i., 284–287.

formulæ, and any slip or mistake, at this or any other
point in the procedure, was fatal to the cause of the
one making it. Apparently, in some matters of small
importance, if the defendant took his oath successfully
the case ended at that point, the judgment being in his
favour. Ordinarily, after the two oaths mentioned,
it was for the court to decide which party should make
proof, and what the proof should be. This was the
real judgment in the case, and was almost the only
point at which the assembly, that is, the judging body,
could make itself felt in any rational way. The proof
was usually awarded to the defendant, and this action,
considering the character of the proof oftenest used,
was, doubtless, somewhat in his favour; but there might
be elements in the situation that would lead to the opposite action. The judgment, then, instead of coming
where we should naturally look for it, came in the
middle of the procedure and before the proof, which, in
a very distant way, corresponds to the modern trial.
This seems less anomalous when the nature of the
proofs is understood.

When once set in motion, the proofs took care of
themselves, so to speak; they needed no attention on
the part of the court except to see that they were
carried out according to the strict letter of the accustomed form. They were of two classes, oaths and
ordeals. In the first class, were the oaths of the
oath-helpers, later called compurgators, and the oaths
of witnesses in those civil suits in which the ownership
of property was in question. The oath-helpers took
their oaths, not because they had any knowledge of
the facts of the case, but because they were willing to
imperil their souls to the extent of swearing with the

man whose oath they were to strengthen. In early times, the oath-helpers were usually required from the party's kindred, a further illustration of the extreme irrationality of the system. Later, this custom passed away, and the idea came in that most of the oath-helpers should belong to the same general class in society as he with whom they swore. The value of their united oaths was measured according to their number and rank, a thegn's oath equalling those of six ceorls. Thus the gravity of the crime was reflected in the number and quality of the oath-helpers, as a result of which it would, of course, happen that a man of low rank must have a much larger number for the same crime than a man of high rank. The result of a successful oath-helping does not seem to have been considered so much a proving that the accused was innocent, although it may have to some extent been that, as something in the nature of a vicarious compensation; there had been an atonement for the crime through the imperilling of the souls of a certain number of men.[1] Doubtless a somewhat more rational way of regarding this form of proof existed in later Anglo-Saxon times; indeed, the changes in the system that have just been noted indicate that this was so. Proof by the oaths of witnesses became common through the practice of having witnesses present when exchanges of property were made.[2] Such exchanges had oftenest to do with cattle, and the presence of witnesses became

[1] Speaking of the early time when kinsmen were oath-helpers, Maitland says: "The plaintiff, if he thought that there had been perjury, would have the satisfaction of knowing that some twelve of his enemies were devoted to divine vengeance."—P. and M. ii., 600.

[2] For instances, see Stubbs, *Select Charters*, pp. 66, 72.

increasingly imperative during the Anglo-Saxon period. Royal decrees upon this matter were frequent and urgent, showing, if other evidence were not abundant, how great a problem cattle-stealing was in these primitive communities. If a man's ownership of certain cattle was called in question and he was not able to bring forward any witness of his purchase, it was practically an acknowledgment of theft. Probably a man would also be allowed to show by oaths of neighbours that cattle had been raised by him; but disputes about such cattle would seldom arise. At first sight, these practices seem very much like our modern witness system, but there is an important difference. These ancient witnesses were not put on oath to answer in court any questions that might be put to them in order to bring out the whole truth about the matter under litigation. They knew beforehand the one set formula to which they would have to swear. There was no elasticity, no equity; it was simply a question as to whether they could take the one oath which was to be the defendant's proof.

The second kind of proof, the ordeal, might, if the court so judged, be resorted to after the fore-oath and oath in rebuttal, or it might follow a more or less unsuccessful oath-helping. In the criminal cases other than cattle-stealing, there was no attempt to use witnesses, compurgation and ordeal being the only proofs. The ordeal was a deliberate appeal to supernatural power and knowledge by men who felt themselves powerless to penetrate the mysteries presented by crime. The ordeals of hot and cold water and hot iron were common. The wager of battle, which was, properly speaking, an ordeal, was not used by the Anglo-Saxons.[1]

In a procedure dealing largely with criminal matters, we naturally look for punishments as likely to follow the proofs; but there was very little punishment of the sort that might be expected. There were no prisons, and executions were rare. Nearly every wrong was righted by a fine, and the system of fines had become so minutely elaborated and definitely fixed by custom that, in imposing them, the court exercised little, if any, discretionary power. If a man was slain, the slayer had to pay a fine, called the *wer*, to the dead man's kin, the amount of the *wer* being determined by the victim's rank in society. A fine which was a compensation for any other wrong was paid to the injured party, and was called the *bot*. Probably, in its broadest sense, the *bot* included the *wer*, the fundamental idea being that it was a private compensation proportioned to the injury done. The *bot* was not a penalty. But in the case of most crimes, a fine, called *wite*, was also paid to the state, this fine being of a penal character. In the shire court, part of this latter went to the ealdorman, part to the king, and perhaps something also to the sheriff. Under the later and stronger kings, as the sphere of the royal peace extended, the magnitude and number of the fines going directly to the king were growing rapidly, and there was perhaps approaching, however distantly, the idea that a crime is an offence against the state.

[1] For a full discussion of the primitive methods of trial see H. C. Lea: *Superstition and Force: essays on the wager of law, the wager of battle, the ordeal, and the torture.*

As to why the wager of battle was lacking in Anglo-Saxon law see P. and M. i., 50, 51.

The system of fines was a mitigation of an older, barbarous system, in which private vengeance and various forms of capital punishment and mutilation were practised. Some of these barbarous customs survived still, especially in dealing with slaves; and some crimes, often those against the king, no one could make good by a fine. Such were known as *botless*.

The last step in the proceedings in most cases was the collection of the *bot* by the victorious party. This, like the initiation of the case, was not attended to by an officer, but by the individual concerned. Here again, however, the act had to be done at a certain time and in a certain way, which had become rigidly fixed by custom. Public authority backed up the individual if he met resistance in his lawful undertaking, even the king sometimes riding forth with his followers to aid in coercing some notoriously contumacious wrong-doer. But, on the other hand, if the man collecting the fine departed in the slightest degree from the prescribed programme, he lost all the benefits of his successful suit. While it may be said that these Anglo-Saxons enjoyed the freedom of living under a law which they themselves had made, and not one that had been imposed upon them by any despotically inclined central power, yet the rigid formalism, which they had developed, was in itself a grievous tyranny and very often defeated the ends of real justice. Although this law was made by the people, the people were very ready to accept something better, when, after the Norman Conquest, the king opened his own court to them.

In concluding the account of the hundred and shire and their organisation, something further should be

said of the shire's two most prominent officials, the
ealdorman and the sheriff. The ealdorman was
theoretically an appointee of the king; he had a distinctly official character, and might be placed over a
single shire or several shires, the latter being usually
the case. He was the shire's chief man, commanding
its military force and having the position in its court
already described. But when ealdormen are first
heard of, they were making successful attempts to
render their positions hereditary, and were identifying
themselves with the interests of their localities rather
than with those of the king. In the late Anglo-Saxon
period, they were becoming a great landed nobility,
and in the eleventh century, now known as *earls*, [1] they
practically destroyed the country's unity and prepared
the way for the Norman Conquest.

At the time when the ealdormen were ceasing to attend efficiently to the king's local concerns, the humbler,
but more truly official, sheriffs were being more and
more generally used for this purpose. We hear of divers
kinds of reeves from very early times, among them,
king's reeves, who seem mainly to have had charge of
the king's landed interests; but the use of shire-reeves,
that is, sheriffs, by the king was not at all general
until the tenth century. The sheriff was appointed
by the king, and had very limited grants of land. Although there appeared in the office of sheriff the same
non-official tendencies that affected the ealdorman, yet,
during the Anglo-Saxon period, these tendencies did not

---

[1] Owing to Danish influence, the word *earl* (from the Danish
jarl) was substituted for *ealdorman*. It should not be confused
with the earlier Anglo-Saxon *eorl*, which was the general word for
the man of noble birth.

have an opportunity to develop far, and the sheriff remained, in a quite real sense, a royal official. The measurably successful maintenance of such officials was the first effective reaching out by the central government to touch and influence the local government. It was a hint, in Anglo-Saxon times, of the long process that made the constitution after the Norman Conquest. Ordinarily there was one sheriff for each shire; he convened the shire court, accounted for the king's share of the fines in the shire and hundred courts, assembled the militia at the king's command, and had the general oversight of the king's property in his shire. He was a substantial link between the centre and the localities.

In estimating the extent to which the king was able to make himself felt locally in the later Anglo-Saxon period, mention must be made of the *king's peace*. Persons or things that were in any special way connected with the king were likely to be considered as falling within the king's peace. It was a serious matter to break the king's peace; deeds of violence against the king's officers or servants or committed in the king's house or on the king's highway were subject to a severer penalty than those against ordinary persons or in ordinary places. Thus there were two kinds of peace in the country: the king's peace, which was very limited in its scope, and the general peace of the local courts.[1] But taking into full account all the efforts of the Anglo-Saxon kings, through the sheriffs or otherwise, to extend their authority in the localities, still the lack of

[1] It is probable that this second form of peace was never thus consciously taken account of at the time, whereas the king's peace was matter of frequent mention.

co-ordination between the central and local governments remained very great, and the local government,
such as it was, would probably have gone on without
serious difficulty if the king had ceased to be. As the
kings grew strong and the country more united under
the West Saxon dynasty, there was a broadening of
the scope of the king's peace; it took in more territory
and covered more persons. But even at the Norman
Conquest, it had not progressed far, and it was left to
the Norman and Angevin kings to hasten to its conclusion a process that had only begun.

3. **Origin and Early History of Boroughs.**—In England,
the urban community, the municipality, bears the name
borough, the term city being applied to those boroughs
which have, or have had, a cathedral church. The beginning of boroughs was the beginning of a special form
of government for the inhabitants of places so called, by
which they were placed in an exceptional position, and
were more or less cut off from the ordinary local organisation. Governmentally and economically they were
little alien units springing up in the hundreds and shires.
Thus there can be no complete knowledge of Anglo-
Saxon local government without taking them into
account, and, as they were to be an essential factor
in the making of the later English constitution, their
primitive and fundamental characteristics are of importance. One is at once confronted by the question
of origins. What was the thing which rendered a place
urban and the lack of which left it simply a village
or township? At first, he is inclined to think of population as being the essential thing: when a community
reaches a certain size, it should be declared a borough
and receive the organisation and rights of one. But

such a conscious, mechanical process could only take place after a considerable number of boroughs existed and people had clearly in mind what was meant by one. What was the origin of these first boroughs?

During the Roman period, there were cities in Britain, as elsewhere in the Roman empire; and these British cities suffered the same devastations from the incoming barbarians as the other cities of the empire north of the Alps. Much of a material character survived and, in several places, there was undoubtedly a continuous population; but it is improbable that any of the governmental institutions of the Roman cities in Britain were in existence after the century and a half of Anglo-Saxon invasion and conquest. Thus the municipal institutions of later times had their origin in the Anglo-Saxon period.

When the first English boroughs emerge from the darkness of the past, the things that distinguish them from the ordinary townships are few and simple. But it is evident that a differentiation had begun: certain communities had started to travel a different road from that of the majority; and, although the divergence was at first small, we know that many of these humble boroughs at length became true municipalities, and, on the way, set the example to many other communities that sought to adopt their forms of government and attain their privileges. But the difficulty is to account for the first distinguishing traits of the borough. Probably these did not spring from the same causes in all cases, and, at present, it is not possible to distinguish between and adequately explain these causes. But the origin of an important group of midland boroughs is known with some certainty.

When Edward the Elder and his descendants were
winning back the territory that Alfred had ceded to
the Danes, they established many fortresses in order
that their hold upon the country might be secure.[1]
In doing this, they might choose an uninhabited spot,
or they might fortify a village or build a fortress near
one. Such fortresses were known as *burhs*, of which
borough is a later form. The *burhs* were, in a special
sense, the king's; they were often thought of as his
places of residence and his peace reigned in them.
Every Englishman's house was his castle, and it was
considered a very grievous offence against him to break
the peace within it; but to make a breach of the peace
in the king's *burh*, to make *burhbryce*, was far more
serious. So a specially stringent peace, enforced by
specially severe penalties, reigned there. Fighters
must be present in these *burhs*, and the burden of maintaining them fell upon the great men of the respective
shires. Where rural communities had, as was often
the case, become fortified places, we see beginning
a strange mixture of population. A well-protected
place and one where a special peace reigned was always
attractive to those whose calling required security:
artisans and traders were attracted, and, if the *burh*
were favourably situated, a market might come to be
regularly held in it. Thus a new and different element
of population was added. Often the shire court was
held in what we may now venture to call the borough,
and increased its importance. But the boroughs more
and more needed courts of their own, and seem to have
had them quite generally by the late tenth century.
Such courts were co-ordinate with the hundred courts,

[1] See above, pp. 18, 19.

and so took the boroughs out of the hundredal jurisdiction. Thus the differentiation was well started,
and yet there was no borough government apart from
the court, which was, no doubt, conducted much as was
the hundred court. And there was no greater unity,
nothing looking more towards modern municipal cor-
porateness, than in any of the rural villages. All the
elements that had gone to form this primitive borough,
the old arable fields of the original settlers, with the
pasture and waste surrounding, and the rural traditions
and customs which these implied, the houses owned
by the great men of the shire, the descendants perhaps of those who maintained the early garrison,
the people who looked to these men as their lords, and,
finally, the later industrial element, that was tending
to assimilate the rest—all these remained clearly discernible, and many traces of them lingered for a
remarkably long while. But what these midland
boroughs had attained was a distinctive name, a court
that enforced a stringent peace, a position of importance in the shire, a somewhat shifting and varied population, and a beginning of industrial and commercial
activity. By no means all the fortresses built to hold
the midlands in subjection were nuclei of boroughs,
but many of them went through substantially the evolution that has been described.

After the conception of a borough, such as we have
been examining, was in existence, there was always
the possibility of its being more or less consciously
adopted by centres of population where no king's *burh*
had been. But it certainly cannot be affirmed that
all the boroughs of later times either began as king's
burhs or received their distinguishing governmental

forms from places that had so started. The fortified residences of great nobles, monasteries, seaports, or any places favourably situated for the establishment of markets were centres about which a considerable population might gather; and, to meet the judicial needs of such centres, especially where much trading was carried on, it seems probable that special courts might arise and the institutional distinction from the ordinary townships be thus established. Populations which gathered about the residences of lay or ecclesiastical lords were drawn by the industrial needs of such establishments. Such needs were very varied. The labourers and craftsmen who met them came often from the servile or semi-servile classes, and the rude towns which they constituted were regarded as belonging to the lords. Such industrial groups might, of course, form upon the king's extensive domains, and, if they developed or acquired the borough qualities, add to the number of boroughs that he already possessed. It is not certain, however, that the midland fortress boroughs were the first places to differentiate from the rural communities, although they seem to have furnished a name that, by some means, became identified with such differentiation. At any point in the later Anglo-Saxon period, there can be found a group of boroughs distinctly recognised as such, the old boroughs. These may have originated in any of the ways above mentioned. There can also be found communities in all stages of progress towards becoming boroughs, and, in the case of some of them, it is impossible to conclude whether they may be properly considered boroughs. This was still the situation at the Norman Conquest. By that time, forces which had been increasing the

powers of the great landholders and depressing the
status of the middle-class freemen were more and more
bringing all boroughs distinctly under lords, who enjoyed various financial and judicial privileges in them.

The tenure by which real estate was held in the
boroughs was known as *burgage* and was based upon a
money rent.   It was a heritable tenure and much like
free socage, which latter was to be the characteristic
tenure of the non-noble freemen.[1]   Burgage has been
described as a sort of town socage.   How a tenure
purely at a money rent arose at such an early time is
an interesting but obscure matter.   Probably it was
originally a commutation of some earlier and more
uncertain service.[2]   Uncertain service was the characteristic of unfree tenure, and when this was com-
muted into burgage tenure by the lord of a semi-servile
industrial group, it went far towards differentiating
that group from an ordinary manor and started it
towards attaining the organisation and privileges of
the more ancient boroughs.

As the boroughs grew in wealth through industry
and trade, it became possible for their lords to derive
a greater income from them; and, as the royal boroughs
were far the most numerous, the king profited most.
The imposition of various tolls was always the accompaniment of a flourishing market upon any lord's
domains.   As the business of the borough courts increased, the fines received by the king from them, as
from the shire courts, increased.   Thus a substantial
revenue was furnished the king from his boroughs, consisting of rents, tolls, and fines.   These items, taken

[1] See below, p. 83 and note 1.
[2] Maitland, *Domesday Book and Beyond*, pp. 198–200.

together, were known as the *firma burgi*, and formed
part of the *ferm* of the shire for which the sheriff was
held responsible. The boroughs were not slow to
recognise that they differed from the other communities, that they had special needs, and that, as
population and wealth increased, so did their power
to obtain privileges from their lords. To gain the right
to pay the sheriff the *firma burgi* in the form of a fixed,
lump sum, instead of running the chance of its constant
increase and suffering the petty annoyance of having
it dealt with in detail, was the first substantial step
towards independence taken by the boroughs. To be
able to deal with the sheriff solely at the gate became a
supreme ambition. But the story of the borough's
strife for independence follows, rather than precedes,
the Conquest. The significant facts to note here
are that the boroughs had come to contain an important, middle-class population; that they had a
form of government peculiarly their own, an increasing *esprit de corps*, and a knowledge of their own
special needs.

4. **Anglo-Saxon Feudalism.**—With the consideration
of the boroughs, there has been completed a brief survey of the Anglo-Saxon local government as it existed
in the earliest times of which we have any important
knowledge. But even while the boroughs were coming
into existence, and, in its beginnings, probably antedating them, a profound change was taking place in
Anglo-Saxon society and local government. It has
been shown that, in their conquest and occupation of
the country, the Anglo-Saxons produced two general
types of settlement: in the east, the free villages;
in the west, the scattered hamlets possessed by the

conquerors and worked by the enslaved natives.[1] By
the end of the Anglo-Saxon period, some improve-
ment in the condition of the slaves had taken place, but
many freemen had lost their full rights in the land and
were lapsing into a condition of more or less dependence
upon great landholders. In the east, certainly, the
land had gotten into the hands of fewer men, and
manors were taking the place of the old free townships.
By a manor, is meant an economic unit of population
in which one man, the lord, owned the land, and the
other men held portions of it under him by various
services and in varying degrees of dependence. The
lord also held a court which the men of the manor were
bound to attend and in which they were tried.

Divers economic and semi-governmental forces shared
in the change which brought forth manors, forces
which, at the start, are hard to distinguish, and which
tended constantly to coalesce. In many parts of western Europe, as well as in England, populations that
had been wandering tribes were becoming stationary, denser, more civilised. As a result, a more efficient government was needed; but it would have
required a long time to evolve a permanent central
power that could furnish this. In the meantime, it
must be supplied by some power that could be created
or developed more quickly, that is, a local power. It
occurs to one that there was already in England a
system of local government, and that it needed only a
fuller development of this to meet the new demands.
However natural this may seem, it was not what took
place, and a little reflection will show that no short
process could have rendered assemblies, constituted

[1] See above, pp. 12–14.

as those of the hundred and shire were, efficient. A rapid change was required, and it meant that the land and the power were to pass from the hands of the many into the hands of the few. This was substantially what has happened, under analogous circumstances, in many parts of the world and at many different times. In a broad sense of the term, it was a *feudal* process; it was the acquisition of economic advantage and some degree of political power by private individuals. Its results in England may be termed Anglo-Saxon feudalism. But the process was far from complete at the end of the Anglo-Saxon period. The forces causing it were neither so great nor so sudden as they have, at times, been elsewhere, and the older local organisation was not without strength and tenacity. Hence local conditions in England, upon the eve of the Norman Conquest, are very hard to understand. There was neither the old organisation and classification of men nor the new; society and institutions were in a fluid condition, and although one can see quite clearly from what and to what they were tending, he must be content with very general ideas as to just what they were.

It is necessary to examine some of the specific processes that effected or constituted this change. *Commendation* was the act by which one man entered into such a relation with another that the latter became his lord. It was a personal relation and for mutual benefit. The lord rendered protection and guaranty, and was often called the *defensor* or *tutor* of his man. In return, he received the value of an armed retainer or some other more or less clearly defined service. The object of the man in getting a lord was to gain, by this private transaction, greater security in troublous times than was afforded by the crude local government, or it was to obtain some economic advantage through connection with a great landholder. Probably in most cases the man acted with a mixed motive. Simple as this relation of lord and man seems, it was capable of great variation: to become the men of some lords, under some circumstances, meant an actual rise in status; there was something honourable, almost ennobling, about the act; on the other hand, commendation often lowered the man's status, and, if it did not mean an immediate loss of freedom, it looked in that direction. There was no technical exactness, and the relation of lord and man might imply almost anything. But one generalisation can be made at this point: the class of non-noble freemen was becoming less homogeneous, it was splitting. The change was that sharper division into classes likely to result from a more settled life and a denser population. No one was at first concerned with furthering it; it took place naturally, for it solved a problem of the times.

One cannot fully understand any medieval relation between lord and man until he knows to what extent the tenure of land was involved, for a man's legal status was closely related to the character of his tenure and was often affected by it. In Anglo-Saxon commendation, land was sometimes involved and sometimes not. The man might bring land to the lord and, in some sort, hold it under him, being able to withdraw the land at any time and "go with it" to another lord, and, in some cases, he might have no such power. Also the land might come from the lord and be granted to the man, in which instance the latter's liberty in disposing of it was probably less. There was no regular scheme, as in the continental feudal system, by which, as between lord and vassal, the ownership of the land always lay with the lord, and everybody must hold his land *of* some one. In the Anglo-Saxon relation, the ownership of the land, as far as there was any conception of ownership, might lie with the man; men held land *under* their lords, that is, under their protection and guaranty, rather than *of* them. And yet, in the frequent lessening of the man's freedom to "go with the land" where he chose, we may see the lord gaining some right in the land, although just what it was may be too vague to express.

After commendation had become well established, the kings took account of it for a purpose of their own, and this resulted in some extension of the practice and added something to its character. As has been shown, a great weakness in the Anglo-Saxon local courts was their inability to make their authority felt; men were not easily gotten to court or held to the court's decrees.[1] It was a police problem. In very early times, when the solidarity of the kin was great, it was natural to look to the kin to hold its members answerable. Later, such police responsibility was in part territorialised, and the hundred was made a kind of police unit and was required to bring to justice those who had committed crime within its bounds. But this solution was inadequate; the state still found it hard to deal with the criminal who had little or no property. The later and greater kings, who were striving to keep the country in order and who saw that greater efficiency in the local courts would increase their own revenue, found in the

[1] See above, p. 23.

new grouping of men under lords a way to meet the
police difficulty. Let the lords, men of substance and
responsibility, be held liable for their men, and let all
men have lords. Let there be no more lordless and
irresponsible men wandering about the country, whom
it was no one's business to bring to justice and from
whom it was impossible to collect fines. Such was the
substance of many decrees of the later Anglo-Saxon
kings. But the police function is a public one, a thing
properly belonging to the state and to be enforced by
the state's officers. The state was here using the power
and position of private individuals at a point where its
own means of meeting a governmental problem broke
down. Such a shifting of a properly public burden to
private shoulders is, in the broad sense of the word, a
feudal process, [1] and thus commendation came to have
a significance that it did not have in its more purely
economic stage. The relation created by commendation gave to the lord no judicial authority over his men.
But placing this police duty upon the lords, albeit in
connection with public courts, may seem the first step
in gaining such authority. As a matter of fact, however, private courts sprang from another source; but
commendation and what went with it brought forth
conditions very favourable to their growth.

Private jurisdiction, the power of a lord to hold a
court for his men and enjoy its profits, had its
origin in grants of *bookland*. In their earliest form,
these were grants made by the king to some church,
that is, to some bishop or abbot, of certain rights and
privileges over a piece of land and the people on the

_____

[1] For a fuller statement of the meaning of the term feudal, see
below, pp. 74–76.

land. The grants were evidenced by a written document, known as the *land-book*, and their permanence was further ensured by the anathema of the church. *Folkland* was land that remained under the folklaw, that is, the unwritten, customary law—land over which no right, based upon a written charter or *book*, had passed. [1] The question, whether the king, in making his grants of *bookland*, bestowed the ownership of the land upon the church, is a difficult one. Did he give the land to the church and thus rob of their ownership all the people living on it?

A satisfactory answer cannot be given because, in the middle ages, there was no sharp distinction between private ownership and the public authority which the state has over all its territory. The Latin word *dominium*, then in common use, generally implied something of both. It seems probable, however, that, in the early grants of *bookland*, the king did not give away the land, the ownership of which, as far as ownership was conceived of, remained where it was already; but he did give away rights which, according to modern thought, no state could part with without destroying itself, that is, distinctly public rights. Yet the king could not carry this beyond a certain point, for, while he remained king, he was king over every foot of soil in his country, and, as such, there was something which he could not give away.

Two questions may now be asked, the answers to which should show the part played by *bookland* in

[1] See Vinogradoff, *Folkland*, English Historical Review, viii., 1–17. Before Vinogradoff's work, it had been the accepted view of historians that *folkland* was public land, the land owned by the folk as a whole.

the changing Anglo-Saxon society. Did the grants establish any abiding relation between grantor and grantee, and, if so, of what kind? What were the specific things which the king gave away? In answer to the first question, it may be said that there was more of the out and out gift and less of the loan or conditional grant in these cases than one, having in mind the relations between the king and his great men at a later time, might suppose. Usually there was some previous obligation on the part of the king or the expectation of future service from the grantee. But there may have been cases where there was no relation between grantor and grantee either before or after the transaction, cases in which the king simply yielded to importunity or was trying to bring better order into some locality by placing more power in the hands of one man.

As to the second question, at least two specific things can be named that the grantee might receive. One was the right, when his men were fined in the courts, to take that portion of the fine, the *wite*, that had before gone to the king. The other was the duty, in cases where a whole hundred had been granted, of acting as presiding officer in the hundred court. When, as was more often the case, only part of a hundred was granted there was no such immediate placing of *bookland* holders at the head of courts; but the taking of the fines that were imposed in the hundred court seems to have been a long step towards it. Soon many holders of *bookland* were presiding over courts in the parts of hundreds that had fallen to them, the old hundred court often surviving, in a reduced condition, for those men in the hundred who were still on *folkland*. The point reached by this process at the end of the Anglo-Saxon period varied greatly from hundred to hundred. There were probably many hundreds that remained practically untouched by it. It will be readily seen how favourable was the state of society produced by commendation to the creation of courts presided over by great landholders. These courts must be regarded as private courts, but the people of the time did not so think of them. Private courts were new, and they must wait some time before contrasting ideas of public and private jurisdiction could arise. It was an institutionally unconscious age. Moreover men were then mainly interested in the financial side of jurisdiction. They were not asking whose courts these were, but who were to get the fines levied in them. They did not think that the king had given any one a court, which was thus changed from a public to a private court, but that he had given some one the right to receive fines in a certain district.

It has been said that the grants of *bookland* were at first made only to churches. Had they remained thus limited, they could not have caused changes of great importance. But their extension was inevitable, for there were nearly as many motives for making such grants to lay nobles as to bishops or abbots. A new class of nobles began to make its appearance from the time of Alfred, the class of *thegns*. The word originally meant household officer (Latin, *minister*), and probably was applied first to officers of the king's household. It rapidly assumed a broader meaning, however, and stood for a class in society about the rank of the later country gentlemen. Whatever its origin, this class finally constituted a nobility of wealth; a man "throve to thegnright" when he had acquired

a certain amount of land. The rank was heritable,
however. To thegns, who seem for the most part to
have been warriors, the kings made many grants of
bookland. Later, churches made them subgrants of
the same character out of grants originally received
from the king, and the thegns soon subgranted to other
thegns or even to churches. This process went on
rapidly from the late tenth century, and was uniting
with the other economic and political conditions, which
have been noted, to produce a change in society, feudal
in character. But Anglo-Saxon feudalism did not have
a chance to work itself out. Before it was at all complete, the Norman Conquest came and brought in new
forces and ideas that immediately dominated.

A sketch has been given of the classes in society before
this feudalising process made itself felt[1]; it is necessary
here to inquire what they were after it had been at work
for some time and as we take our last look at Anglo-
Saxon local conditions. At the bottom, were the
slaves or serfs, as before; and here there had probably
been less change than elsewhere. But some change
there had been, and it was all in favour of the serf.
In England, as on the continent, Christianity had
been doing something to better the serf's condition
by persistently regarding him as a human being, and,
wherever opportunity offered, by attempting to increase his rights. As early as the seventh century,
the church was insisting, albeit with little success,
upon the serf's right to the personal property which
he had himself acquired. What has already been
said about the difficulty the medieval mind found in
forming clear-cut ideas of slavery of course applies

[1] See above, pp. 16, 17.

here, as at the earlier time.[1]   But despite this, there
was probably a clearer line of demarcation between the
legally free and unfree than anywhere else in society.

Above the serfs, are found the names of classes and
subclasses, the status and relations of which are very
hard to understand.   All within these classes technically freemen, their actual freedom varied infinitely;
and this is much the same as to say that there was
no uniformity in the conditions upon which they held
and cultivated land.   It was the size and character of
their holdings that, more than anything else, determined
their status.   We come first to the small class of *boors*.
The *boor* received land, cattle, and tools from his lord,
and to his lord these reverted on his death.   He paid
for the use of the land in fixed amounts of labour and
in the products of the soil.   Above the *boors*, was the
very broad class of *villeins*.   This word had different
meanings at this time.[2]   In the use just made of it,
it approached in inclusiveness the old English word
ceorl, and covered everything between the *boors* and the
sokemen.   In the villein class, there were three subclasses: the villeins (the term used here in a narrower
sense), the *borderers*, and the *cotars*.   But these
terms were vague and the names of the subclasses
varied much from place to place.   The holdings of
this class varied greatly in size, the normal holding of
a man of the first subclass being about thirty acres,
while the *cotars* probably had little or no land.   The
villeins (in the broader sense) paid for the use of their

[1] See above, p. 16.

[2] *Villein* is from the Latin *villanus*, signifying one who lived in
the *villa*.   In England, this was, of course, simply a borrowing of
the continental term, and does not imply a continuance of the
Roman villa system.

land in labour and in kind, often in money also. The land passed from father to son, and the holder could not be evicted while all the regular services were performed; but he probably had little freedom to dispose of any of his land. As to whether he had the right to quit the soil, it is hard to make a positive statement, for he probably seldom made the attempt. This whole class shows clearly the effects of the feudalising movements. While legally free, and distinguished quite clearly from the serfs, these villeins, owing to the hold the lords had gotten upon their land and services, and the jurisdiction which, in many cases, the lords had over them, were practically quite unfree. Above the villeins, was a class of men described by a great variety of terms, of which, probably, *sokemen* was used for the greatest number. The term freemen, *liberi homines* (used in some narrow and special sense), was also common. Both terms were used oftener in the north and east than elsewhere. They indicate no sharp distinction from the villeins; probably in many cases, men who were called *sokemen* in one shire would have been called villeins in another. Taken as a whole, the class stood a little higher in the scale of actual freedom; in one way or another, the *sokemen* were a little less dependent upon their lords. Some of them were lords themselves, but they were not, of course, noble. Above the non-noble freemen were the nobles, the great landholders. These were the thegns, the earls, and the great ecclesiastics. It will be seen that, with fairly definite lines marking off the servile from the free, and the noble from the non-noble, there lay between the servile and the noble a vast body of men over whom a change was passing, a change that had gone just far enough to blur the old characteristics, but not far enough to bring out clearly any new ones. But the class was certainly dividing; some may have been "thriving to thegnright," but surely a much larger number was on its way to the class below.

It will be noticed that in discussing these changes nothing has been said of the Danish settlements and conquests of the ninth, tenth, and eleventh centuries. The question naturally arises whether there were no relations of cause and effect between the Danish invasions and Anglo-Saxon feudalism. There is so little direct evidence upon the subject that no detailed statement can be made; and, probably, it would be easy to overstate the Danish influence. The Danes, who came from the continent in much the same condition as to society and institutions as their Anglo-Saxon predecessors, doubtless retarded for a time the manorialising process in those districts in which they became dominant; they tended to reproduce the earlier conditions of the Anglo-Saxon settlers in the east. As to the rest of England, the coming of the Danes seems to have had just the opposite effect; it placed a burden of war and defence upon the south and west, a burden that always depressed a peasantry; and it brought on a period of disorder and unrest favourable to the growth of private powers at the expense of the state.

4

SECTION III

1. **The King.**—Like most of the other Germanic peoples that invaded the Roman empire, the Anglo-Saxons entered Britain under the leadership of a king or kings.[1] But this is not to ascribe a pre-conquest origin to all the petty royal lines that we hear of in England in the seventh and eighth centuries. The necessity of leadership, of united action, of military efficiency, was the great source of kingship among these early peoples. In the slow movement from east to west in Britain, there was a great opportunity for disintegration, independent action, and the formation of new groups. In the petty leaders of tribes or groups of kin, was the stuff out of which kings were made. The word king itself probably meant "son of the family."[2] It would not be long before a heroic halo would gather about these primitive chiefs and a divine extraction be created for them. They were symbols of tribal or national unity and consciousness; they were military leaders, and there were very many of them. One is in

[1] For evidence of early kingship among the Angles, see Chadwick, *The Origin of the English Nation*, ch. vi.

[2] "The word *cyning* is in form a patronymic and would seem originally to have meant 'son of the family' (*i. e.*, presumably the royal family or family of divine origin). If this suggestion is correct it would appear that *cyning* was originally not a title of authority, but rather equivalent to the modern word 'prince.'"—Chadwick, *Studies on Anglo-Saxon Institutions*, p. 302.

constant danger of associating with the word king
ideas that may not belong to it in the special time and
place under consideration. The content of the word
expanded greatly during the Anglo-Saxon period, as
the number of the kings decreased, until the idea that
the king should be the civil head of a centralised state
was clearly present, though far from realised. The
kingship of Edgar or Cnute was vastly different from
that of Ceawlin or Ini.

The royal succession was regulated by that combination of heredity and choice which was characteristic
of most of the early Germanic kingdoms; from a family
that had, in some way, become recognised as the royal
family, the most eligible member was chosen. The
direct line of succession was not generally departed
from unless there was some good reason, like a minority,
for doing so. But in certain instances, the designation
of the last king seems to have had some weight, and
it was not unusual for a king to associate his natural
successor with him. It is particularly important not
to read modern constitutional ideas into the act of
choosing these early kings. At no time during the
Anglo-Saxon period was there a body of men that
was conscious of any constitutional right to elect the
king. There might be a somewhat formal acceptance,
by the great men, of him whom heredity or conquest
had pointed out as their lord and leader; and such
warriors and populace as had naturally gathered at the
time and place at which a new sovereign was to be
proclaimed might show their approval by acclamation. But these men, great and small, were acting in
a purely personal capacity, not as standing for the
nation. However, no presumptive king could feel at all

sure of his throne until he had received this recognition. [1]

No detailed account can be given of the growth of kingship during the Anglo-Saxon period.   In the early days, there were many small, distinct peoples with their petty kings or chiefs.   But throughout the period there was a tendency to coalesce into larger and larger groups.   The well-known seven kingdoms, often called the heptarchy, represent one of the more prolonged stages in this process.   These kingdoms were very unequal in size and strength, and it was inevitable that, sooner or later, the strong should begin to lord it over the weak, and that finally one kingdom should attempt to rule over all the others.   In the seventh century, the Northumbrian kings ruled more widely and effectively than any before them; this supremacy passed to Mercia in the eighth century; then to Wessex early in the ninth century, where it remained with the descendants of Egbert until the Danish conquest.   The smaller kingdoms gradually lost their status and Kent, Essex (much reduced in size), and Sussex became shires [2]; East Anglia soon shared the same fate, being divided into two shires.   Northumbria and Mercia lost their identity as kingdoms during the great Danish invasions and settlements of the ninth century, most of Northumbria and half of Mercia becoming the Danelaw.

It was during the period of struggle among the seven kingdoms that Christianity spread throughout England; and Christianity had much to add to the primitive Teutonic conception of king, as well ideas derived from the Old Testament as those of a strictly Christian

[1] See Chadwick, *Studies on Anglo-Saxon Institutions*, pp. 357–366.
[2] See above, p. 19.

origin. Kingship was strengthened and made more grand and inviolable; for the missionaries and other clergy understood, from the start, that the central power was their natural ally against the forces of disorder and division. The consecration of the king, which included the anointing and the coronation, became a religious ceremony, almost a sacrament, performed by the clergy. Although the crown existed in heathen times, yet there was nothing that could properly be called coronation; the rude custom of lifting the accepted king upon the shields of the assembled warriors differed very widely from the solemn and dignified procedure after the church had invested kingship with its sanction and its glamour. Probably the Anglo-Saxon king owed less to this religious sanction and to any semi-religious or priestly character which he might derive from the consecration than was the case in many countries, France for instance. He always retained much of his old character of the accepted lord or war-chief of his people. But the contribution of Christianity was substantial and the content of the word king was beginning to broaden.

With the Christian religion, there came into England some Roman ideas of government, probably in not very distinct form or in very large numbers. But in Ethelbert of Kent's crude codification of the law we see beginning to work the idea that a central power should be something more than a military leadership. And the codification itself, which had a notable effect upon the legislative work of his successors, was certainly the result of Roman influence. Several specific instances are known in later Anglo-Saxon history where continental and ultimately Roman influences powerfully affected the action and ideals of kings. In the long-continued, and apparently fruitless, attempts, repeated in almost the same form generation after generation, to bring criminals to justice and bolster up the weaknesses of the local courts, we see a somewhat blind struggling of kingship towards a higher realisation of itself. Some promptings and suggestions were certainly received from Rome; and it was in this general and vague way, rather than through the more tangible gifts of laws or institutions, that Rome touched the Anglo-Saxon government. The idea that they could be something greater reached the Anglo-Saxon kings from the continent, but they employed only crude, Teutonic methods in striving to realise it. The large differences between the late Anglo-Saxon kings and the early may, then, be thus summarised: the late kings ruled over much larger and more diversified populations and had to deal with new and complex problems in government—they were no longer petty kings; they had become Christian, and were strengthened and exalted by the church's conception of monarchy; they regarded themselves as civil rulers who were bound to keep order and promote their people's welfare. [1]

The powers and privileges of a typical sovereign of the house of Alfred were very strictly limited by the customs of the kingdom. But it cannot be said that the function of enforcing this limitation was vested in

[1] The fact should not be overlooked that much of the activity in making the local courts more efficient had a selfish, revenue purpose behind it. But most governmental progress has lain in the operation of intelligent selfishness. However, a society that could train the heathen Cnute into the kind of king he came to be was not without its ideals. It also had not been without some substantial attainments in centralised government.

any clearly defined constitutional way in the king's council. This council, known as the *witan*,[1] an assembly of the great and wise men of the realm, certainly exercised, at times, much power. The part that such men played in the choice of king has already been noticed, and we know that the king's continuance in office often depended upon their favour. In the performance of any important act, their sanction conferred an added authority. But the relations of king and witan were never made clear, and hence great variations in practice were possible; when the king was weak, the witan seemed to do all the governing; when the king was strong, its share in government appeared insignificant. On his accession, the king had to take a notable oath. It was a threefold promise: first, that the Christian church should be kept in peace; second, that all sorts of injustice and violence should be forbidden all men; third, that, in his judgments, he would exercise justice and mercy that he might hope for the same from a just and merciful God.[2] The Anglo-Saxon king was no irresponsible potentate; the people of the time had no conception of such a ruler. Their sovereign must not violate the customs and traditions of the country, and, if he did not, there seems to have been little to prevent his attaining much actual power; if he did, the people resisted him irregularly and personally rather than constitutionally.

As regards his property, the king was, in many ways, situated like a private individual; but probably

---

[1] See below, pp. 57–61.

[2] This old Anglo-Saxon coronation oath suggested, after the Norman Conquest, the form in which the first great charter of liberties was cast. See below, p. 256.

no private individual ever had as much.   There was no
land belonging to the state as contrasted with that
which the king held personally, just as there was no
distinction between the public treasury and the king's
private purse.   There was not governing enough
done at the centre to make an elaborate and expensive
machinery necessary; all was primitive, personal, and
on a small scale.   The king's revenue consisted, in
the first place, of what was paid him by the tenants
on his land, just as in the case of any landlord; in the
second place, of his judicial income, the penal fines
imposed in the local courts; in the third place, of
purveyance.   All medieval kings travelled much, for
much of their income was paid them in kind and
might have to be collected and used on the spot.   In
their endless progresses through the kingdom, the
kings were conveyed and maintained largely at the
expense of the districts through which they passed.
Besides these more important sources of revenue,
there were many of a minor character, such as the
proceeds from mines and salt-works, wrecks, treasure-
trove, various special tolls, etc.

It will be noticed that no mention has been made of
taxation.   In its usual and specific sense, a tax is "a
charge or burden laid upon persons or property for the
support of a government."   There was something of
this, no doubt, in purveyance, but necessarily only
in an irregular and obscure way.   There was only one
true tax in the Anglo-Saxon period, the Danegeld.
This was a land tax and was levied for the first time
in 991; but throughout the reign of Ethelred II., it
was a tax, in the strictest sense of the word, only
from the point of view of incidence, assessment, and

collection. It was not a regular levy to pay the expenses of government, but purely a matter of emergency with nothing of the sort preceding it and with no thought of its continuance in any form. But Cnute did continue it and began its transformation into a regular charge for the support of government. It was only upon its revival by William the Conqueror, however, after an interruption during the reign of Edward, that this transformation was at all complete. It must be understood, moreover, that, neither in the Anglo-Saxon time nor for long after, did the people of England grasp the idea that upon them rested a direct financial obligation to support their government. The king had his revenue; let him live on that; let him "live of his own," to use the common expression of a later time. To the end of the Anglo-Saxon period, central government was so personal and so slight that it was never thought of as something in which all the people had an abiding and vital concern.

2. **The Witan.**—The Anglo-Saxon kings governed in conjunction with a body of men known as the *witan*, the wise men. [1] The origin of this assembly cannot be traced with entire certainty. Tacitus states that the German tribes which he knew had two assemblies: one was a general meeting of the armed freemen of the tribe and dealt with the more important matters; the other was a meeting of the chief men of the tribe, and determined lesser things and discussed in advance the more important concerns, the final decision of which lay with the larger body. Some writers, who have

---

[1] *Witenagemot* (*witena*, genitive plural of *witan*, plus *gemot*, assembly) "does not appear to have been an official term."— P. and M. i., 40, note 4.

been zealous to prove that the Anglo-Saxon kingdoms were never without democratic, deliberative assemblies, have regarded the witan as a decreased and degenerate survival of the larger of the old assemblies, arguing that, whereas only the great men ordinarily attended the meetings, the whole body of freemen continued to have the right to do so; and adducing as proof of this, instances in which large concourses of people were spoken of as being present.   This proof is unsatisfactory since such instances were rare, and, what is of more importance, were occasions upon which the populace would naturally gather, such as the acceptance of a new king, the issuing of some great edict of war or peace, or the like.   It is not necessary to explain the gathering of a crowd at such times by a theoretical right to attend the meetings of the witan; and there is not the least evidence that these crowds became, in any sense, part of the witan or engaged in any deliberations.   Furthermore there is no proof that the primitive Anglo-Saxons ever had a national assembly either in England or upon the continent.   But it is certain that the early kings had councils consisting of members of the royal family, officials, and great warriors, bodies that correspond to the smaller assemblies described by Tacitus. From such councils, without doubt, the later witan was descended.

The make-up of the witan cannot be clearly defined. The name itself is vague and indicates a shifting personnel rather than one based upon any strict theory. The king might determine largely who should attend. The witan ordinarily included the royal family, the great lay and ecclesiastical officials, such as ealdormen, bishops, and great abbots, and men whose wealth,

influence, or attainments made the king desirous of
their presence or afraid to do without it. As a general
thing, the presence of a large number of men who held
no official position was indicative of the king's power.
Most of those whose influence was irksome or threat-
ening to the king would be in an official or semi-official
position. [1]

The functions of the witan were various and undifferentiated, but, as has been said, the character of the
king largely determined its influence in government
at any given time. In the very late Anglo-Saxon
period, its authority was decreasing. The power
accumulated in the hands of the two or three great
families of earls undoubtedly affected it. One should
be especially careful not to ascribe to the witan any
of the traits of a modern parliament. The witan was
not a representative body, and was not standing for
the people's rights as against the king's power or in
any other capacity. In most that it did, it acted in conjunction and harmony with the king; and, as far as it
stood for anything opposed to the king, it would be
primarily for the aristocratic interests of its members.
Only when, in the case of some very broad abuse or
despotism, the interests of all classes for a time coincided, may it have acted in the people's interest. The
witan did kinds of work that would now be termed
executive, legislative, and judicial; but there was then
no consciousness of such division and hence no attempt
to classify business. Its sessions were not long and,
in the early days, there seems to have been little
regularity in its time of meeting; later it met, with

[1] For a detailed discussion of the composition of the witan,
see Chadwick, *Studies on Anglo-Saxon Institutions*, ch. ix.

some uniformity, three times a year, on the three great festivals of Christmas, Easter, and Whitsuntide. It was very seldom that over a hundred men attended.

Of the legislative and judicial work of king and witan, a word further must be said. While most of the law of the country was a local, unwritten law, unconsciously made by the people and administered by them in the local courts, it is worthy of notice that the king and witan at times did some important legislating. They passed laws, called *dooms*, which, of course, were written, and which applied to all parts of the country over which the king ruled. This lawmaking began with the *dooms* of Ethelbert of Kent and Ini of Wessex, which have come down to us, and those of Offa of Mercia, which have been lost. There was then an interval of nearly a century in which no written laws were made. Legislation was, in a sense, refounded and made a normal function of the central government by Alfred. A very important series of laws was put forth by the powerful descendants of Alfred in the tenth century. But the highest point in Anglo-Saxon legislation was reached under the foreigner, Cnute, who issued a code of laws of a very advanced character for the time. Law-making lapsed in the reign of Edward the Confessor, but was again revived after the Norman Conquest. These *dooms* were much like the *capitularies* of the Carolingian sovereigns, but were not contemporaneous; they began just as the Frankish legislation was declining, and continued during a time when, on the continent, no laws were being made by a central power—an evidence of the comparative compactness of the English territory and power of the English rulers.[1] King and witan also constituted a high court of justice. This was not a court of appeals, but a court of first instance for cases of great importance and for the few that, for various reasons, had failed to receive a judgment in the local courts. But despite these rather high-sounding functions, it must be remembered that the quantity of the work was small, that the central power came into little actual contact with the people, the real governing of whom lay in that nexus of local popular, and growing private, powers, an account of which has been attempted.[2]

It has been incidentally shown that the central government was not in a healthy condition at the close of the Anglo-Saxon period. Economic forces were creating a strong landed nobility. As the kingdom grew larger and the demands upon government greater, kings were constrained to make grants of immunity and semi-jurisdictional authority and utilise the strength and position of private individuals for police purposes. Thus the higher nobility was coming into the possession of a dangerously large public power. The old official class of ealdormen was necessarily affected by these changes. The almost inevitable medieval transformation was taking place—the local official was becoming the local potentate. This was helped on by the king whose reign is often taken as marking the highest point reached by the Anglo-Saxon central government. Edgar was confident of his own ability to control any element in the realm; and, seeing inefficiency of executive authority every-

---

[1] P. and M. i., 18–21.
[2] See above, Pt. I., § II., 2, 3, 4.

where and having, for his time, high ideals of government, he sought by placing more power in the hands of the earls, to obtain his end by the easy but dangerous method of utilising private ambition and local family pride. He sowed the wind and his successors reaped the whirlwind. Under the weak Ethelred II., this policy resulted in a marked decentralisation; each earl regulated the affairs of his locality to suit himself, all concerted action was destroyed, and a situation was created that made possible the conquest of England by the Danes. Under the strong Cnute, the earls were kept under control, but the system of local powers, as established by Edgar, was not rooted out; and under Edward the Confessor and Harold, power was concentrated in the hands of a smaller and smaller number of families. Since the Danish invasion of Alfred's time, a racial distinction had existed between northern and southern England. This division was now intensified by coinciding roughly with the territories controlled by great families of earls. The existence of a north and south England and the final bitter jealousy between the houses of Leofric and Godwin constituted the principal negative cause of the Norman Conquest. Apparently too great a strain had been placed upon the Anglo-Saxon system of government; that which served in Northumbria, Mercia, or even Wessex was found wanting when applied to all England, especially in time of war and rapidly changing economic conditions. England seemed destined to pass through a stage of feudal disintegration, resembling that which befell the Frankish state in the ninth century, when she was rescued by the extraordinary results of the Norman Conquest.

SECTION IV

THE ANGLO-SAXON CHURCH

THE Anglo-Saxon church was in peculiarly close relations with the civil government, both central and local. It is for the purpose of accounting for and explaining these relations that its history is touched upon here. The kingdoms of the heptarchy were Christianised in the seventh century by missionaries, largely monastic, coming either from the continent or from one of the kingdoms that had already accepted the new religion. It was the practice of these missionaries to gain at first, if possible, the adhesion of the king and the great men, trusting that the people, in large masses, would accept, with little question, the religion of their leaders. Such acceptances *en masse* were quite common, and, in general, the Anglo-Saxons adopted Christianity readily. Where any long resistance was made, it was usually on political grounds, the prejudice naturally felt against the religion of an enemy, whether that enemy were the native British or some neighbouring Anglo-Saxon kingdom. Christianity was not at first preached, to any great extent, to the lower classes; it was, from the start, the religion of those in authority, whether in the central government or in the local courts. But as time passed, it worked its way downwards and touched larger and larger numbers of people.

There was little organisation in the newly established

63

church; in each little kingdom or subkingdom, at some natural centre, perhaps a favourite royal residence, there would be some sort of church establishment with a bishop at its head, and with a heterogeneous group of clergy usually living under some monastic rule. From this point of light, maintained under royal protection, missionaries were sent out into the unconverted parts of the kingdom. It was a system suited only to a half-Christianised country; it was on a purely missionary basis.

The change from this primitive organisation to one suited to a fully established and permanent church was largely the work of one man. This was Theodore of Tarsus, who was archbishop of Canterbury from 668 to 690. With but a few important later changes, the church remained what he made it up to the time of the Danish invasions and conquests late in the ninth century. His greatest work was the creation of the dioceses. The diocese, the territory over which a bishop had control, was the fundamental division in the Roman church polity. It is sometimes said that Theodore divided existing dioceses into smaller ones; but, as has been shown, the existing small kingdoms, considered as fields for missionary effort, were about the only ecclesiastical divisions before his time. Even granting that early churchmen sometimes took account of the smaller, tribal divisions in organising their work, it would be doing violence to later ideas to call these dioceses in more than one or two instances.[1] It had been the purpose of Pope

[1] The dioceses of Canterbury and Rochester correspond to the ancient divisions of east and west Kent. In very early times, these territories often had different kings.

Gregory I., when he planned the Christianising of England, to have two co-ordinate archbishoprics established, one in the south and the other in the north. This was not carried out, however, and Theodore made his organisation upon the basis of one metropolitan church, that at Canterbury. It seems to have been owing to the influence of Bede in behalf of northern England that the bishop of York was made archbishop early in the eighth century.[1] For a short time in the last half of the same century, owing to the political supremacy of Mercia, Litchfield was recognised as an archbishopric. But the normal arrangement, from the time of Bede to the disruption of the church in the north by the invading Danes, was a division into two archbishoprics and seventeen bishoprics, the latter often coinciding with old tribal or national boundaries. The bishops of these dioceses had their residences, for the most part, in small places instead of in the large centres of population, as was the practice upon the continent. The English bishops, in a very real sense, ruled over districts or peoples and were far less bound to locality than were the continental bishops. The division of the dioceses into parishes has been ascribed by tradition to Archbishop Theodore; but the parishes grew gradually and naturally, and were not created by any superior authority. The parish was usually merely the township regarded ecclesiastically, the region under the care of a single priest. In the wilder and more thinly settled part of the country, a parish often included several town-

[1] A bitter rivalry often existed between the two archbishops, leading sometimes to the most undignified quarrels. The question of precedence was not satisfactorily decided in Anglo-Saxon times.

ships or hamlets, and, in some cases, has always continued to do so.

In the little that can be said of the government of the early church, we note especially how it was related to the state. General church assemblies or synods, held primarily for legislative purposes, were either national or limited to one of the archiepiscopal provinces. The meetings were very irregular, both as to time and place. They were always attended by the bishops and by many of the abbots; but besides these ecclesiastics, a king or kings and a varying number of ealdormen or other laymen of importance attended. Just as churchmen attended the great lay assemblies, so laymen attended these synods; and, although we do not know the details of their procedure, there is reason to believe that, in both cases, the element that might at first seem foreign and unnecessary was regarded as integral and important. Church and state worked together and in harmony, for they had the same end in view, the maintaining of an orderly unity in the country. Theoretically the English church, like the other churches of western Europe, was under the control of the pope, but in practice, that control or any papal interference amounted to very little. It must also be remembered that this church was just as national and as much a unit when England consisted of seven separate and hostile kingdoms as after some permanent unity had been attained under the rule of the West Saxon kings. England was regarded as an ecclesiastical unit from the start; considerations of geography and race made it natural. But it was vastly important that it should have been so, for it was through the organisation of the church that English-

men from all parts of the country were first lead to
think of themselves as forming one nation. The great
political service of the Anglo-Saxon church was in thus
furnishing an ideal and example of unity.

In judicial matters, the union of church and state
was even closer. The clergy were amenable to the
hundred and shire courts in all matters of which these
courts took cognisance; they were under their jurisdiction to the same extent that laymen were. Hence
the propriety and necessity of the presence of bishop
and priest. In criminal cases, a special procedure
was necessary in the case of clerks, and the bishop
was in the court, "in the relation of lord and patron,"
to declare authoritatively what this procedure was.
But the bishop was also regarded as a learned and
necessary member of the court with respect to its
jurisdiction over laymen, especially in matters touching
morals. There were certain distinctly clerical offences,
breaches of ecclesiastical regulations, heresy, and
the like, that "would not come before the popular
courts, for they were not breaches of the secular law;
and they were not crimes for which the penitential
jurisdiction alone was sufficient. For such, then, it is
probable that the bishops had domestic tribunals not
differing in kind from the ecclesiastical courts of later
ages."[1] In its penitential system, the church had
a power of a semi-judicial character, which exercised
a restraining influence, in matters of morals, over both
clergy and laity.[2]

Monasticism was an important institution in England,

[1] Stubbs, *Constitutional History of England*, § 87.

[2] It should be remembered also that bishops or abbots who had
received grants of *bookland* had, over the people on the land,
that kind of jurisdiction, that has been described above, pp. 42–45.

as elsewhere in the early church. As we have seen, England was Christianised largely by monks, and, in very early times, monastic establishments were the chief centres of Christian influence. The seventh and eighth centuries were the glorious period of Anglo-Saxon monasticism. The houses by no means conformed to one rule, and the rule of St. Benedict, which was becoming universal upon the continent, was quite exceptional. In fact, there was from the beginning too much irregularity in the English system to ensure a long period of purity and usefulness. But in the first flush of enthusiasm, when many great men and women of the nobility aided in founding monasteries and actually entered and managed them (a source of corruption in the course of time), there was a short period during which the good far outweighed the evil. At this time, indeed, the whole Anglo-Saxon church, and especially that of Northumberland, stood for greater sanctity and learning than was to be found elsewhere in Christendom, with the possible exception of Ireland.

The Danish conquests of the ninth century threw large parts of England back into heathenism. Four or five dioceses ceased to exist, and several were, for some time, in a precarious and unsettled condition. The province of York of course suffered most; and, even when the newly settled regions had been reclaimed to Christianity, the northern archbishopric stood aloof from the southern, and there was really less unity in the church than there had been in the earlier centuries. This was simply a reflection in the church of the political separation of north and south which the Danish invasions and settlements served

to initiate.[1] In the south, church and state were
brought into even closer relations than before; witan
and ecclesiastical synod were so remarkably alike in
make-up and business that it is hard to distinguish
between them. In this later time, are found the first
instances of archbishops of Canterbury playing the
part of statesmen and of advisers and intimate friends
of kings, something which became more common after
the Norman Conquest. Spiritually the church declined after the Danish invasions. It lacked recuper-
ative power. The monastic abuses became greater,
and the efforts of Dunstan and other great churchmen
of his time to bring into England the principles of the
Cluniac reform bore no permanent fruit. England
had been sending missionaries and scholars to the
continent, and had been regarded as a leader in religion and learning; now the relations were exactly
reversed. Cut off so completely from papal leadership
and influence at a time when much of value might
have been gained from them, the English church, on
the eve of the Norman Conquest, presented a peculiar
and provincial aspect. Owing to its isolation and the
ravages of the heathen Danes, it had dropped behind
in the general forward movement of Christendom.
An intimate connection with the state, rural bishops
living in close contact with the people, an irregular
and decadent monasticism, an undignified rivalry
between its two archbishops, great independence of
the pope, some antiquity and barbarity of custom and
ceremony—these were the leading characteristics of
the pre-conquest church.

[1] See above, p. 62.

PART II

The Norman Conquest—its more immediate Results

1066–1100

SECTION I

NORMAN INSTITUTIONS AND IDEAS AT THE TIME OF THE CONQUEST

IT is the judgment of most scholars that the Norman Conquest had a more profound influence upon English history than any other single event. Its effect upon the constitution was perhaps greater than upon any other phase of the national life. A particularly careful study of this event is therefore essential if one would understand the later institutional growth. As has been already stated, we have, up to this point, been treating only a portion of the material that went to the making of the English government; now there came from the continent the last considerable gift of institutions and ideas. The method of studying this conquest should resemble, in general features, that followed in studying the Anglo-Saxon conquest. [1] Having already seen something of the public life of the country to be invaded, we turn now to a very brief examination of eleventh century Normandy, after which will follow the more vital consideration

[1] See above, p. 7. Although the Norman Conquest came six centuries later than that which gave to the English the island of Britain, and we have of course much fuller evidence of all sorts respecting it, there are nevertheless some problems connected with it that remain wholly or partially unsolved. But there is a much better prospect of the satisfactory solution of these than of many of the older ones.

of the coming together of Norman and Anglo-Saxon institutions. [1]

The circumstances of Normandy's origin and her uniformly able and masterful dukes had given her an independence and power possessed by no other part of France north of the Loire river.   One may expect therefore to find there some exceptional conditions and institutions.   As in all the other parts of France, feudalism prevailed in Normandy.   But this statement alone tells very little; many questions immediately present themselves.   The feudal practices of one place may differ greatly from those of another, and the feudalism of one time differs from that of every other time; yet the use of the same term implies that there must be certain fundamental principles that

---

[1] Our knowledge of Norman institutions is very incomplete. We know much of what may be called the external history of the duchy, of its relations to the French kings and other neighbouring powers, and of its general reputation and characteristics.   But Normandy possessed not a vestige of written law at this time, and there has remained little evidence of any sort that throws light upon its internal organisation.   But we are not simply concerned with Norman institutions.   It must be remembered that the Normans were not an isolated people, having a knowledge merely of the institutions inside their own duchy.   They constituted a vassal state of France and were acquainted with all the varying feudal relations by which the numberless big and little powers which made up France were held together, and with the peculiar position of one of those feudal powers that held the royal title.   Moreover, it is to be noticed that the Normans did not go to England simply to reproduce their own duchy there; their duke was to become king, and the Norman nobles were to be the vassals of a king, hoping to gain all the independence and power that that seemed to them to imply.   It is not without some knowledge of the institutions in the north of France in general, as well as in Normandy, that we can get any clear notion of what the Normans carried with them to England.   For the best short account of Norman institutions and law, see P. and M. i., book i., ch. iii,

remain stable. Feudalism, in a broad, loose sense of the word, there has been in various parts of the world and at various times; but *the* feudal system, historic feudalism, that feudalism which is usually meant when the word is used without adjective or explanation, is that which originated in France in the early middle ages and spread thence in western Europe. This feudalism differs from every other in that it was based upon the fusion of specific Roman and German institutions, which, obviously, can have been exactly paralleled at no other place or time. [1] Institutions more or less analogous, however, have existed in all feudal systems, since all have arisen from the same general condition and to meet the same general needs. The feudalism of Normandy was of course a type of French feudalism, but the system seems to have been in an earlier stage of development there than in other parts of northern France at the time of the Conquest; some features of the system that had become quite hardened elsewhere were still in a doubtful and fluid condition in Normandy. [2] In this respect, Norman institutions were like the Anglo-Saxon institutions with which they were about to come in contact; but, as has been shown, Anglo-Saxon feudalism

[1] It is impossible in this work to enter into a discussion of the vast subject of European feudalism. But much will be said of it incidentally and considerable knowledge of it taken for granted. For the origin of feudalism see Adams, *Civilisation during the Middle Ages*, ch. ix.; for the developed feudal institutions, see Seignobos, *The Feudal Régime*, and Emerton, *Medieval Europe*, ch. xiv.

[2] But it has recently been shown that the duke's vassals probably owed him specific numbers of knight's services in the eleventh century.   Haskins, *Knight Service in Normandy in the Eleventh Century*, English Historical Review xxii., 636–649.

was not derived from the continent; it was of indigenous growth, and lacked those features that the continental system drew from Rome.   A clear perception of these facts is most needful in beginning the study of the Norman Conquest.   To summarise them: in England, there had been forming a feudalism of purely Germanic origin, which, at the date of the Conquest, was only half grown and peculiarly vague and complex; in Normandy, there was an undeveloped type of continental feudalism; but the Normans knew thoroughly the north French feudalism of their time.[1]

The substance of what is known of Norman society and government may be quickly told.   The peasantry was in a better condition than elsewhere in northern France; there were few slaves.   Among the upper classes, most land tenures were tending to conform to the feudal type; the vassal held land *of* his lord (implying that, as between the two, the superior claim lay with the latter) and by a definite contract of honourable service.   The service was generally military. It is doubtful whether this system had existed long enough or generally enough to give rise to a hard and fast theory that all free tenures must be of this type. Of the extent of private jurisdiction, little is known; but it certainly existed.   Part of it was the jurisdiction of the landlord over his peasantry, and part feudal jurisdiction, that of the lord over his vassals.   All private courts in Normandy were limited by the unusual number of cases reserved by the duke for

---

[1] The Conquest, which was a wonderfully many-sided event, resulted in much more than can be explained by simply conceiving of one feudal system as coming in and displacing another; but this is the feature of the event concerning which one is most likely to go astray.

his own consideration; all crimes, for instance, punishable by death were tried at the duke's court. In Normandy, there was more corporal punishment, and consequently less composition by fine, than in England. There was therefore a more rigorous repression of crime, and, in this respect, Normandy must be regarded as more advanced. The Truce of God existed in Normandy for the same reason that it did elsewhere on the continent, the mitigation of private warfare; but the stern rule of the dukes rendered it less necessary than in most other places.

The duke, in governing, took counsel with a body of men who formed his *curia* or court and who were usually known as *optimates* or *proceres*. These great men were ordinarily his immediate vassals, and an important question respecting the *curia* is whether or not it was simply the duke's feudal court of tenants-in-chief. It was, practically that, and would, doubtless, soon have become that in theory; it was a council of an older sort, resembling the Anglo-Saxon witan; but it had, by this time, become quite thoroughly feudalised.[1] The Norman church, in the separation of its organisation from that of the state and in its close relations with Rome, differed from the Anglo-Saxon church as all continental churches did. As in England, however, the lay power was in thorough sympathy with the church and perhaps exercised a greater control over it.

[1] "What we know is that when the time for the conquest of England is approaching, the duke consults or professes to consult the great men of his realm, lay and spiritual, the *optimates*, the *proceres* of Normandy. He holds a court; we dare hardly as yet call it a court of his tenants-in-chief; but it is an assembly of the great men, and the great men are his vassals."—P. and M. i, 73.

SECTION II

NORMAN AND ANGLO-SAXON INSTITUTIONS COME TOGETHER

THE Norman Conquest, considered from any point of view, is a difficult subject. Institutionally considered, it is, perhaps, especially so. The initial difficulty lies in the vagueness and intricacy of the previous institutions of both Anglo-Saxons and Normans, but there were in the Conquest itself many sources of institutional influence and development. The time and circumstances of the undertaking and the personalities and doings of the Conqueror and his principal followers, as well of his sons have to be taken carefully into account. At a time when there was little that was hard and fast about institutions and when the upheaval of an invasion gave opportunity for change, very small things could mightily affect the future. It is, of course, out of place here to give a narrative account of what took place. It is the purpose rather to examine the conditions of government and society after the Conquest had wrought its first great change. There is some difficulty in determining at what precise point to make this survey, since the Conquest so profoundly affected all later English history. There has seemed, however, to be a propriety in regarding the reigns of the first two Norman kings as containing what may be most properly considered immediate results. In the reign of Henry I., a development began which was introductory to all the institutional growth of the twelfth century; hence this reign, notwithstanding the formidable hiatus of the anarchy under Stephen, connects itself with what followed rather than with what went before. We shall, therefore, be mainly concerned here with the latter part of the Conqueror's reign and with the reign of William II. ; but the consideration of some matters will make it necessary to trespass occasionally upon a later time. As in the Anglo-Saxon period, the distinction between the local and central governments must be made prominent, the first three subdivisions of the subject dealing with the classes of men and their relations and activities in the local institutions, and the last three with the new central power and the church.

1. **The Classes of Men and the Introduction of Feudalism.**—It was no purpose of the Conqueror to make changes in English law and custom beyond what were necessary in the creation of a powerful and effective monarchy. He intended to rule in the fullest sense of the word, but he had none of that pettiness of purpose which would lead him to arbitrarily make changes for the mere pleasure of lording it over a conquered people. Moreover, he had no idea that it was necessary to make any general substitution of Norman or French institutions for Anglo-Saxon. He was to rule as an English king, and he believed that there were many good features in the English system, and, doubtless, felt the expediency of leaving undisturbed many things, which, while they had nothing in particular to recom-

mend them, might occasion discontent and heartburning in the removal. This, as nearly as it can be interpreted, was the Conqueror's initial attitude; but as years passed, more change and severity were necessary than he at first supposed, and many things came to pass that could not have been foreseen.

In violent and sudden changes, the lower classes of men and the smaller local institutions are the ones least affected at first. We have reason to believe that, in the early years after the Conquest, the Anglo-Saxon serf, villein, and *sokeman* lived on very little disturbed in their relative positions. The large tenures, those of their lords or lords' lords, might be changing hands and changing in character very fast without immediately affecting them. But a change did reach them, at just what time it is impossible to say, the beginning of which must be noticed here. The status of the lower classes, that strange complexity of nomenclature and condition where freedom faded imperceptibly into unfreedom, was beyond the comprehension of the new Norman lords of the soil. Perhaps they did not feel that it was worth while to try to comprehend it, or they may have been largely unconscious of it. Vague as were many things in continental status, the line between the servile classes and those above them was usually quite distinct. Moreover, when the Norman mind acted freely, it was likely to produce what was clear-cut; and the Norman lawyers of the twelfth century had many of the principles of the Roman law to help them. A process began in England, which, in the course of time, drew a tolerably clear line between freedom and unfreedom. The large, inchoate, Anglo-Saxon class was being cut in two;

a part, and that probably much the smaller, was to pass into a better recognised condition of freedom, while more were to become, by a gradual depression, a part of the servile class. The process was not complete for a century or more after the time we are now considering, but it is possible at this point to see the beginnings of future, well-known classes, whose character fundamentally affected the English constitution. The unfree class came to be known after the Conquest as the villein class, and was made up of the pre-conquest slaves whose status had been raised, and the pre-conquest villeins, whose status had been lowered. It was much larger than the servile class before the Conquest, but not so abjectly servile.

That this simplifying process greatly improved the legal position of the serf can hardly be doubted. We need not indeed suppose that the *theow* or servus of earlier times had been subjected to a rigorously consistent conception of slavery. Still in the main he had been rightless, a chattel; and we may be sure that his rightlessness had not been the merely relative rightlessness of later days, free against all but his lord. Indeed we may say that in the course of the twelfth century slavery was abolished. That on the other hand the villani suffered in the process is very likely. Certainly they suffered in name. A few of them, notably those on the king's manors may have fallen on the right side of the Roman dilemma "aut liberi aut servi," and as free men holding by unfree tenure may have become even more distinctly free than they were before; but most of them fell on the wrong side; they got a bad name, and were brought within the range of maxims which described the English *theow* or the Roman slave. Probably we ought not to impute to the lawyers of this age any conscious desire to raise the serf or to debase the villein.

6

The great motive force which directs their doings in this as in other instances is a desire for the utmost generality and simplicity.   .   .   .   They reck little of the interests of any classes, high or low; but the interests of the state, of peace and order and royal justice are ever before them.[1]

The class, thus formed, bore some peculiar characteristics; its members had a distinctly servile side and a distinctly free side.   The former was shown in their relations to their lords, in which were present the usual servile disabilities.   The villein whose daughter married outside the manor must pay the *merchet*, or marrying fine, to his lord; and the latter had many petty and vexatious rights over the property of his villein, which proves, however, that the villein did have personal property that was recognised as his. The villein was bound to the soil and to certain services, payments in labour and in kind, which were determined by the custom of the manor and which varied in their amount and certainty in individual cases.   To his land and to his services, the villein could be strictly held; if he fled, his lord had the right to bring him back by force.   On the other hand, to all persons except his lord, the villein presented his free side; as against them, his right to have his property and personal safety protected was practically the same as that of the freeholder upon the same manor. As the system of king's courts developed, its attitude towards the villein became a matter of great importance as affecting his status.   In a word, and by way of anticipation, it may be stated here that the villein could be a presenter of criminals in a royal court, and,

[1] P. and M. i., 430, 431.   For the depressing effect of post-conquest taxation upon the middle classes, see below, p. 105.

by the early thirteenth century, stood on a practical equality with the freeman in such court in all matters relating to its criminal jurisdiction. But it was not for him a civil court; he could bring no action there.

The men above the villeins, the non-noble freemen, are known usually as freeholders. As the mass of Anglo-Saxon tenures became somewhat simplified after the Conquest, this class held normally by one of the socage tenures, tenure in free socage, the ancestor of the modern freehold, being the most important. [1] The normal manor contained a number of freeholders in addition to its villein tenants; but a freeholder might have a manor with freehold and villein tenants of his own. The services of the freeholder were much the same as those of the villein, but possessed a kind of definiteness that left him who rendered them less at his lord's disposal. The freeholder lacked also the ascription to the soil and the more personal incidents of servitude. But any general description is likely to make the distinction between the freehold and villein classes appear clearer than it actually was. The more the investigator deals with details, the more difficult he finds it to obtain a sure touchstone of demarcation; even such obviously servile marks as the payment of the *merchet* become vague and unsatisfactory as guides. What at first seems a less clear-cut test, definiteness of service, has been found, in the long run, the best. It is true that the villein's

---

[1] Free socage was the most important of a group of Anglo-Saxon free, non-noble tenures. The origin of its name is obscure. After the Conquest, free socage was more widely used and often by people of higher rank than in Anglo-Saxon times. See Maitland, *Domesday Book and Beyond*, pp. 66 *ff*. This tenure was commonly known as *fee farm* from the Conquest to Edward I.

service was often fixed as to its sum total, but he did not know from day to day what his lord would have him do; he was at his lord's disposal.

A matter which greatly complicated the relations of all classes was what has been termed the divorce of tenure and personal status. At a time when ideas of land ownership were very vague and several individuals of different status ordinarily had rights in the same piece of land at the same time, it was impossible for the land to take its character from its tenants; they were too numerous, heterogeneous, and shifting. Hence it became the practice to identify a certain piece of land with certain services; it always owed villein services or it always owed freehold services, etc.;

. . . service due from each particular piece of land came to be everything, and the actual status of the holder of the land a matter of comparative indifference. It is scarcely possible to overrate the effect of this manner of holding land in breaking up the social system of the middle ages. Great nobles thought it no degradation to hold land on socage tenure of mesne lords far below them in the social scale, or even to undertake the more precarious liabilities of the unfree villein holder. [1]

In general, there seems to have been no limit to the number of different tenures by which the same individual might at once hold different pieces of land. Where there was divergence between tenure and status, it was usually the man of higher status holding the lower tenure, and the ordinary freeman might be in danger of losing his free status by too long identification with villein tenure. But notwithstanding the various sources of confusion among classes, a great body of the unfree,

[1] Medley, *English Constitutional History*, pp. 34, 35.

the tenants in villeinage, stands out clearly enough from the freemen; and of the latter, there was a large class of holders by socage tenure, the personal status of most of whom was non-noble and free. The existence after the Conquest, of a substantial non-noble, free class was a very important condition of later constitutional development. [1]

In turning to the consideration of the nobility, we come upon an important and immediate result of the Conquest. Owing to the initial resistance at Hastings, which the Conqueror was pleased to consider treasonable, there was a very extensive confiscation of land in the south. The protracted resistance in the midlands and north brought equally sweeping confiscations there. Hence almost all the land in England either changed hands or was regranted on new terms to the old holders. It was through this process that the principles of continental feudalism entered England. The land was granted upon feudal terms by no special design, but because the Conqueror was acquainted with no other. It was now held *of* the king, that is, the proprietorship lay with him and not with the grantee, and it was held by definite contract for some honourable service, ordinarily military service. Then the men who held directly of the king, his tenants-in-chief, might make subgrants of land to others, who would hold of them upon the same conditions. But all the tenures in England did not become feudal. When new grants were made to nobles, they were invariably feudal, but the lower holdings within these grants remained as before. However, the feudal principle that all land must be

[1] See below, pp. 306, 307; 311, 312.

held *of* someone began to affect the non-feudal tenures. The socage tenures, while remaining throughout their later history unchanged in essentials, acquired after the Conquest a feudal tinge that gave them for a time a somewhat anomalous character. [1]

The unit of military service was that of the single knight, the warrior fully armed according to medieval fashion. Hence the unit of military tenure was a holding of such value as to support a knight. When the new feudal tenures were created, they were reckoned in terms of knights' services. The Conqueror might grant to one of his followers an extent of territory from which forty knights were required, to another, a holding furnishing twenty or thirty knights, and so on. The number of knights' services were almost always reckoned in multiples of five. Although there was, of course, a relation between the amount of land granted and the number of knights required from it, yet no very accurate measuring unit seems to have been used; the Conqueror probably fixed the numbers very arbitrarily. In many cases, certainly, the number of knights required was much below what the land might have furnished. Comparatively few tenants-in-chief owed over fifty or sixty knights, and the sum of all was about five thousand. It has been contended by some writers that this system of knight

---

[1] This feudal tinge appears in the universality with which all lands were held of some lord, all rendered some kind of service, and all tended to assume some of the more characteristic feudal dues, such as the regular aids and the relief. But they lacked the essential feudal characteristic of being held by an *honourable* service. Free socage tenure became increasingly popular, being a free tenure, with a definite, non-military service and usually lacking the more vexatious feudal incidents, as wardship and marriage. Burgage, the characteristic tenure in boroughs, was a sort of "town socage."

service was simply a continuation, under another name, of what is often called the *thegnage* of Anglo-Saxon times. There was, however, an essential difference, which is an illustration of the fact, already insisted upon, that England before the Conquest did not possess the principles of continental feudalism. What had been growing in England was a more or less complete territorialising of military service. The old militia idea that every freeman could be called upon to render military service to the state no longer existed in its purity; the attention and emphasis had been shifting from the individual to the land. A certain amount of service had, from time immemorial, been rendered from a certain extent of territory; hence, except in cases of extraordinary emergency, just so many men and no more were required from it. [1] There was even appearing a general rule that five hides was the normal amount of land from which to require one fully armed warrior. It is, moreover, likely that the large land-holders were, to some extent, held responsible for the number of men their lands were to furnish. But this practice was growing, as we have seen so much else in the Anglo-Saxon system, without any theory or underlying principle to suit the facts; indeed, the facts were, at that time, so varied that they can be made to square with no principle whatever. They had broken away from an old principle or principles, but had not as yet reached uniformity enough to give rise to a new one; there had not been in England, as on the continent, any pre-existing principles derived

---

[1] This territorialising of military service is precisely analogous to the process through which the duty of attending the shire court was passing. See above, pp. 21, 22.

from an older civilisation that might serve as hints and guiding forces in the yet complex and imperfect facts. The thing that had been lacking and that came in at the Conquest was the idea of a definite contract understood as existing between lord and man. In the grants made by the Conqueror to his followers or to the restored and pardoned Saxon nobles, such contracts were made, and the land was recognized as coming from him and its proprietorship as remaining with him. This system of knight service remained for a century after 1066 the chief means of recruiting an army. The Norman kings, however, did not abandon the old right of the Anglo-Saxon kings to enforce a general levy of all freemen in case of great necessity; and in the survival of this right, the military system of England differed from that of the continent, where military service had been entirely appropriated by the feudal idea.

It has been often represented that, when William brought feudalism into England, he consciously modified it in several ways in the interest of his own power. This has been found to be an inadequate explanation of the facts. In the first place, there can be ascribed to William no thought of introducing a new system; it was not a time of institutional self-consciousness. In the second place, several things, necessarily resulting from the Conquest itself, had an effect upon the feudal holdings and made them differ from the continental type. The most prominent of these was the scattering of the large fiefs, which has often been ascribed to a deliberate plan of William to make it difficult for his great nobles to concentrate their forces. But it was an inevitable result of the piecemeal conquest of the country; William conquered first the south-east and, shortly after, the south-west, and must hasten to reward his clamorous followers in those regions; then came the series of uprisings in the north, the confiscation of most of the land, and the consequent new grants there; and, last of all, the country about Chester and the Welsh border was subdued, and many of the Norman nobles, who had begun to get their allotments in the south-east four or five years before, received their final holdings in the regions last conquered. Moreover, when a Norman was, in any part of England, put into the place of a rebellious Saxon lord, he was likely to find the lands of his predecessor very irregular and scattered; for the majority of the Anglo-Saxon nobles had never gone far in rounding out and perfecting their holdings.

A second effect of the Conquest was a sharper defining of feudal obligation and incident. This resulted from the rapid creation of so many new holdings. On the continent, where the feudal system of landholding had grown step by step through centuries, all sorts of anomalies and relics of earlier forms of tenure remained; in conquered England, where things were being made over new and the king was strong, there was a tendency to push the feudal theory to its logical conclusion and work out details. In the reign of William II., there was a deliberate attempt to exploit the feudal relations in the interest of the king, which resulted in carefully elaborating and defining the feudal obligations. Erelong, as far as feudal law was concerned, especially feudal land-law, England was leading Europe. It may be remarked in conclusion that the Salisbury oath, which is likely to strike one as a marked assumption of power upon the Conqueror's part, was not a new kind of oath. There is evidence that such an oath had been required at other times during his reign, and he and his ancestors seem to have habitually required the same in Normandy. It established in England the important principle that every man's oath to his lord was taken saving his allegiance to his king.[1]

2. **The Local Courts, Communal and Private.**—The Anglo-Saxon local judicial system remained for some time after the Conquest little changed. Its usefulness was probably recognised by the new king, who certainly had nothing worthy to replace it. The private jurisdictions, which have been noted as seriously cutting into the hundred courts, were now, in most cases, the jurisdictions of Norman instead of Saxon lords, and the old conception that they were still in some sort public courts with changed presiding officers probably soon passed away. But notwithstanding the substantial continuance of the old system, certain important changes did begin and certain new conceptions inevitably arose in the early Norman period.[2]

The duty of attending the shire court became more and more attached to certain holdings of land.[3] This change was of very slow and obscure growth and resulted in many anomalies. The largest holdings did

---

[1] Though William I. did not consciously modify the feudal system, it must not be supposed that he was neglectful of his own interests; but he cared for these in an eleventh century manner and not in the manner which some modern writers have ascribed to him. See below, pp. 100-102.

[2] These are to be briefly outlined here, and this consideration will serve as a starting point for the consecutive study of the creation of the English judicial system in Part III., §I.

[3] Maitland, *The Suitors of the County Court*, English Historical

not always owe suit of court, and the actual make-up of
the court under this system must have been a curious
jumble of high and low, rich and poor. Soon after the
Conquest, the earl and the bishop ceased to attend
the court, leaving the sheriff as the only presiding
or constituting officer—a change that was to fundamentally affect the court's future history. Earl began
to be a title of nobility instead of signifying an office.
This was a result of preceding Norman history, during
which the control of the dukes had been so complete
that no great official power had been allowed in the
hands of a local nobility; the counts, who, in some
respects had corresponded to the Anglo-Saxon earls,
were few in number, practically confined to the ducal
family, and with no such relation to a local court as
that held by the earls. The bishop withdrew from
the shire court as a result of William's separation of
ecclesiastical from lay jurisdiction.[1] The court met,
as formerly, twice a year; but it could be summoned
oftener by the king when he had any special business
that he wished it to transact. The time of meeting
and the make-up of the regular hundred court[2] underwent no change in the early Norman period; by that
time, it was held either by the sheriff or by some
deputy directly responsible to him.[3]

Review iii., 417–421. The territorialising of suit of court probably
began in the Anglo-Saxon period, but this has not been proved.
See above, pp. 21, 22.

[1] See below, p. 116.

[2] On the specially full meetings of the hundred court in Henry
I.'s time, meetings that were really becoming king's courts, see
below, pp. 168–170.

[3] In the obscure and unreliable *Leges Henrici Primi*, we read
of the possibility, if neither a lord nor his steward could attend court,

In the reign of William II., the holding of the hundred and shire courts fell into irregularity and abuse. To some extent, the king was manipulating them in his own interest through his officer, the sheriff; but undoubtedly the chief abuse was by the sheriff himself. The courts were summoned capriciously, and unusual or extortionate fines were levied. This would have been impossible in the Anglo-Saxon period when bishop and earl sat with the sheriff, and the essentially popular character of the courts was safeguarded by this balance of officials. Henry I., early in his reign, ordered that these courts be held as they had been before the Conquest, thus correcting the sheriffs' abuses of his brother's time. This was but a small part of what Henry did in a judicial way. As has been remarked, his reign opened the great period of constitution making, and, more particularly, the twelfth century judicial development. Hence we do not consider in this section the later fortunes of these ancient courts.

As to private jurisdiction, the Conqueror had, of course, always known it upon the continent and must have regarded it, in some form, as a part of the natural order of things. It was growing rapidly in England in Edward the Confessor's day, a growth that must have been fostered by the incoming continental ideas. As the vague and illogical Anglo-Saxon conceptions of

---

of the lord's being represented by the priest or reeve and four men from the manor. If such a system actually prevailed in the ordinary hundred and shire courts, it is impossible to say what the functions of these representatives were. The reeve and four men would ordinarily be villeins, and it is clear that they were not regarded as suitors, that is, could not act as judges in the courts. As to their connection with the frankpledge and later jury system, see below, pp. 137, 147, 148; 169–171.

private courts played no part in later history, it is necessary here to grasp clearly the main ideas brought from the continent. The principle that a man had jurisdictional rights over the unfree tenants of his land had its origin in the Roman empire. Such rights can certainly not be regarded as having originated in governmental grants. On the other hand, private jurisdiction over freemen grew upon the continent at a later time and as a result of the breakdown of the central government. This took place in three ways: the sovereign, in his weakness, made to private individuals grants that either expressed or implied judicial authority; men who had been *bona fide* officials in earlier times continued to exercise their judicial functions, essentially upon their own private responsibility, after the state had broken down; and there were out and out usurpations.[1] It was natural that a recovering central power, especially one under the sway of the Roman idea that the sovereign was the source of all legislative and judicial authority, should assume that all such power in private hands had passed there by royal grant, and hence could be resumed whenever the king saw fit. The Conqueror and his early successors did not do much theorising upon this matter, but the lavish judicial grants which they sometimes made certainly implied that they had a good deal to give; and where they found any one exercising a jurisdiction so great as to be prejudicial to themselves, they were very fertile in practical means to limit it.[2] But there came a time when an English king set himself to theorise upon the subject, and it

[1] See Adams, *Civilisation during the Middle Ages*, pp. 210–214
[2] For conditions in pre-conquest Normandy, see above, pp. 76, 77.

will be useful, in that connection, to have in mind the actual historical facts.[1] The Norman Conquest was responsible for the first clear formulation in England of the idea that the king was the source of law. It also brought in the principle then obtaining on the continent, that a man had, by virtue of the feudal relation, some degree of jurisdiction over his vassals. These two ideas, at bottom contradictory, must sooner or later clash.

As the classes of men and the classes of courts after the Conquest have now been considered, it may be useful, by way of recapitulation, to note in what courts the three classes, serfs, non-noble freemen, and nobles, would ordinarily appear. The serf was entirely under the jurisdiction of his lord in the manorial court; his lord's steward presided and his fellow serfs and probably the freemen on the same manor were his judges. The non-noble freeman was under the jurisdiction of his lord, where such jurisdiction belonged to the latter of ancient right or had been acquired through the new disposition of the land, or he might still be subject to the hundred court. In the lord's court, he was judged by the other freemen of the manor, probably not often by the villeins. The natural working of the continental idea of the lord's judicial authority over his tenants was undoubtedly reducing the sphere of the hundred and shire courts, and this process might have reached its logical conclusion had not a new and mightier force interrupted and changed it. The noble, the man holding upon condition of honourable service, was under the jurisdiction of his lord and was amenable to a court over

[1] See below, pp. 178, 179.

which the latter presided, and in which his fellow vassals, those holding of the same lord, were his judges. In a very literal sense of the word, he was judged by his peers. This court was not held at a fixed time or place like the manorial court. It was characteristic of the strictly feudal jurisdiction to operate irregularly, simply as occasion required. It had an even less flourishing and lengthy career in England than the other form of private jurisdiction. The highest suzerain of all, the king, had his feudal court made up of his tenants-in-chief, in the same manner as any other lord with vassals. It was the Curia Regis, or king's court. [1] But he was king as well as suzerain, and a mighty king at that, and, from the beginning, his feudal court did some extraordinary and unfeudal things in the way of arbitrary interference in cases either in the communal or private courts. The king's court was soon to be the most prominent factor in English judicial history.

This sketch of the local powers and jurisdictions just after the Conquest must include a mention of the palatine earldoms. The well-known object of these was to erect a specially centralised, efficient, and interested power on the dangerously exposed frontiers. William, whose conquest had done so much to rid England of overpowerful earls, perhaps did not at first feel ready to do entirely without this favourite resource of immature governments; but it is more likely that he accepted something of the sort as a matter of course and that the traditional locations of some such powers in Anglo-Saxon times was of influence. Certain earls were given large, compact pieces of

[1] See below, pp. 102-104.

territory which were made practically exempt from
all governmental interference, as far as internal affairs
were concerned. Chester, Durham, and Kent were
the three palatine earldoms established. As Kent
was only granted for life, little account need be taken
of it. The two others lasted long and had many
important consequences. Several other holdings, especially those on the Welsh border to the south of
Chester, fell only a little short of these in point of size,
compactness, and immunity from state interference.
But when these greatest of private powers after the
Conquest are compared with the houses of Godwin
or Leofric in Edward's time, the contrast is so striking
as to need no insistence.

3. **The Boroughs.**—Although the Norman Conquest
resulted finally in greatly stimulating all commercial and
industrial interests in England, its early effect upon the
boroughs was depressing. We have seen that in the late
Anglo-Saxon period the boroughs were more and more
regarded as being upon the domain of some lord, and
that the king had by far the largest number.[1] Under
the influence of continental ideas, all boroughs became
lords' boroughs soon after the Conquest. When the
citizens of the struggling continental municipalities
of this period were regarded individually, they were
always classed as servile, and most of them were of
servile origin. It was natural that the new Norman
lords of the English boroughs should regard the burgesses in the same way. This could not but tend to
lower their status, but the idea was so contrary to
fact in England that its logical results in the treat-

[1] See above, pp. 35, 36.

ment of burgesses were far from completely realised.
However, the somewhat arbitrary levying by the
lord of a payment called *tallage* from his boroughs
certainly originated in it. Tallage is to be carefully distinguished from the old *firma burgi*, made up
of the rents, tolls, and court fines.[1]

The boroughs also suffered severely from the extended devastations which William I. found necessary
to the complete conquest of England.[2] But the stable
peace which the strong Norman and Angevin kings
gave the country and the commercial advantages
of the closer connection with the continent soon began
to affect the boroughs favourably. This was noticeable
as early as the reign of Henry I., and from that time
the boroughs entered more regularly upon the struggle
for liberties and immunities which began slightly
before the Conquest. The specific things they were
seeking varied somewhat according as they were
king's towns or those of ecclesiastical or lay lords,
but may be grouped, in a general way, as follows: they
wanted their *firma* fixed at a lump sum, and, in the
case of the king's towns, paid directly to the king without the sheriff's intervention; they wanted to be free
from tallage and Danegeld; they wanted as little
interference as possible from outside in choosing their
officers and in jurisdiction, every burgess being amenable only to the borough court; they strove to mitigate
the network of tolls by which they were surrounded
and which hampered the ingress and egress of traders.
Henry I. granted a charter to London which may be

[1] See above, p. 37.
[2] "The civic population recorded in Domesday fell from 17,000
to 7,000."—Medley, *English Constitutional History*, p. 423.

7

regarded as inaugurating the boroughs' great twelfth century struggle for independence. The privileges conferred by this charter were great, considering the time, and it served as an important incentive to other boroughs. "The privileges of the citizens of London are not to be regarded as a fair specimen of the liberties of ordinary towns; but as a sort of type and standard of the amount of municipal independence and self-government at which the other towns of the country might be expected to aim." [1]

The logical outcome of what the boroughs were aiming at, just as in the case of continental municipalities, was complete political independence. In all countries where the feudal régime was supreme, the municipalities felt themselves to be alien units in uncongenial and hostile surroundings. They were, in many respects, the advance guards of the modern in the midst of the medieval. They learned early the particularity of their interests; their hand must be against every man as every man's hand was against them; the interests of the feudal warrior and of the citizen were antipodal. Any possibility of the towns' profitably sharing in the general government of the country was denied by every condition of the time. Rather it was their purpose to wall themselves off, literally and figuratively, from all governmental surroundings and, while profiting by the growing industrial demands and by commerce, work out their own institutional salvation. They soon learned the most effective ways to use their increasing numbers and wealth. To buy privileges was their great method, but they knew how to use force upon occasion. These conditions were

[1] Stubbs, *Select Charters*, p. 107.

much the same in Germany, France, and England in the twelfth century. In Germany, owing to the break-down of the central government, the logical conclusion was finally reached, in many cases, in the free cities. In France, it was measurably reached, for a time, in the communes of the north and south; later, all liberty, inside the city walls as well as out, was lost in the absolute power of the king. In England, the boroughs never reached political isolation, nor were their political rights taken away from them by an absolute king; a unique set of conditions and series of events broke down the barriers between them and certain important elements of the outside population and eventually made it possible for the burgesses to take part in the general government of the country.[1]

4. **The Central Government—King and Curia Regis.**—The most important and far-reaching constitutional result of the Norman Conquest was the strengthening of the central government. We have seen the Anglo-Saxon constitution stronger in the lower part of the structure than in the higher; now, without damage or violent change in the lower part, the higher was transformed and strengthened and the way prepared for the union between the two, which is the key to most of the later constitutional growth.

In the Anglo-Saxon period, the central government consisted of king and witan; after the Conquest, it consisted of the king and king's court, or Curia Regis. The word king, as applying to the first two Norman rulers of England, had a larger content than it had ever had in Anglo-Saxon times or than it had had in France. And it was not to remain long unchanged after the

[1] See Part III., § III., 4, 5, 6.

Conquest; from reign to reign and century to century, one has to carefully revise his conception of the English kingship. It is, perhaps, needless to say that when William conquered England he did not trouble himself about a theory of royalty. He knew its practical limitations in both England and France, and he determined to rid himself of these as far as possible. The substance of power was what he wanted. He certainly did not purpose to emphasise any break in Anglo-Saxon policy caused by the Conquest; he was the successor of Edward rather than a conqueror introducing new and strange notions. He laid much stress upon the promises of Edward and Harold, and, in the coronation ceremony and the important coronation oath, he followed the Anglo-Saxon form. But he immediately began to rule as no Anglo-Saxon king had ruled, and the introduction of feudal tenure and the ambitious expectations of his followers did not reduce him to the empty kind of suzerainty held by the king of France. English kingship changed because there had been a conquest and because the Conqueror was what he was, and it remained changed because his successors were, for the most part, strong men with a similar determination to rule. Had he been succeeded by weaklings, there is no reason to suppose that it would not finally have fallen back where it was in the person of Edward the Confessor. The Norman kings had no well-defined conception of absolutism; they thought it possible to obtain sufficient power under the old forms. The facts preceded theory; new conceptions dawned slowly in the middle ages, and before any distinct theory of absolute monarchy got lodged in people's minds the king's power began to be limited in a new way, and a new set of ideas, destined to be permanent, began to form.

Notwithstanding this general precedence of fact over theory, there was brought in from the continent by the Conquest at least one important idea concerning kingship that had only in the vaguest way been in England. It was the idea that the sovereign was the source of all legislative and judicial power. It had passed into Frankish kingship, as had so much else, from Rome. It is easy to get a wrong impression of the vividness with which this had ever been present on the continent; we see it quite clearly in Charlemagne, but after him it had certainly lost all reflection in facts. This Roman idea was an important factor in the creation of the English judicial system.[1]

The best concrete example of the great power that the Conqueror was exercising by the end of his reign and, doubtless, his most original piece of work, was the Domesday survey. While it had no technical bearing upon his relations to his people, either as feudal lord or sovereign, it was of immense practical value in putting the resources of the newly acquired country at his command. The Domesday survey was really a census, undertaken on a scale of magnitude and precision, which, for times when anything of the sort was almost unheard of, testifies, as nothing else does, of the organising genius and energy of its author. William had conquered him a country; it lay open and subdued before him, giving him an unmatched opportunity to do with it as he chose. He would know his new acquisition to the smallest details, its resources, its population, its local conditions and history.

[1] See Part III., § I., 1.

The resulting Domesday Book gives us a knowledge of England in the eleventh century such as is possessed of no other European country for the same period.[1]

The early Norman king governed in conjunction with his feudal court, which, for more than a century after the Conquest, was known as Curia Regis or Consilium.[2] So many important parts of the English government have grown out of this body that there has, not unnaturally, been much interest manifested in its origin. Many scholars have felt great pride in tracing all the best products of England's later constitution to something primitively Anglo-Saxon, and hence have discussed this question with a considerable amount of bias. The cause for pride seems so obviously to lie in the successful development of the primitive institution into a thing of permanent value to all mankind that one ought to be able to approach the question of origins with an open mind.

The term Curia Regis was applied to a small, permanent body of officials and barons in attendance on the king, and to a larger body of counsellors, who, in early times, met three times a year on the three great

[1] Documents 3 and 4 in A. and S. are characteristic entries in the Domesday Book. The chief matter of constitutional interest in connection with the Domesday survey is not the fact of the survey itself but the method by which it was made. See below, p. 140 *ff.*

[2] In the Latin of this time, there was but one word for counsel and council, namely, *consilium;* hence it is hard to tell in what instances the word signified a distinctly recognised body of men. It seems to have more frequently meant counsel, and it is safer not to regard it as indicating any specific form or differentiation of the Curia Regis until a much later time. See below, pp. 287–289.

church festivals when the king wore his crown.[1] It
is impossible to make a clear distinction between the
work of these bodies. One is, perhaps, inclined to
think of the smaller Curia Regis as administrative
and the larger as deliberative or legislative, but these
are ideas entirely foreign to the times. Little deliberation took place, and the assent of the barons to the
king's ordinances seems to have been much a matter
of form. Work that we should consider judicial and
administrative occupied most of the time of the
Curia Regis, the larger meeting especially devoting
itself to the former; but, as far as can be judged, there
existed at the time no conscious distinction between
either the functions or the powers of the two bodies.
It is more correct to say that there were not two bodies,
but larger and smaller sessions of the same body;
when the larger Curia Regis was in session, the smaller
ceased to exist.

The question that next arises concerns the composition of the larger Curia Regis. Was it made up on
the same principle as the Anglo-Saxon witan? The
principle of its composition some half or three quarters
of a century later is very evident, and the specific
question here is as to how soon after the Conquest
this principle began to operate. The Curia Regis
of Henry II.'s time was made up, for the most part,
of the king's tenants-in-chief. The officials and members of the king's household might, obviously, attend
on other grounds, but most of the great officials were
vassals of the king. The king might invite persons

---

[1] An exact date for this bifurcation of the Curia Regis cannot be
assigned, but there are certainly traces of it before Henry I., in
whose reign it became permanent and important,

whose attendance he wanted for some special and immediate purpose, as was often the case with papal legates; and it must not be supposed that the lesser tenants-in-chief all attended or were expected to attend. But the principle existed that the great majority attended because they were king's vassals. This means that the Curia Regis was the king's feudal court. Now was it a feudal court immediately after the Norman Conquest or did it only gradually become so? It is foreign to the spirit of the time to suppose that William consciously changed the witan into a new kind of council. But as the feudal tenure began to prevail, most of his counsellors would naturally be those who held from him in chief. William brought in the continental feudal organisation because he knew no other and, when he had done so, he was bound to have a feudal court made up of his tenants-in-chief, just as every other lord of vassals had. Thus we may believe that the king's feudal court, the Curia Regis, came into existence in England almost as soon after the Conquest, and with about as much conscious creation, as the Norman-French language.

5. **Taxation.**—The Normans brought into England no ideas on taxation that were in advance of those already there. In fact, the Danegeld under Cnute probably approached more nearly a true tax than anything known to the Normans. Hence what has been said of the conception of the royal revenue as being the proper and sufficient support of king and government, the idea that the king should "live of his own," applies long after the Conquest.[1] But a change in the Danegeld

[1] See below, pp. 56, 57.

and some changes in the ordinary sources of revenue and the ideas connected with them, changes that formed starting points for later development, need to be noted here.

The Conqueror renewed the Danegeld, which had been dropped by Edward the Confessor, and trebled it. This made it a tax of six shillings on every hide of land.[1] It was levied regularly, and Cnute's use of it as a regular payment for the support of government was made permanent. From the Conquest, there has always been a land tax in England. William's use of the Danegeld is an excellent example of his adoption of an Anglo-Saxon institution that seemed likely to prove of value to him. The trebled Danegeld was oppressive, resting heavily upon the Anglo-Saxon middle class, and probably contributed to the depression of status in that class which was the final result of the Conquest.[2] The desire for more accurate knowledge of the wealth of his country, to serve as the basis for the assessment of this tax, was an important cause of William's Domesday survey. The data obtained served for the assessment of the land tax for over a century.

Under feudalism, some of the requirements of state were provided for in a precarious fashion by means of the nexus of private contracts. Thus, if all these were kept, the king would be able to lead into the field as many knights as the land of the country was reckoned as owing him. Where feudalism was thorough-going, there was no possibility of anything like modern taxation, for the king was in immediate

[1] The hide averaged about 120 acres.
[2] See above, pp. 80-85.

relations only with his tenants-in-chief. From them, the payments known as the aids were, in theory, voluntary gifts to the overlord on certain exceptional occasions when he was in special need of money— ransoming his body when taken captive in war, the knighting of his eldest son, and the first marriage of his eldest daughter. If an aid were to be taken upon any other occasion, the consent of the vassals must be expressly given.[1] When the king was able to take such unusual aids with some frequency and regularity, their original character was passing away and they were approximating taxation. This change can be clearly seen in the thirteenth century, but the limited number who could be concerned in the aid prevented its becoming the germ of any form of national tax.

From his vassals the king also received a considerable revenue through the so-called "incidents" of feudal tenure, the most important of which were *relief, wardship,* and *marriage.*[2] In the reign of William

---

[1] What is said of aids or any other element, expressed or implied, in the feudal contract applies, of course, to any lord and his vassals as well as to the king and his vassals.

[2] At the death of the vassal, the possession of his holding reverted to the overlord as a result of the latter's abiding proprietorship; when the heir of the deceased vassal took possession of the land, the payment of the relief was an acknowledgment of this fact. When the heir was a minor, the lord was his guardian during minority and received more or less of the land's income during that time. The lord must have a voice in disposing of the hand of an heiress in marriage, as her husband would become his vassal. She was often given to the highest bidder. It is not always easy to distinguish exactly between the normal and necessary use and the abuse of these incidents. Although their true propriety had long before passed from them, they and other minor incidents remained as a source of revenue until the abolishing of feudal tenures in the reign of Charles II.

II., came the well-known abuse of those incidents, but it should be remembered that much was done at that time in the way of developing and determining them. While for a long time valuable to the king and to every feudal overlord as a source of revenue, they had no element of taxation in them; they were incidental to a special form of private contract. But these contracts served the state in a really public manner when they supplied an army. That this was recognised is shown by article eleven of Henry I.'s coronation charter: "To those knights who hold their land by the cuirass, I yield of my own gift the lands of their demense ploughs free from all payments and from all labour, so that as they have thus been favoured by such a great alleviation, so they may readily provide themselves with horses and arms for my service and the defence of my kingdom."[1] It was felt in Henry I.'s days that the prelates who held from the king by barony, but who, owing to their ecclesiastical character, might not serve personally in the field, should make a payment of money instead. This was the origin of *scutage*, or shield-money. It was the commutation of a service owed on the basis of private contract; but Henry I. was so much a sovereign as well as suzerain that, as in the article of his charter just quoted, one feels that the public character of the service provided for in this private manner was being much emphasised. This was still more the case in Henry II.'s reign, when scutage was extended to laymen and became a system for commuting personal service that the sovereign manipulated much to suit himself, and from which he derived much money for

[1] A. and S., p. 6.

hiring mercenaries on the continent. In the hands of John, it became so regular and frequent a levy that we can no longer think of it as a commutation of anything private or public; it had become a tax. But as was the case with the feudal aids, scutage concerned a class of men rather than a kind of property, and hence, in the fading out of feudal distinctions in the late thirteenth century, it came to an end.

A source of revenue that has the appearance of a tax was the tallage levied upon his boroughs by the king; but, as has been shown, this seems to have had its root in two continental conceptions: one, that a lord had the right, on occasion, to take something arbitrarily from the property of his unfree tenants; the other, that the citizens of a municipality were unfree.[1] The king tallaged his boroughs as a lord of tenants, not as king; hence he tallaged only those on the royal demesne. Other lords could tallage their boroughs; but it finally became an established practice that they should tallage only when the king did. Here again, it was only a class that was reached, and that in a private rather than a public way. Tallage practically ceased in the fourteenth century. Thus for long after the Norman Conquest there was no system of national taxation and no conception of taxation, in any proper sense of the word. The king had various sources of revenue. It goes without saying that, as in the case of Danegeld, the Norman kings retained any important means of supply that had attached to Anglo-Saxon kingship. As a matter of fact, the Danegeld was a tax, but it had been the offspring of accidental necessity

[1] See above, pp. 96, 97. The term tallage was not applied to this payment until the reign of Henry II.

and had been retained, as any source of revenue, however originated, was always retained.[1]   An actual tax had preceded any idea of taxation.   Generally speaking, throughout the twelfth century, the king "lived of his own."

6.   **The Church.**—The effects of the Norman Conquest upon the English church were many and fundamental. It not only brought the primitive, insular church into vital touch with continental conditions, but it did this at a time when centralising tendencies, the exaltation of the papacy, separation of church and state, and the strengthening of the former at the expense of the latter were the ruling influences at Rome and at many important ecclesiastical centres.   The Cluniac movement had reached its height and was soon to be surpassed by the Hildebrandine principles, which, carried to their logical conclusions, would have made Europe a theocracy.   Hildebrand had not become Gregory VII. in 1066,[2] but was, and had been for some years, the most influential individual in the Roman *curia*. It was a time of unprecedented opportunity for the growth of papal influence in Europe, and Hildebrand knew how to take wonderful advantage of it.   In

[1] The Danegeld, under that name, ceased early in Henry II.'s reign, but something corresponding to it was levied occasionally throughout his life.   In 1194, a new basis of assessment for the land tax came into use; the *carucate*, or 100 acres of ploughland, took the place of the hide, which had become an ill-understood and antiquated unit.   The tax levied on the carucate was known as *carucage*.   It was destined to a brief existence, coming to an end under Henry III.   The origin of what may be properly termed national taxation will be considered in connection with the origin of parliamentary control of taxation.   See below, pp. 358–361.

[2] He became pope in 1073.

France, Spain, Hungary, Bohemia, and even Scandinavia, local conditions were most shrewdly utilised
for spreading the Cluniac reforms, and especially for
emphasising the authority of the pope—where possible,
in the concrete form of a papal overlordship of the
feudal type; where not, in any form that presented
itself.[1]

Most significant at just this time were the papal
relations with the Normans who were establishing
themselves in southern Italy.   In 1059, Pope Nicholas
II. granted to Robert Guiscard the title of duke of
Apulia and Calabria, but on condition that Robert
do him homage and hold his dukedom of him upon
a strictly feudal basis.   In 1064, Pope Alexander II.
sent a consecrated banner to Roger, Robert Guiscard's
youngest brother, who was engaged in the conquest
of Mohammedan Sicily.   It was looked on as something in the nature of a crusade against the infidel,
and, as the conquest of Sicily had been vaguely taken
into account in the negotiations of 1059, there was an
expectation on the part of the pope of holding the whole
of south Italy and Sicily, the future kingdom of Naples
or the two Sicilies, as a vassal state.   Here were Norman adventurers who won for themselves a powerful
state, with no shadow of legal right save what may be
thought derivable from papal grant and sanction, and
who then became vassals of the church.   There was
a certain propriety in the fact that Norman rulers were
coming into this personal relation with the papacy,
for Normandy stood for very advanced ideas in church
reform; its monastery of Bec was known throughout
Europe as a sort of second Cluny.   When, therefore,

[1] See Stephens, *Hildebrand and his Times*, ch. viii.

at this very time, the duke of Normandy proposed to conquer England, a country over whose church the papacy had almost no control and from whose chief archbishopric the Norman Robert of Jumièges had been recently and uncanonically driven, it is no wonder that Hildebrand was interested, and regarded William's undertaking as a parallel on a grander scale of that of the Norman Roger in Sicily.

The word Crusade was not yet heard in the Christian world, nor was it to be heard till near thirty years later when Peter the Hermit at the Council of Clermont was to utter his fiery declamation against unbelievers; but a virtual crusade was preached against Harold and his adherents, and all Europe knew that when William's shipbuilding should be ended and he should be ready to sail, his troops would march to battle under the protection of a banner consecrated by the successor of St. Peter.[1]

One of William's chief advisers and his closest friend was the great Lanfranc, who had been made prior of the abbey of Bec in 1045 and was later abbot of a great monastery in Caen, and was thus identified with the most advanced continental thought on church reform. Lanfranc had also been for many years famous as a theologian. His relations with William increased the pope's expectations of church reform in England. But the expectations did not stop with reform. Why should not the Norman kingdom in England follow the example of the Norman dukedom in Italy, and guarantee its continued co-operation with the pope by the close, vassal relation?

[1] Hodgkin, *The History of England from the Earliest Times to the Norman Conquest*, p. 476.

We have now to consider William's attitude, after the Conquest, towards the pope and towards the English church, and how the changes necessarily wrought in the church by the influx of continental ideas affected its relations to the state. William had been very willing to profit by the moral support and the prestige which the pope's patronage had lent his undertaking, but he did not intend to allow the pope to gain any hold over England that would at all diminish his own power. His policy was like that of his ancestors in Normandy, who had favoured a pure and vigorous church and under whom Normandy had become prominently identified with church reform, but who had been masters of everything in their duchy. About 1076, the demand, which must have been expected,[1] came from Hildebrand, now Gregory VII. It was that William should do homage to the pope for England. The papal legate, who brought this demand, bore also the request that the old English payment to the pope, known as Peter's Pence, be more diligently collected and sent. William readily acceded to the latter, but to the demand that he become the pope's vassal for England, he replied that he had never promised it, and that his predecessors in England had never entered into any such relation with former popes.

William's specific policy with respect to the church

[1] "It is quite within the limits of possibility that, in his negotiating with Rome before his invasion of England, William may have given the pope to understand, in some indefinite and informal way, that if he won the kingdom, he would hold it of St. Peter. In accepting the consecrated banner which the pope had sent him, he could hardly fail to know that he might be understood to be acknowledging a feudal dependence."—Adams, *The History of England* (1066–1216), p. 49. See *ibid.*, pp. 38–50 for an excellent general account of the effect of the Conquest upon the English church.

in England is stated in the well-known rules that have generally been ascribed to him. He would allow no one in his kingdom to acknowledge a pope as true pope except upon his authority [1]; no letters were to be received from the pope that he had not first seen; the national synod of the church was neither to enact nor prohibit anything which was not in accord with his will; no bishop could excommunicate or bring to trial any of the king's barons or ministers except at his command. Whether these rules were formulated by William or the chronicler who recorded them, there is reason to believe that they represent William's purpose and practice. Their enforcement meant royal oversight of the relations between England and Rome and a strict royal control of internal church polity. This clear-cut, masterful attitude of the Conqueror undoubtedly had an influence upon the relations of church and state in England at many later times, and worked itself into the English tradition that shared in producing the important anti-papal legislation of the fourteenth century.[2]

Of the changes necessarily wrought in the English

[1] In a time of frequent anti-popes, and when the attitude of a country towards claimants of the papal office might have many political bearings, this was a necessary principle for a sovereign who would really rule.

[2] Why Gregory VII., who must have been offended at what he probably considered William's ingratitude and bad faith, never used coercive measures in order to gain from the conquest of England the advantages which he had looked for, is an interesting question. The answer probably lies in the greater importance the contest with the Emperor must have had in the eyes of a pope of that period; and the practical difficulty of dealing with so distant a country as England, filled with the traditions of an independent church and having such a self-willed sovereign as the Conqueror, must have been great.

8

church by the Conquest, enough can be seen in the early post-conquest period to make clear the general character of the continental influence; but it created some conditions, the results of which to church and state showed themselves very gradually. The old problem of the relations of the two English archbishops [1] faced Lanfranc as soon as he became archbishop of Canterbury. While his authority was questioned in the province of York, he could not carry out the thorough-going reorganisation and reform which seemed to him imperative. That province coincided roughly with the old Danelaw, the part of England that, under Edwin and Morcar, had held aloof from Harold, and was the hardest for William to subdue. It threatened the unity and good government of the church as well as the state. William naturally favoured the claim of Canterbury; the question was referred to Pope Alexander II., who, however, refused to decide and referred it back to an English council. In 1072, a council was held that judged unequivocally for Canterbury. As the decision was based on historical grounds and much documentary proof was adduced, it seems likely that it was intended to be final.[2] Though this was far from the case, it is important to note here that it settled the matter for Lanfranc's lifetime [3]

[1] See above, p. 65, note 1.

[2] The documents were, for the most part, forgeries by Lanfranc. See Adams, *The History of England* (1066–1216), p. 44, and Böhmer, *Die Fälschungen Erzbischof Lanfranks von Canterbury*, cited by Professor Adams.

[3] It was again violently disputed in the reign of Henry I. In 1127, the real matter at issue was dodged by the archbishop of Canterbury's applying for, and receiving, the office of papal legate, on the basis of which he could exercise authority over the archbishop of York. This proved the final, though logically unsatis-

and gave him the coveted opportunity to deal with the church as a whole.

As Norman barons were given the lands of Saxon earls and thegns, so Norman prelates filled the vacancies in the English church, and many vacancies were made for them. During the first three or four years after the Conquest, the church was left quite undisturbed; here as elsewhere it was William's disposition to let things remain. But it became increasingly clear to him and to Lanfranc that a general overhauling of the church was necessary. Probably they did not at first realise how serious were the differences between the English church and that which they had always known; its ignorance and its married clergy must have surprised them as much as its archaic customs and its isolation. About Easter of 1070 a council met at which three papal legates were present. The removal of Stigand, archbishop of Canterbury, whose irregular supersession of Robert of Jumièges had helped win the pope to the support of William, was its first work. From this beginning, the process of displacement and filling of vacancies went on rapidly until, at the end of the year, only two or three English bishops were left. While the reign of William covered the period of the great conflict between Gregory VII. and the Emperor Henry IV. over the manner of investing prelates, William did not abate in the least his participation in the ceremony. With this wholesale creation of Norman bishops and the consecration

factory, solution of the problem; for in 1221, Stephen Langton, archbishop of Canterbury, succeeded in establishing it as a principal that the office which he held necessarily carried with it the legatine power, and that an archbishop of Canterbury was papal legate from the moment of the pope's confirmation of his election.

of Lanfranc as archbishop of Canterbury in August of the same year, the transformation of the English church was well under way.

In the early years of William's reign, as in the Anglo-Saxon period, it is hard to distinguish a general synod of the church from a state council. There seems to have been one important trait, however, that marked off the early Norman from the Anglo-Saxon synod; whereas it was summoned by the king, and barons as well as clergy were present, the final decision in church matters lay with the clergy alone. The church made its own laws. In the course of time this real legislative independence reflected itself in the personnel of the legislative body and the synods were attended by clergy only.[1] While this change was taking place, there was being created the practically new diocesan synod. This was a democratic assembly of the clergy of the diocese. It was very important at a later time in connection with the origin of the representative system in Convocation.[2]

About 1070, came William's famous edict separating the lay and ecclesiastical jurisdictions; the bishop ceased to be a necessary member of the shire court, and thereafter any one who was to be "impleaded by the episcopal laws for any cause or crime" was to go to the bishop's court.[3] Perhaps this was the most

[1] Adams, *The History of England* (1066–1216) pp. 44, 45. It is interesting to note, in view of later history, that under Henry I. the archbishop of Canterbury began to hold his provincial assembly at the same time that the king held his court. See below, p. 338.

[2] See below, p. 332.

[3] A. and S., document 1. Just what was done here and its relation to later judicial history will be discussed in Part III., § I., 5.

striking and sudden introduction of continental practice. But changes were appearing rapidly. When
the new bishops and abbots received their endowments
of land, it was made clear in each case that a part of
the land was held as a barony; that is, the bishop or
abbot held land as a vassal of the king, and the number
of knights owed from each allotment was fixed. [1] Thus
the English prelates came to have the two clearly distinguishable sides, the feudal and the ecclesiastical, that
one usually associates with the medieval clergy. The
new bishops also conformed to continental practice
in the matter of residence. The rural seats were
abandoned and the bishops lived in the largest towns
in their dioceses. The urban seats required more
attending clergy, and a development and better
organisation of the cathedral chapters resulted. The
new bishops moved about less and came in less personal
contact with the people of their dioceses, a change
that came naturally from their continental training
and baronial rank.

The effect of the Conquest on the parish priests was
marked, though more gradual. The marriage of
priests was common before the Conquest, notwithstanding some attempts at reform in the time of
Dunstan; and the ordination of the sons of priests,
a dangerous abuse, looking as it did towards the
formation of a clerical caste, was not uncommon.
Celibacy of the clergy was a leading principle in the
Cluniac programme. Far-sighted church reformers
saw that the transmission of church property by
heredity and the building up of family interests among
the clergy would militate against the undivided

[1] See A. and S., document 5.

devotion to the church and the centralisation under the pope for which they were working. This might seem, then, a natural place for Lanfranc to begin his reforms and push them with vigour. But he was very shrewd and moderate in his dealings with the lower clergy. By ruling that for the future no priests should marry and no married clerks be ordained, he accomplished his end slowly and without upheaval. The Conquest unquestionably resulted in bringing the lower clergy under better order and control.

In all countries where the reform movements had taken deep root it had frequently come to pass that the right to present to the parish church was vested in some neighbouring monastery; usually one of the monks received ordination for this purpose, and the church in question was said to be "reformed." In this way, the monastery gained a control over the income of the living and over the incumbent that was very complete. This undermined the power of the bishop and tended to make the priesthood the servant of the monasteries. It was part of the long conflict between the secular and regular clergy, in which the latter, whose interests were always identified with centralisation and the papacy, were strengthened by every monastic revival. In England, lay patronage had been almost universal before the Conquest, although a few parishes had been "reformed." After the Conquest, many lay patrons, with their continental penchant for making pious gifts to monasteries, parted with their rights of patronage. This and the general effect of continental ideas upon the church depressed somewhat the status of the parish priest, who, before the Conquest, ranked with the thegn in the social scale. From this beginning lay patronage suffered many invasions in the following centuries when the national character of the English church was being seriously attacked by powerful and ambitious popes.

The reform movements that were affecting the whole Christian church had had their source and inspiration in monasticism. So quite naturally the English monasteries underwent a great change and renewing of life after the Conquest. The appointment of abbots from the continent who brought in the new standards of monastic life, the struggle of the monasteries to free themselves from episcopal control, and the founding of colonies of the great Cluniac "Congregation" were important immediate changes. But England was now open to all continental developments; one after another, the new monastic orders of the twelfth and thirteenth centuries were introduced and most of them grew vigorously.

In general the Conquest incorporated England closely . . . with that organic whole of life and achievement which we call Christendom. This was not more true of the ecclesiastical side of things than of the political or constitutional. But the church of the eleventh century included within itself relatively many more than the church of to-day of those activities which quickly respond to a new stimulus and reveal a new life by increased production.[1]

[1] Adams, *The History of England* (1066–1216), p. 47.

PART III

The Period of Constitution Making

1100–1485

SECTION I

THE MAKING OF THE JUDICIARY

THE last four centuries of the middle ages were the period of the most rapid and important creation in the history of the English constitution. Following a period distinctly introductory in character and succeeded by a time of confirmation and gradual development, there were in these centuries sketched out in the rough all the main features of England's judicial, legislative, and, with one important exception, administrative systems.[1] In studying these centuries, then, one is interested in watching the rapid and virile growth of a set of institutions destined to be of the greatest value to the world; in succeeding periods, he sees the same institutions, constantly perfecting, suiting themselves to later and more complex conditions, and successfully passing through crises that proved their abiding value and capacity for adaptation.

Although in studying the growth of institutions it is impossible to make use of chronological divisions that approach exactness, yet it may be said that the great work of the twelfth century was shaping the main features of England's judicial system, though much of importance was left for the thirteenth and even

[1] Even the exception, the system of cabinet government, was clearly foreshadowed in the fifteenthc entury. See below, pp. 294, 296, 297.

later centuries[1]; with the same caution, we may
identify the thirteenth and fourteenth centuries with
the creation of the legislative system[2]; and during
the latter period, the conception of a strictly limited
executive power was evolving and taking firm hold
of the minds of the English people. Thus we study
in these centuries the making of the English constitution in its three parts, judiciary, executive, and
legislature. These are to be considered in the order
named.

**1. Origin and Early Development of the Three Central,
Common-Law Courts and the Circuit Court System.—**
As soon as the early disorder and upheaval resulting
from the Norman Conquest had subsided, some
attempts were made to bridge the gap between central
and local government that lasted on from Anglo-
Saxon times. Kings who had a conquered country
before them, who felt their strength, would not be
long in finding occasion to interfere in and modify
the local institutions. William II. brutally and directly
seized wealth and power. Neither he nor his famous
minister was a statesman, and, although they accomplished some things of permanent importance in their
application of feudal principles to the church and
in developing the details of feudal obligation,[3] their
expedients, for the most part, appear gross and tempor-

[1] "Of all centuries the twelfth is the most legal.   In no other age,
since the classical days of the Roman law, has so large a part of the
sum total of intellectual endeavour been devoted to jurisprudence."
—P. and M. i., 111.

[2] "In the natural course of all constitutional history the judicial
precedes the legislative."—Shirley, Preface to *Royal Letters* [Rolls
Series] ii., p. xviii.

[3] See above, p. 89.

ary. A king and a minister of a different sort followed them. The combined work of Henry I. and Roger of Salisbury, his justiciar, was the foundation of the constitution. Their aim was the orderly, peaceful, and efficient government of the whole country and the strengthening and aggrandising of the central power.

The king had more and more work to do and the king acted officially through the Curia Regis. Hence this feudal court felt keenly the pressure of business. In the earlier reigns, it had been a comparatively simple and undifferentiated body, but as it had more work to do it developed rapidly. This development was the institutional manifestation of the increasing activity and effectiveness of the central government, and was along four main lines that may be briefly summarised. There was a more adequate organisation for transacting the king's business throughout the year; the smaller Curia Regis was made a more efficient and regular working body.[1] A classification of business, that had probably begun in the preceding reigns, was brought to a state of some maturity and efficiency; twice a year the smaller Curia sat for financial business and received the revenues that were brought from the counties by the sheriffs; the Exchequer was in embryo.[2] For the purpose of giving better attention to the king's interests in the localities the Curia Regis became itinerant; certain members were sent out upon

[1] See above, pp. 102, 103.

[2] The primitive Curia Regis transacted any kind of king's business just as it happened to come up. Pressure of work taught it the economy of time and labour in doing all of one kind at one time. Financial business was the first so classified. For an account of the organisation of the Exchequer in the reign of Henry I, see Adams, *The History of England* (1066–1216), pp. 184–186.

circuits, or "iters," that they might from close, personal inspection accomplish what they could not from a distance. The judicial work of the court began to extend beyond cases in which the king was personally concerned, and limitless possibilities of judicial growth were opened when cases between man and man began to be entertained. The two last-named developments require further discussion here.

The practice of sending members of the Curia Regis into the localities to transact the king's business was fitful and uncertain at first and was used only when there was something exceptional to be attended to; but before the end of the reign it had become an established custom.[1] The things that these itinerant members did were the same in purpose as those done by the central body; they looked after wardships and escheated property, inspected arms, took oaths of fidelity to the king, saw whether any one had left the kingdom or built a new castle, saw that the king had his rights in such judicial matters as he might be concerned in, attended to all matters touching the royal revenue—in short, they did all the royal business that they were instructed to do when they were sent out. As it has been aptly expressed, they carried the Curia Regis down into the locality and did a little branch business there. They remind one strongly of Charlemagne's *missi*, and though they were probably not institutionally derived from these, the same general causes brought them forth. Charlemagne was suspicious of the loyalty and efficiency of his counts and the *missi* were designed to check and supplement the

[1] There were occasional instances of this practice in the earlier Norman reigns and even before the Conquest.

counts' work. Henry I. was suspicious of the sheriffs, and in the English *missi* were the means by which the sheriffs' shortcomings might be made known and remedied. These king's messengers were erelong known as itinerant justices, but the word justice must not be understood to signify any exclusively judicial function. It was nearly two centuries before that was the case. The itinerant justices might be sent out in Henry I.'s reign on purely judicial business, and toward the end of the reign were probably so sent with some regularity; but their more normal work was of a general administrative sort. Their increasing judicial business however leads us to inquire about the judicial development of the body of which they were members.

The judicial work of either the Saxon witan or the early Norman Curia Regis was small; it was confined to "great men and great causes." The Curia Regis, as the king's feudal court, was where his tenants-in-chief were tried. But many cases in which the property rights of the king were more or less directly concerned would come up for trial in the local courts. A few instances are known in which, even before the Conquest, the king sent a representative into a local court or imposed his order upon that court to the end that a matter in which he was involved might be speedily and satisfactorily concluded. After the Conquest, this royal interference became more frequent. It was natural that it should, with the stronger king and the continental idea that the king was the source of law. Logically the next step in extending this kind of interference would be to draw the case entirely out of the local court and try it in the king's court, or what was virtually the king's court owing to the presence and influence of the king's representatives. And so, as we have seen, itinerant members of the Curia Regis might be sent to perambulate a district trying royal pleas.[1] For the better prosecution of all their work, but especially the judicial, the itinerant justices probably had the counties before them in specially full meetings of the county courts.

But the king might become interested in a case owing to the position or influence of one of the parties, and where he had no property concern whatever. The plaintiff, despairing of speedy or satisfactory justice in the local court, might be in a position to secure royal interference. The king was restrained by few theories regarding the boundaries of jurisdiction. He was the source of law and he was strong, and he would interfere where there seemed to him good reason for doing so. As such interference became more frequent, the payment of a sum of money by the plaintiff became the commonest means of securing it. When the intervention had been purchased, the king sent an order to the defendant bidding him right the supposed wrong. If this order were disobeyed, the natural result was the bringing of the defendant before the king's court to show cause. This amounted to evoking the case from the local court, where it would ordinarily have been tried, into the king's court. The commoner such a practice became, the less likely was the defendant to be awed by the royal command, which thus became the first step in a regular procedure. The royal order, being formal and important, was written. Hence it was called a writ, a name which, up

[1] See A. and S., documents 2 and 6.

to that time, had borne no special legal sense. The cases that were being thus dealt with were civil cases and so the rule became established that every civil case tried in the king's courts must originate with a writ. [1]

With the opening of such a possibility as this, men would try to get their cases into the king's court if there were any regular advantage to be derived from the change. There was an advantage in the better law and better methods employed there. The ancient procedure retained in the local courts was clumsy and inflexible; owing to its punctilious formalism, it often failed to render justice and was not fitted to meet the rapidly changing conditions which followed the Conquest. The king's court began to supply what was essentially an equitable jurisdiction; it was employing a law that was free from the trammels of the old formalism and was rendering justice by the most direct means possible. It was a court composed of Frenchmen, where the French language was used; but it did not simply transfer French or Norman law to England. It made use of any principles, French or English, which best suited its need, and it did not hesitate to strike out upon new lines. [2] But men who

---

[1] For a primitive writ belonging to the reign of Henry I., see A. and S., document 9.

[2] "Of the law that this court administered we know little, only we may guess that in a certain sense it was equity rather than strict law. On the one hand the royal tribunal cannot have held itself straitly bound by the old English law; the men who sat in it were Frenchmen, few of whom could understand a word of English. On the other hand it must often have happened that the traditional Norman customs would not meet the facts, for a Norman count and a Norman bishop would be quarrelling over the titles of their English *antecessores*, and producing English land-books. Besides

wanted to have their cases tried in this new court had to pay for the privilege, they had to buy the originating writs. There was thus a transaction profitable to both parties. Men liked to get their cases into the king's court, for they felt surer of justice there; the king liked to have them buy the privilege, for it swelled his revenue.

The central government was in an exceedingly vigorous and promising condition at the close of Henry I.'s reign. Almost any future seemed possible for the fertile and adaptable Curia Regis. But it was a very critical point in the history of this central machinery. The system was very young and lacked

---

the king did n't mean that England should be another Normandy, he meant to have at least all the rights that his cousin and prede-cessor had enjoyed. . . ." His jurisprudence was "flexible," "occasional," "dealing with an unprecedented state of affairs, meeting new facts by new expedients, wavering as wavered the balance of power between him and his barons, capable of receiving impressions from without, influenced perhaps by Lombard learning, modern in the midst of antique surroundings. In retrospect it would appear to a man of Henry II.'s day as something so unlike the *laga Edwardi* that it must be pronounced distinctively un-English, and therefore distinctively Norman, and Norman in a sense it was. It was not a jurisprudence that had been trans-planted from Normandy; but it had been developed by a court composed of Frenchmen to meet cases in which Frenchmen were concerned; the language in which men spoke it was French, and in the end so far as it dealt with merely private rights, it would closely resemble a French *coutume*."—P. and M. i., 107–108.

"Among the most permanent and momentous effects of that great event " (the Norman Conquest) " was its effect on the language of English lawyers, for it is not a small thing that a law-book produced in the England of the thirteenth century will look very like some statement of a French *coutume* and utterly unlike the Sachsenspiegel, nor is it a small thing that in much later days such foreign influences as will touch our English law will always be much rather French than German."—*Ibid.* i., 87.

the hard and fast qualities of one of long standing, well
known and taken for granted by the people. It still
required the guiding and sustaining of those who had
made it. When these were suddenly withdrawn by
Henry's death and his successor's ill-advised quarrel
with the administrative family, and the country
experienced a long period of civil war and general
anarchy, the promising governmental beginnings passed
away. That Henry II. had a genius for government,
that he came to the throne while his grandfather's
system was still easily remembered, and that he
himself had been trained to understand and appre-
ciate it, were vitally important conditions of England's
later institutional growth, especially along judicial lines.

Henry II. was a born lawyer, and his reign stands pre-
eminent in the legal history of England. When he came
to the throne he saw lawlessness everywhere. His
ambition, like that of the Norman kings, was to gain
for himself the substance of power, to really rule
England. The first step was to bring the lawlessness
to an end. He did not legislate upon any large scale;
the creation of new law came in a more incidental
and unconscious way. To his mind, new law was not
needed so much as the enforcement of the old. But
he found the old judicial machinery inadequate for
the kind of enforcement that he proposed; it was not
indeed sufficient to renew that of his grandfather's
time. Henry II.'s great work was the devising of
new methods to meet practical judicial exigencies,
and for this he displayed a genius that has perhaps
never been surpassed. So permanent and fundamental
did his new schemes for enforcing the law prove that
they profoundly affected the body of the law itself,

and what is most characteristic in English law and procedure either originated or was in some way foreshadowed in his reign.

Henry II.'s work has been tersely summarised thus: "The whole of English law is centralised and unified by the institution of a permanent court of professional judges, by the frequent mission of itinerant judges throughout the land, by the introduction of the 'inquest' or 'recognition' and original writ as normal parts of the machinery of justice."[1] The discussion of this work may be introduced by briefly describing, in chronological order (as far as that is known), Henry's chief judicial innovations. In the Constitutions of Clarendon,[2] 1164, we find a method of determining whether a certain piece of land, about which there was some litigation pending between an ecclesiastic and a layman, was a lay holding or an ecclesiastical holding, or, in the technical language of the time, whether it was lay fee or alms. If the latter, the case was to be tried in the church court; if the former, in the king's court. Hence the preliminary question was one of importance and Henry ordained that it should be determined by putting on oath twelve men of the locality where the land lay and causing them to state whether it was lay fee or alms. But this question might frequently arise when it was preliminary to no further question about the land, and this method of determining it developed into a regular action in the royal courts, known as the assize *utrum*. It became the normal action, touching the proprietorship of land, in use by parish priests. There is some evidence that before Henry's time the same method had been

[1] P. and M. i., p. 138.   [2] A. and S., document 13.

occasionally used, but he made it normal. In the Constitutions of Clarendon, Henry also claimed successfully for the royal courts cases involving the right to present to churches, debt cases, and the punishment of criminous clerks who had been tried and convicted in the church courts.

Two years later, he created an action far more important than the assize *utrum*. In the disorderly state of society produced by the preceding reign, violent and unjust disseisins were common; men were thrust out of the seisin or possession of their lands by the strong hand and left to the doubtful and dilatory justice of the old courts to recover it. To remove this abuse and bring order into society, Henry determined to protect possession, as such, by a summary process in his own court. Suppose *A* had been recently turned out of land, of which he had been in possession, by *B*. *A* could now obtain a writ from the king ordering his justices to summon twelve men of the locality where the disseisin had taken place, put them on oath, and ask them this question: Did *B* at such a time disseize *A* of such a holding? If the answer was in the affirmative, *A* was restored to his possession. To be sure, *B* may have had a better right to the land notwithstanding *A's* possession of it, but this must be shown in the courts and a judgment obtained. It was Henry's purpose to have no more people turned out of their land except on the basis of judgment regularly rendered in court. This new process was known as the assize of *novel disseisin*. Old disseisins could not well be taken account of; an arbitrary date was fixed, all disseisins anterior to which were not considered *novel*. The assize of *novel disseisin* was a possessory assize, which means that it dealt only with the question of possession, not with the question of right. This was the first of the three famous possessory assizes created by Henry. In the document known as the Assize of Northampton,[1] 1176, is found the first intimation of the assize of *mort d'ancestor* (death of the ancestor). The design of this assize was to protect heirs, to prevent violent and unlawful confiscations by overlords or others upon the death of a property holder. The principle contained is this: if a man died possessed of real estate and some one claimed that he had had a better right to the property than the dead man, he could not prevent the latter's heir from taking possession until he had received a judgment in his favour by regular legal process. The question of fact, whether the ancestor died in possession of the property, was answered by the statement under oath of twelve men of the locality. The third possessory assize had to do with the presentation of clergymen to livings. Such presentation was known as advowson. If a question arose as to which of two persons possessed the advowson of a certain church, twelve men of the locality were summoned and put on oath to tell who presented to this church last, and he who had done so was given the privilege of presenting this time. But the claim might be made that, although he did present the last time, he had had no right to. In that case, remedy might be sought in the king's court; but the determination of a question of best right was always likely to be a long process, and, in the meantime, the church must neither be kept vacant nor he who possessed the advowson, in virtue of his

[1] A. and S., document 16, article 4.

having made the last presentment, be turned out of his possession. The new action in the king's court by which the possession of the advowson was determined was known as the assize of *darrein* (last) *presentment*.[1]

Acting on this same principle of protecting possession and very likely at about the same time that the *novel disseisin* was instituted, Henry began to interfere in actions determining best right. He declared that no man could call in question a tenant's right to his free tenement without beginning his proceedings by obtaining a royal writ. This writ was known as the *writ of right*, and, although it did not necessarily bring the trial of the case into the king's court, it gave the tenant decided advantages and extended a royal procedure. The tenant had his choice between accepting the demandant's offer of the wager of battle, or, as it was termed, putting himself upon the *grand assize*.[2] By this latter mode of proof, the question at issue was determined by the sworn statements of free men of the neighbourhood taken before the king's justices. The writ *præcipe*,[3] which came into use in the same reign, marks a still further royal interference in proprietary actions. In it, the king ordered the tenant to restore the land which the

---

[1] For illustrations of the three possessory assizes, see A. and S., document 24.

[2] The word assize, originally denoting a sitting or session, was at this time rapidly assuming restricted and somewhat technical meanings. From a session of the Curia Regis, it passed to the set of decrees issued at that session, then to certain actions instituted by those decrees, and finally to the procedure by sworn inquest which was the distinguishing feature of those actions.

[3] A. and S., document 20.

demandant claimed or, if not, to appear in the king's
court "to show cause wherefore he has not done it."
Henry II. seems to have issued this writ whenever
he chose, and by this means an action which involved
the question of best right to land could be brought
bodily into the king's court. In the proprietary
actions concerning advowson, that we have seen
drawn into the royal court, the same choice was given
the possessor as in the case just considered. In these
instances, the king was getting control of, and changing,
old actions; the possessory assizes he created.

Henry II.'s third great judicial innovation was
the use in his courts of a new method of learning of
suspected criminals. The first mention of the method
in this reign was in another connection. In article
6 of the Constitutions of Clarendon, the king was correcting what he considered an abuse in the church
courts, as well as providing a means for bringing to
trial those whom individuals dared not accuse. Men
were not to be brought to trial on vague and unsub-
stantiated rumour, but if some individual were not
ready to come forward and make the accusation,
twelve freemen of the suspected man's neighbourhood
were to be put on oath before the bishop and state
their belief as to whether he ought to be tried for the
matter in question. The sheriff, at the bishop's request,
was to bring these men before him. Two years later,
in the Assize of Clarendon, [1] this machinery of accusation received its epoch-making extension. It is a
notable instance of Henry's boldness and originality
in dealing with the difficulties and disorders which
he found in the country. The problem of bringing

---

[1] A. and S., document 14.

criminals to justice had remained practically unsolved to this time, and crime of all sorts had increased with impunity in the preceding reign. With his hands freer from continental matters than at any previous time, Henry now addressed himself to this problem. His method was to make regular in his own court the already slightly used machinery for accusing suspected criminals, and to impose new and cruel punishments upon those convicted. Quick and terrible retribution was to impend over every murderer, robber, or thief, or those who harboured such. Twelve men from each hundred and four from each vill were to give information on oath, based either on their own knowledge or on common report, whether there were at that time in their localities murderers, robbers, thieves, or the receivers of them. The men thus accused were put to the old form of proof, the ordeal. The Assize of Clarendon, whose first article instituted this new procedure in the king's courts, was drawn up in view of an immediate peregrination of the justices throughout the land. But the new method of detection was not confined to the use of the justices; the sheriffs were also to use it, and, when the old shire court had declined and lost its criminal business, it became the basis of a new, but limited, criminal jurisdiction of the sheriff.[1]

In the Assize of Northampton,[2] ten years after the Assize of Clarendon, the king was still fighting crime by the same method, but forgery and arson were added to the crimes that were thus being drawn into the royal courts and the punishments were still more cruel. It should be noted here that there is a slight

---

[1] See below, pp. 170, 171.   [2] A. and S., document 16.

inaccuracy in calling the men who presented suspects accusers; they did not in a formal way accuse any one; they did not commit themselves to a belief in any one's guilt. Nor were they witnesses; they gave no testimony touching crime. They simply constituted a searching means of getting at popular report and belief; this they were under oath not to conceal, and if such report reached justice or sheriff through another channel they were liable to fine for non-fulfilment of their duty. The representatives from the vills were probably largely from the villein class; they would know the suspects of their own class and be posted on all local rumour. They reported to the twelve men of the hundred, most of whom would be knights, and the latter made what use they chose of this information in the final statement to the justices.

In this summary of Henry II.'s judicial changes, two institutions have been mentioned that require further explanation, the writ and the group of neighbours put under oath to answer questions at the royal command. A few words will suffice for the first. The general meaning of the word writ in the reign of Henry I. has already been noticed; also the fact that it had begun to have a special, legal use in connection with the written orders sent out by the king to ensure and hasten justice in cases in which he was interested. [1] In Henry II.'s reign, the writ was a well-recognised institution and began to differentiate and become technical. In each of the possessory assizes, the first step was to obtain from the king a special form of

---

[1] See above, pp. 128, 129.

writ applying only to that particular action. There were also writs suitable for opening each of the proprietary actions over which the king's court was getting control. A proprietary action for land, the commonest and most important, was begun by the writ of right or the writ *præcipe*. As actions became regular and frequent, their appropriate writs became stereotyped in form; but as new actions passed under the jurisdiction of the king's court, new writs were made to suit them, which, in the course of time, became stereotyped also. These common, regular forms of writs were known as *writs of course*. Writs were sold and became an important source of royal revenue; many people were willing to pay well for the better law and procedure of the king's court. The drawing up and issuing of writs was a difficult and important function, which, already in the twelfth century, was being assumed by the Chancellor and his staff. Every civil case tried in the royal courts originated with the purchase of the appropriate writ; hence these writs have become known as *original writs* to distinguish them from writs issued for any purpose after the actions had begun. The manufacture of new writs by the Chancery was, under a strong king, a most adaptable and efficient means of extending the royal jurisdiction.[1]

[1] "The metaphor which likens the chancery to a shop is trite; we will liken it to an armory. It contains every weapon of medieval warfare from the two-handed sword to the poniard. The man who has a quarrel with his neighbour comes thither to choose his weapon. The choice is large; but he must remember that he will not be able to change weapons in the middle of the combat and also that every weapon has its proper use and may be put to none other. If he selects a sword, he must observe the rules of sword-play; he must not try to use a cross-bow as a mace."— P. and M. ii., 561.

In this lies the great importance of the original writ in the judicial history of the twelfth and early thirteenth centuries.

The group of neighbours who gave the king information under oath will be readily recognised as a primitive jury. It is necessary here to make some inquiry into the origin and early history of the jury system. When William the Conqueror wanted to get information about some local matter, commonly something relating to the value of land as bearing on the royal revenue, he sent an official to the locality or an order to a local official to summon a number of men who would be likely to know what was wanted, put them on oath, and question them. Their answers were written down and sent to him. This process was known as *inquisitio*, which may be translated inquest or inquiry. It was thus that William gathered the vast mass of local data contained in the Domesday Book. This sworn inquest was the institutional germ out of which the modern jury and the House of Commons have grown.

It has naturally been a question of great interest whether William made use here of an institution which was Anglo-Saxon in origin or one which he brought with him from the continent. English scholars have been loath, in this, as in the case of some other institutions, to abandon a native origin. But at present no scholar denies that the jury came from the continent; William was simply continuing to use in England a machinery for getting local information which he and preceding dukes had been accustomed to use in Normandy. Like many other Norman institutions, this had been derived from the Frankish state. It is

known that the Carolingian sovereigns of the eighth
century used this method in learning about lands and
permanent rights. Between this eighth-century Frankish institution, then, and that of the first Norman king of
England there was an unbroken line of connection.

If the inquiry into origins be pushed a step further,
a difficult problem is encountered. It may be stated
to begin with that, like all Frankish institutions, the
sworn inquest was either primitively Teutonic or
else Roman in origin. All Teutonic peoples, of whose
early customs we have any considerable knowledge,
had institutions which bore a superficial resemblance
to the one under discussion. In dealing with the hundred and shire courts of the Anglo-Saxon period, three
institutions have been briefly described that must be
mentioned again here.[1] These were the suitors to the
local courts who acted as judges, the compurgators,
and the sworn witnesses. Their analogues are found
among other Teutonic peoples, and in looking for a
possible germ of the jury these institutions first
attract attention. Here were representative men of
the community, and, in both civil and criminal suits,
their neighbours' fate lay largely in their hands. Are
they not, then, like a jury? Although this is looking
at the matter in a summary and superficial way, there
is a slight element of truth in the suggestion. The
developing English jury of the thirteenth and fourteenth
centuries derived some of its sanction and spirit from
the Teutonic notion of a popular and local source of
justice, which doomsmen,[2] compurgators, and sworn

[1] See above, pp. 21, 24–26.

[2] The name given to the group of suitors who often exercised the
judging function for the whole body.

witnesses all illustrate. But this is a matter quite apart from the question of the jury's institutional origin. In returning to that, it will be useful to contrast briefly the sworn inquest of William I. with these three institutions. The suitors of the local courts were judges largely in their discretionary application of the *proofs* to the cases in hand. The compurgators were men who swore with the plaintiff or defendant, basing the oath however upon no knowledge of the facts of the case. The witnesses were brought into court to swear to a set formula, the nature of which they knew in advance. The inquest was a royal institution by which men of a locality answered upon oath questions put to them by some one acting under the royal command, and about a matter, usually relating to land and revenue, in which the king was interested. The contrast is sufficiently obvious to need no insistence. It can not, perhaps, be dogmatically denied that the early Frankish kings had adapted to their own use and developed the Frankish institution that corresponded to the Anglo-Saxon sworn witnesses, but there is no evidence to prove it. There is no possibility of the inquest's having been derived from either of the other two institutions.

There existed, however, in the later Roman empire a custom the same in all essentials as the one whose origin we are discussing. It went by the same name, *inquisitio*, was used by the central government, and for the same general purpose. For the interval between the fall of the empire and the eighth century no evidence has been found, so that it cannot be positively asserted that this was its origin; but in view of the amount of borrowing of this sort that is known to have taken place, it is more probable that the Frankish kings took the institution from Rome in just the form in which they so long used it than that they made over a practice of the native, local courts into an instrument of central power.

The regret which some writers have evidently felt at having to abandon an Anglo-Saxon, and even a Teutonic, origin for the jury seems uncalled for when the matter is properly considered. The sworn inquest was an existing institution which English kings, courts, and people chanced to seize upon, and which, in the course of centuries and through many unforeseen influences, they made over into something that was in many important respects radically different. The primitive inquest was a piece of administrative machinery which had nothing to do with a court system, central or local; throughout its known history, it had been an instrument of royal power, and probably often, as in the hands of William the Conqueror, of royal oppression. The matured judicial jury has done its service and won its renown in safeguarding the liberties of the people from the encroachments of monarchy; while the jury as developed into the House of Commons has become the mainspring of the English constitutional system. On the continent, the sworn inquest had no such development. From Charlemagne to William the Conqueror, it had remained almost unchanged, and everything which has since made it a notable or admirable institution it has gained on English soil.

There was little change in the inquest until the reign of Henry II. William I. and succeeding kings had occasionally used it in connection with judicial

matters,[1] but there was no regularity or special purpose
in such use; if the king were interested in a certain
case and wanted to get the facts involved, he would
use this method, just as in other subjects of local inquiry.
When Henry II. made use of it in determining whether
a disputed holding were free alms or lay fee, he was
not applying it to a new subject matter; but when this
preliminary procedure in the king's court grew into the
assize *utrum*, this royal method of ascertaining the
truth necessarily became the most important part of
the procedure in the new action. The same thing
was true of the other new actions of this reign; and,
in the old actions that were drawn into the king's
court, the jury trial became optional with one or both
parties to the suit. It became quite naturally the
normal method of trial in civil cases in the king's court,
superseding the old proofs.

The jury of accusation, however, the jury which
presented suspected murderers, robbers, and thieves,
seems something new, for it did not answer the old
questions about property or revenue; it was essentially
the same machinery, but employed upon a different
subject-matter. It was not however new, for, though
not the normal use of the inquest, the Frankish kings
of the ninth century had employed the sworn statements of men in the localities to find out about delin-
quent officials or serious crimes, matters that threatened
the country's peace. A use of the inquest similar
to this had, at some time, passed into the Frankish
church, probably by royal grant; and, in certain places,
this so-called synodal jury had become a well-known
institution. There is no conclusive evidence, however,

[1] For an early example, see A. and S., document 2.

that an accusing jury had existed in either England
or Normandy before the time of Henry II.[1] In the
Constitutions of Clarendon, is a provision which suggests an accusing jury for cases in the church courts
where "the accused be such that no one will or dares
to accuse them." A similar provision, applying to the
Norman church, had been made in 1159. In these
instances, Henry was probably reviving a custom that
had fallen into disuse. The great thing that he did
in the Assize of Clarendon was to incorporate this
decadent piece of procedure in his own rapidly growing
court.[2] Since then, there has always been in the
English court system a jury for presenting criminals;
it was the foundation of the modern grand jury.

There were thus in the reign of Henry II. three clearly
distinguishable uses of the jury: the old, non-judicial
use, in which the king employed the sworn inquest

[1] Regarding the famous and anomalous case of the twelve senior
thegns in the reign of Ethelred II., Maitland says: "There is however
one law that must cause some difficulty. It is a law of Ethelred
the Unready, published, so it would seem, in the year 997 and
applicable only to the Danish district. In it we hear how a moot
is to be held in every wapentake, and how the twelve eldest thegns
are to go out with the reeve and to swear upon the relic that he puts
into their hands that they will accuse no innocent and conceal
no guilty man. Certainly this looks like a jury of accusation; but
the context will make us doubt whether we have here a law of any
generality. There seem however to be good reasons for believing
that some of the Scandinavian nations came by a route of their own
to something that was very like the jury. . . . We cannot say *a priori* that there is only one possible origin for the jury,
we cannot even say that England was unprepared for the introduction of this institution; but that the Norman duke brought it
with him as one of his prerogatives can hardly be disputed."—
P. and M. i., 142, 143.

[2] A suggestion of what lead Henry to do this and what gave
his machinery of accusation its particular form will be found
below, pp. 169, 170.

to get local information; the trial jury in the civil cases which the king was drawing into his courts; the accusing jury. This reign may be regarded as the starting point of the history of the judicial jury in England. Two main changes or developments which appeared soon afterwards have left the institution substantially as it exists to-day. The first of these was the evolution of the trial jury in criminal cases; the second, the process by which trial juries became judges of fact capable of protecting the liberty of the people. The need of a jury to try criminals was distinctly felt in Henry II.'s reign. When accusing juries presented murderers and others suspected of serious crimes before the royal courts, the king found himself unwilling to abide wholly by the result of the old form of proof, the ordeal. His object was to rid the country of criminals and he did not propose to be deterred by an antique procedure which shifted the responsibility of finding the truth from man to God.[1]   After ten years' experience in dealing with criminals in his courts, Henry instructed his justices in these words:

And if he [the suspect] shall have been to the water whole he shall furnish sureties and remain in the kingdom unless he has been accused of murder or other infamous felony by the community of the county and of the lawful knights of the country, of which if he has been accused in the said manner, although he has been to the water safely, nevertheless within forty days he shall depart from the realm, and take with him his chattels saving the rights of his lords, and at the mercy of the lord king he shall abjure the realm.[2]

[1] See above, p. 26
[2] A. and S., p. 21.   See also article 14 of the Assize of Clarendon.

This not only shows dissatisfaction with the ordeal, but gives a hint of what may in time take its place; it was because a man's neighbours believed in his guilt that he was to be banished; and, when neighbours were regularly and formally summoned to state the facts, the trial jury in criminal cases was existent.

It is impossible to give a detailed, chronological account of how the new procedure grew. Our knowledge of how criminal actions were conducted in the late twelfth and early thirteenth centuries is scanty. But this was pre-eminently the time of jury growth; the simple but adaptable inquest machinery was being used by the king for very many purposes, and it would have been strange if some form of it had not finally met the new want which was being felt in the criminal procedure. For a long time, there was no conscious creating of a new form of jury, but a tentative use of one or more of the old forms. The presenting juries of the townships have already been mentioned; it early seemed that such juries from the four townships adjacent to the scene of the crime would be a fit body to traverse the presentment which perhaps they had already had their share in making. The duties and methods of a new local official, the coroner,[1] may have furthered, perhaps suggested, this practice. The coroner early ceased to be a justice, even in petty cases, but his right to empanel a jury remained a relic of his original and higher position. He became a keeper of the pleas of the crown,[2] by which was meant that

---

[1] See below, pp. 187–190.

[2] The idea of crown pleas appears for the first time with any distinctness in the reign of Cnute. A small number of serious cases was reserved for the king, but it is hard to find a principle upon which the choice was made, except, perhaps, a consideration of

he held preliminary inquiries and kept records that were to be used later by the visiting justices. Now the juries which the coroners had used in such inquests were supposed to have made some investigation of the crimes; they would naturally have been drawn from the adjacent townships, and might be resummoned to give their information to the justices. It was also not uncommon to hold the accusing jury of the hundred to answer concerning the guilt or innocence of those whom they had presented. It was commoner, perhaps, to turn to the jury of another hundred and make it the traverse or petit jury in these cases; but as it would not be likely to know the facts, it became, during the reign of Henry III., the practice to join several juries together and regard them as one trial jury. These were often the hundred jury that had presented the criminal, the jury of some other hundred, and the juries from the four adjacent townships. Probably from very early times there was some sense of the impropriety in calling upon a man's indictors to pronounce upon his guilt or innocence. Yet it must not

---

the revenue to be gained from the fines and the limits imposed by the old conception of the king's peace. The Norman dukes also had their reserved cases. In the private and unauthorised collection of laws in Henry I.'s reign, known as the *Leges Henrici Primi*, there is a long and very heterogeneous list of crown cases, and, by the large grants of jurisdiction which they sometimes made, the Norman kings of England certainly implied that they possessed a very inclusive jurisdictional power. With the drawing of the important criminal cases into the royal court in the reign of Henry II., the idea was rapidly taking shape that these crimes, wherever and whenever committed, were breaches of the king's peace. The king's peace was becoming coterminous with the country, and all important breaches of it were crown cases. For the older conception of the king's peace, see above, pp. 30, 31, 33; for further discussion, P. and M. i., 44–46.

be forgotten that the presenting juries did little more than state popular rumour and might thus address themselves to the second duty quite disinterestedly. It was not till 1352 that a statute was passed barring a man's indictors from serving upon the jury that tried him.

The use of a second jury in criminal cases at first merely supplemented the old procedure; it served to bring out more clearly the accused's local reputation. Formally the ordeal was still the proof, but if a man came through the ordeal successfully after a jury of his neighbours had pronounced him guilty, it went hard with him. The order of the pope in 1215 that the clergy should no longer take part in the ceremony of the ordeal met an immediate and complete response in England; the ordeal disappeared forever.[1] This meant no exceptional obedience to the pope on the part of England, though the last year of John and the minority following was a time of great papal influence; but it meant that the English courts had a new and better procedure ready to put in the place of the old. It was no small thing, however, to make such a complete and conscious change at that early date, and for a long time there is evidence of the perplexities and difficulties that it cost. Although it had apparently recommended itself as a more rational method of proof, the jury was nevertheless regarded as a lower type; it was not of immemorial antiquity like the ordeal, and it rested on a purely human basis. Largely on these grounds, it appears, grew the idea that it could not

---

[1] This did not include the trial by battle, which was, in principle, a true ordeal, for the clergy had no official connection with the ceremonies attending it.

be forced upon any one as a method of proof. Except in the four recently created assizes, in which a man consciously chose jury trial when he selected his assize, parties to a civil suit had the option of a jury or one of the older forms of trial. These were compurgation or trial by battle, according to the nature of the suit. In the case of a felony in which a man was brought to trial by the appeal of some individual, the appellor offered trial by battle and the appellee might either accept it or put himself upon the country, as choosing jury trial was usually termed.[1] But when a man was indicted at the suit of the king,[2] that is, presented to the justices or the sheriff by a jury, there was no option left after the ordeal was abolished. The state was confronted by what seemed an insoluble problem; the prejudices just mentioned made it loath to force a man to put himself upon the country, and yet, if he refused to do so, there was no form of proof available. The experiment was tried, in 1221, of forcing jury trial upon notorious felons, but the completeness with which it was abandoned shows how thoroughly it ran counter to the ideas of the time. The state handled minor suspects, who refused a jury, by forcing them to give pledge or even leave the country;

[1] This option was gradually acquired during the thirteenth century.

[2] "The judges began to favour the indictment and to discourage the appeal by all possible means. They required of the accuser a punctilious observance of ancient formalities, and would quash his accusation if he were guilty of the smallest blunder. Still throughout the middle ages we occasionally hear of battles being fought over criminal cases."—Maitland in Traill's *Social England* i., 293. See further in this reference for an interesting account of the famous Abraham Thornton case in 1818 and the abolishing of trial by battle in 1819.

but it was not considered that a conviction had taken place. Thus when suspected felons refused a jury, they remained technically unconvicted and their property could not be confiscated nor their blood attainted; the consequences of their crimes could not be visited upon their heirs. There was thus a strong motive for continued refusal in instances where conviction was a foregone conclusion. In these cases pledge or exile was insufficient; the state could do nothing but keep the men in prison until they consented to put themselves upon the country. There was reason therefore for making that imprisonment as terrible as possible, and from the "strong and hard" prison of the thirteenth century there came by a natural evolution the horrible *peine forte et dure* which was not abolished until 1772. It should be understood that, in the vast majority of cases, those indicted for crime willingly accepted jury trial.

We come now to the second important matter in jury history subsequent to Henry II.'s reign. How did it come to pass that the judicial jury became in England a means of protecting the liberty of the people, while on the continent the same parent stock brought forth the canonical inquisition, an institution so opposite in character? The early thirteenth century was a critical time for the English jury; the young institution was very pliable, and the influences and circumstances of that time largely determined its whole future history. It but narrowly missed travelling the road of its continental cousin. The most prominent trait of the primitive jury, judicial or non-judicial, was its supposed or actual knowledge of the facts inquired into; and when such a jury became a regular part of judicial procedure, one is likely to think that it was nothing more than a group of witnesses and that the justices were engaged in obtaining and weighing testimony. A good many details might be collected from the early practice in favour of such a view, and if the judges had at that time been a little more inclined to deal with the jurors separately, questioning them solely on the facts of the case and keeping to themselves all discretionary or judging functions, there would have been an inquisition in England instead of a jury. But though it may be granted that the early English jury was nine-tenths witness, the one-tenth something else was very important, for it was this which received the development. It is the purpose here to inquire what this element was and why it persisted and grew.[1]

Except in the four petty assizes, where it was an original and necessary part of the procedure, the jury was at first regarded merely as one among other methods of proof. If the litigants chose it, they must abide by the result; and the court would no more have thought of inquiring into the action of the jury than of questioning or criticising compurgation. The thought of the judges was to reach a conclusion by some of the known methods of proof rather than to inquire into the processes. They deemed the jury in some respects preferable to the older proofs, but the habit of thought was still too much dominated by the immemorial practice of appealing to supernatural powers in judicial matters for rational distinctions to have become prominent. The older proofs furnished

[1] The discussion of this subject is based upon the admirable account in P. and M. ii., 622–627.

speedy and unequivocal answers; the jury was expected to do the same. It would have been impious to question how God reached the conclusions which he manifested in the trial by battle or the older ordeals; there was little disposition to inquire how the jury reached its unanimous answer. It was usually speedily reached; it was the "voice of the country"; the litigants had placed themselves upon the country; it was what was wanted. The jurors drawn from a limited district, the neighbours of the parties to the suit, embodied in themselves when they came into court something that would have seemed more valuable to the court, could the comparison have been made, than the product of any rational taking and weighing of evidence. The fact that the jury reached its verdict in its own way and returned a complete and final answer shows that there was likely to be at least a slight judging element in what it did. Moreover the jurors were not to be content with the knowledge of the facts which they happened to have when summoned; they were expected to make inquiries and inform themselves as best they could before coming into court. This entailed some weighing and judging of evidence. They were not mere mechanical transmitters of fact like modern witnesses, but were embryonic "judges of fact" from the outset.

Upon these characteristics depended the triumph, in the course of the fourteenth century, of the principle of unanimity in the jury. Its early position as one among several kinds of proof tended to make it like them; if they spoke unequivocally, the jury must. "The *veredictum patriæ* is assimilated to the *judicium Dei*." Moreover, the jury being the voice of the country, that itself implied unanimity. The majority dogma was not clearly formulated for two centuries yet, and if the country were to speak, it must be through unanimity. And the judging element favoured a unanimous verdict, for the juror did not have to stand strictly upon his own personal knowledge; he might be persuaded to change his opinion, or he might accept the fuller information of his associates. The judges regarded unanimity not only as the most natural but the most convenient requirement, and often used much pressure to obtain it. There were many exceptions to the rule in early times but the tendency was decidedly in favour of unanimity, and that as the result of the primitive characteristics of the English jury and the circumstances of its early use in the courts.

It may be impossible to state fully why the traits of the jury just discussed persisted and triumphed over those which at first seemed more obvious and important. Two considerations, however, may be brought forward with confidence. England was quite uniformly orthodox during centuries when heresy trials were growing frequent upon the continent. The peculiar nature of the crime of heresy led very readily to the separate examination of witnesses and the secret collection of testimony accompanied by torture— an inquisitorial procedure. Had such trials been common in England, the jurors might soon have become mere witnesses, and there would have been in the hands of the state an engine of tyranny instead of an institution which guarded the liberty of the subject. The second and more important consideration is that the possessory assizes were made with a jury as a necessary part of the procedure, and that too a

jury tinged with those traits of the older forms of
proof that we have been noting. Now these assizes
exactly met the needs for which they were designed;
they grew very rapidly and struck deep root in English
soil. From these, the jury spread quickly but voluntarily into other civil actions.[1] At the critical period
of jury history in the thirteenth century, when it was
being determined whether it should triumph over
other forms of proof, and, having so triumphed, what
should be the line of its own development, its necessary
use and its character in the possessory assizes were
decisive influences. These popular actions were working by their very presence, tacitly but powerfully,
for the spread of the jury, and that jury like their own.
"Much was at stake during those wakeful nights in
which the Novel Disseisin was being fashioned."

If, then, juries were to be finally judges of fact and
not witnesses, there would soon come a time when true
witnesses would be needed. It was far into modern
times before the idea entirely disappeared that the jury
should itself furnish at least a part of its facts. Throughout the thirteenth and even in the fourteenth century,
care was often taken that some of the jurors, owing to
the locality or class whence they were drawn, should
have information which would be useful in the trial and
which they were expected to impart to their fellows.
But this had to be supplemented more and more; the
apparatus of informing the empanelled jury was developing, and the witness was an important part of it.

---

[1] "Before the twelfth century was at an end, the inquest in one
form or another—sometimes it was called an assize, sometimes
a jury—had become part of the normal procedure in almost every
kind of civil action."—Maitland in Traill's *Social England* i., 289.

In the earliest practice of the thirteenth century, it is possible to discern a shadowy distinction between what we would call a juror and a witness; but this was long before they were distinguished in name or consciously placed in separate categories, when, as it has been expressed, the witness served on the jury. But as the jurors became judges of fact, this distinction of necessity grew; it was a century and a half however before it was clearly understood and stated. Of the intervening steps, we know almost nothing. Shortly before the middle of the fourteenth century, it was ordered that witnesses, in contradistinction from jurors, were not to be challenged; that witnesses "should say nothing but what they know as certain, that is, what they see and hear," while jurors, placed under no such limitation, were "to tell the truth to the best of their knowledge." This must have ended any serious confusion between the two.

In this connection care must be taken not to ascribe to the medieval jury too beneficent and modern a rôle. The jury to-day seems thoroughly democratic; by it a man receives the verdict of his equals; but the state of society made this impossible in the middle ages. Except in the manorial courts, jurors could only be drawn from the class of freeholders and the whole mass of the peasantry was below that; in civil actions in the manorial courts, the peasant might have a jury made up in part, or occasionally wholly, of his class, but in criminal cases, which would not be tried in these courts, his verdict was rendered by a class much above him. On the other hand in the case of men of standing and influence in the community, it was very difficult, owing to the principle of

unanimity, to obtain from a jury an adverse verdict
in any serious matter.[1]

With this discussion of the jury, is concluded the
account of the new business and the new methods which
the king's court was assuming in the late twelfth and
early thirteenth centuries. But the increased business
had a most important influence upon the court itself;
its old structure and organisation had become insufficient, and it is necessary to consider next how
it adapted itself to the new demands. The king had
been rapidly making the judicial business of the country
his own; an important specialisation of his court
for judicial business resulted; a court was created in
the modern sense of the word out of the king's court,
Curia Regis, where the word court has its broader
and earlier meaning. Certain specialisations of the
Curia in the reign of Henry I. have been noted.[2]
These were all revived at the beginning of Henry II.'s
reign, but no one of them was a thorough-going judicial
specialisation, a court. But during his reign and the
century following, two of them, the itinerant justices

[1] "After some hesitation our law had adopted its well-known
rule that a jury can give no verdict unless the twelve men be all
of one mind. To obtain a condemnatory unanimity was not easy
if the accused was a man of good family; one out of every twelve
of his neighbours that might be taken at random would stand
out loyally for his innocence. Bribery could do much; seignorial
influence could do more; the sheriff, who was not incorruptible,
could do all, since it was for him to find the jury."—Maitland in
Traill's *Social England* i., 294. This author thinks that if it had
not been for the drastic calling of jurors to account by king and
Council in the time of the Tudors and Stewarts the institution
might not have survived.

[2] See above, pp. 125–131.

and the Exchequer, underwent a development along judicial lines that transformed them.

The Assize of Clarendon marks an important turning point in the history of the itinerant justices. After that, the criminal cases that were being drawn into the king's court and the new possessory actions formed the principal part of their business, and one hesitates no longer to call them judges. They might not now all be members of the central Curia, but some of each group almost always were. In either case, however, they were doing, as formerly, Curia Regis business; the court which they held was Curia Regis. Long after Henry II.'s time, they did king's business of a non-judicial character, often along with their judicial work, but it is not surprising that in this legal reign the English *missus dominicus* was becoming a specialist in judicial matters. If a constantly increasing number of actions were to be tried in the king's court, that court must become to some extent itinerant, unless litigants and juries were to bear the burden and expense of long journeys. This new need seized upon the already existing itinerant justice system and the circuit court was created. After the Assize of Northampton, which in 1176 still further extended the work of the itinerant justices, they were almost constantly used to the end of the reign. There was at this time little regularity in sending them out, in the extent or location of their circuits, in their personnel, or in the contents of their commissions. The king seems to have apportioned his increasing business between Curia Regis at Westminster and Curia Regis in the localities as its varying amount and nature from year to year or month to month suggested.

The century following Henry II. was still a time of experiment and gradual development in the itinerant justice system, or the system of commissions as it may perhaps be more properly called. There came to be two main classes of commissions, those of a minor character and the general iters. The more important minor commissions were for gaol delivery or the possessory assizes. The individual commission of gaol delivery applied to a specific gaol named therein; it did not order an inquiry through a jury of accusation, but dealt simply with those persons found in the gaol at the date named; it might, however, involve the trial of some of the greatest criminal cases. This commission was often entrusted to knights resident in the shire concerned, in which case, of course, there was nothing itinerant about it. For the possessory assizes, many commissions were issued every year. The general practice was to entrust them to at least one permanent judge, a member of the central court, who associated local knights with himself. The growing use of knights in the administration of royal justice was a very characteristic and important development of this period. The local gentry in England were destined, in one way or another, to do much governing.

The general iter of this period, the iter *ad omnia placita*, was in a special sense *the* iter or eyre. Of this, the famous iter of 1194 may be taken as an early example and prototype.[1] The justices who were sent out on such visitations had tremendous commissions; they not only tried all sorts of cases, but were still, as in the earlier time, collectors of revenue, and might be charged to attend to any kind of king's business.

[1] A. and S., document 21.

Henry III. got a great revenue by their means. They put local juries on oath for a great variety of purposes, their visitation being a prolonged inquiry into every matter that could possibly concern the king. The later scheme, by which business might still go on at Westminster for a certain locality after a commission had been issued for that locality, the cases coming on at Westminster until the justices were actually in their local session, had not yet been thought of. The moment a commission was issued, all business included in the commission stopped for the entire circuit to be visited; and if commissions were issued for all England, all the business named was forthwith suspended at the centre. This lead to a glut of work in the local sessions of the justices and greatly increased their length. Thus these general visitations were altogether formid-able and burdensome [1]—"those tedious old iters," Maitland calls them. They became one of the standing grievances against Henry III., and the people were outspoken in their complaints. It became a sort of unwritten law in his reign, apparently as a result of the general outcry, that they should be made only once in seven years. This remained the practice until they ended in the next reign.

One of the great legal reforms of Edward I. had to do with the itinerant justice system; the statute of Westminster II., 1285, inaugurated a new régime that in some of its principal features has lasted to the present day. It reorganised one of the minor com-missions, that of Assize, and instituted the *nisi prius*

---

[1] Speaking of the justices who were about to visit Cornwall, a chronicler stated that *quorum metu omnes ad silvas fugerunt.* Cited in P. and M. i., 202.

principle. The commission of Assize replaced the old
general iter, and the justices were relieved of the
mass of non-judicial business which had so long been
a relic of their earliest history. This commission at
first included only cases concerning real property, but
before the end of Edward III.'s reign it had expanded
so as to include almost every action, criminal as well
as civil. However, the very rapid contemporary development of the justices of the peace[1] so reduced the
work of the itinerant justices that their visitations
were never of the old prolonged or burdensome character. To the same end, worked the *nisi prius* principle.
Cases were put upon the docket at Westminster and
were tried there unless before (*nisi prius*) the appointed
date the itinerant justices had come into the county
concerned. Thus for any circuit, judicial business might
be done at the centre and in the locality at the same
time. The commissions of Assize were always entrusted
to sworn knights of the king's central court, but as these
justices went on their circuit from county to county
they associated with themselves a certain number of
knights from each. With these changes, the system
of commissions assumed the chief features that it has
since borne. Its history in the thirteenth and fourteenth centuries shows how rapidly the king's courts
were absorbing the judicial business of the country
and how necessary it was that much of that business
be done in the localities.

The second of the Curia Regis specialisations of
Henry I.'s reign, which began to receive important
judicial development in the reign of his grandson, was
the Exchequer. This institution had little about it

[1] See below, pp. 194, 195.

at the start that suggests a court—the smaller Curia
Regis sitting spring and fall before the chequered
table to balance the king's accounts with the sheriffs.
It was an administrative body of a special sort, a financial bureau.   In the course of two centuries, it became
also a court; it was always Curia Regis.   The primitive
Exchequer controlled the king's treasure; nothing could
be paid out without its authority, for there was no
treasury department in any way distinct from it.
It received all moneys due to the king; at Easter and
Michaelmas, the sheriffs made their reckoning with
this body for all sums due from their respective shires
and had their accounts audited.   It dealt with the
king's debtors.   It was through a development of this
last function that it first did judicial work.   In dealing
with debt cases, it developed a summary procedure
peculiarly its own; while aiming to deal impartially
between king and subject, its position as guardian of the
king's financial interests made it especially careful that
the king should receive his due.   It could also entertain the case of one who had a claim against the king.
The king could not be sued, but king and Curia might
accept the claimant's petition that the case be in-
vestigated.   This was an extension of the Exchequer's
judicial work, and it was supposed to associate with
itself the two chief justices when questions of law
were involved.   After it had to all intents and purposes become a court of law, its administrative work
and its traditions hardly allowed it to be so considered;
the Barons of the Exchequer knew the "course of the
Exchequer," not the common law.   But finally, despite
this supposition, it began to entertain cases between
subject and subject, and thus did violence to any

existing theory of its functions. These cases were
for the most part debt cases, and the persistence with
which they were taken to the Exchequer, rather than
to the law courts where they belonged, is only to be
explained by the benefit to be derived from the speedy
and severe methods which the Exchequer had evolved
in collecting the king's debts. In the reign of Edward
I., the Exchequer was forbidden by statute to accept
such cases; but the prohibition seems to have been
little heeded, and, partly by the use of legal fiction [1]
and partly by the express permission of the king, it
drew to itself more and more of the common pleas.

This change of function was accompanied by a
change in personnel. When, as in the reign of Henry
I., the Exchequer was merely the smaller Curia Regis
sitting for financial business, it of course contained
such great officials as the Justiciar and the Chancellor;
but with the increased judicial business of Henry II.'s
time, a process of specialisation began. The Chancery,
the writ-issuing department, became separated in the
reign of Richard I., and both Chancellor and Justiciar
ceased to attend early in Henry III.'s reign. This
left the Treasurer as the presiding officer of the Exchequer, and a Chancellor of the Exchequer was
appointed as the keeper of its official seal. But more
important in showing the transition from the old
feudal to the new official régime, is the fact that the
king now appointed its members, the Barons of the
Exchequer. It was no longer a feudal body or part

[1] The plaintiff usually claimed that he was indebted to the king
and was prevented by the defendant from discharging his debt.
This brought the case technically within the competence of the
court by making it a concern of the king's revenue, and the court
allowed the defendant to make no denial of the plaintiff's claim.

of a feudal body. It was a body of appointed officials, whose work was rapidly becoming judicial, but who, owing to their non-judicial origin, were never called judges. In the reign of Edward I., the Treasurer ceased to have anything to do with the Exchequer's judicial business, and a Chief Baron became the presiding officer of the court.[1] With but slight changes, the Court of Exchequer remained as it was organised in this reign down to its absorption in the High Court of Justice in 1873. In the early seventeenth century, the treasury department had become completely separated from it. But it should be remembered that this department is as straight a descendant from the original Exchequer as the court, and that the term Exchequer is as properly applied to it.

It was the great extension of the king's judicial business in the reign of Henry II. and the period following which developed a common-law court out of the original Exchequer. The same cause brought forth the other two common-law courts. The first definite and purposeful move towards the creation of a central court in the modern sense of the word was when Henry II. designated from his Curia a body of about five men, clerks and laymen, who, with the king or without him, were to devote themselves exclusively to doing justice. It was a specialisation[2]; the increasing judicial work could not be left to the

[1] The Chancellor of the Exchequer also never became a common-law judge; he is connected only with that Exchequer which is a revenue department.

[2] It was not a complete specialisation to begin with; any of the five might at the same time be Barons of the Exchequer and attend to various kinds of king's business.

occasional and unskilled performance of tenants-in-
chief. This body of five judges soon became known
as the Bench, from the nature of their seat when
doing justice. Until the reign of John, there was little
further development of the court. This king often
had, when travelling, a party of justices in his train
who did justice in his presence *en route*, while the Bench
remained at Westminster. Thus arose a distinction
between the body of judges who habitually did justice
in the king's presence (*coram rege*) and those who remained at the centre and usually did justice without
the king. That this distinction was clearly recognised
before the end of John's reign is shown by the well-
known clause in Magna Carta: "The common pleas
shall not follow our court, but shall be held in some
certain place."[1] So many were seeking justice at the
king's court that it had become a matter of importance
to know where the judges were to be found who tried
the common pleas, the cases between man and man.
During the long minority of Henry III., there was no
coram rege court as distinguished from the Bench
at Westminster; but upon the king's coming of age,
or very soon after, the same differentiation appeared
as in the preceding reign, and from that time there
was, besides the Exchequer and the Bench, another
central court, the characteristic of which was the
king's presence. This was the beginning of the Court
of King's Bench, a court which quite naturally came
to deal with the important criminal cases, the pleas
of the crown.[2] As the later medieval kings gradually
ceased their peregrinations, this court, like the others,
became stationary at Westminster. The Bench always

[1] A. and S., p. 45.   [2] See above. p. 147, note 2.

remained the technical name for the court whose main business comprised the civil suits between man and man, but it came to be more generally called Common Bench or Common Pleas. Thus before the end of the thirteenth century the Curia Regis had thrown off the three common-law courts, Exchequer, King's Bench, and Common Pleas.[1]

To begin with each had its proper business; the King's Bench, the pleas of the crown, including all breaches of the king's peace; the Common Pleas, the ordinary civil actions; the Exchequer, matters touching the royal revenue. This is but a rough statement; really the spheres of the King's Bench and Common Pleas overlapped, and this facilitated the practice of stealing work from the Common Pleas which was begun by the King's Bench and adopted by the Exchequer, for more business meant more money. In the end it came about that while each court had some work all its own, each could entertain any of the common civil actions.[2]

---

[1] For a very useful diagram illustrating these and other developments of the central Curia, see G. B. Adams, *The Descendants of the Curia Regis*, American Historical Review xiii., 11–15.

[2] Maitland, *Justice and Police*, p. 35. The differentiation of the King's Bench from what might, at the end of the thirteenth century, be termed the king's council (see below, pp. 286–290) was very gradual. "For ordinary purposes" the King's Bench consisted "of a few professional judges, . . . but at any moment this court can be afforced by the presence of the king, of his councillors, of numerous barons and prelates"; in either form this was the old *coram rege* court. But in the reign of Edward I., can be noted the beginning of the final complete separation of the King's Bench, a limited court of professional judges, from a larger and vaguer Curia Regis or what stood for that at this later date. But when that separation had taken place and the Curia Regis had brought forth its third judicial offspring, we find that neither in its smaller nor its larger form, neither as Council nor as House of Lords, had that body divested itself of all its judicial power. And the judicial

2. **The Displacement of the Old Local Courts by a New Local System of Royal Courts.**—The immediate effects of the Norman Conquest upon the old local courts, both communal and private, have been discussed.[1] We begin here with the situation as found in the early part of Henry I.'s reign. Private jurisdiction was increasing under the impulse of continental thought; Henry had attempted to correct the irregularities in the hundred and shire courts for which the sheriff had been largely responsible in his brother's time, and the sheriff, a royal officer, had become the only presiding and constituting official in those courts. This last fact, taken in conjunction with the continental conception of the king as the source of law and the masterful character of the post-conquest sovereigns, leads one to look for an early and fundamental change in the local courts. There are many clear indications that the change was beginning under Henry I.

There were meetings of the county court that required such full attendance and entertained such a class of cases as make it clear that they were different from the ordinary meetings. Their composition was strikingly like that of the later itinerant justice courts; cases in which the king was specially concerned were tried there, and also cases between the vassals of different lords, such as on the continent would always have been carried before a suzerain's court. When

---

power which remained was of a higher order than that which it had transmitted. "A court which is to stand above the king's bench is being evolved out of the old court held coram rege."— Maitland, Introduction to *Memoranda de Parliamento*, pp. lxxx.- lxxxi., *passim.* See also below, pp. 200, 201.

[1] See Part II., § II., 2.

the king ordered this specially full attendance for doing this kind of business and the presiding sheriff was perhaps more emphatically the king's representative than wont, the shire court had, for the time, become a king's court. It is probable also that in the course of the reign itinerant justices were sent out with some regularity and that such courts were summoned to meet them.[1]

In the same reign, there is evidence of specially full meetings of the hundred court, held twice a year when necessary, whose main purpose was *view of frankpledge*. The frankpledge system was a continuation by the Norman kings of a thoroughly established Anglo-Saxon principle and the rapid extension of an application of it that was probably first made shortly before the Conquest. The principle was that every man of the lower classes, who could not be readily reached through his property and held responsible for his misdeeds, be provided with a *pledge* who must produce him at court in every suit in which he was concerned. This was the animus of the decrees of Anglo-Saxon kings that every man must have a lord; they were essentially police regulations.[2] But it was hard to find a pledge for every man, and the burden upon individual pledges was often great. The late application of the principle was to make a group of the man's neighbours his pledge; a fixed body of men was thus held responsible for bringing any one of its members to court. This group was called a tithing.

---

[1] For a discussion of this point, based upon a study of Henry's writ concerning local courts and some passages in the *Leges Henrici Primi*, see G. B. Adams in *American Historical Review* viii., pp. 487–490.

[2] See above, pp. 41, 42.

The tithing, like the hundred, had had a long and obscure history before it was put to any judicial use—a history that would lead into fields of discussion that cannot be entered here. Suffice it to say that in southern England the tithing was identical with the township, while in the centre, where it seems not to have existed before the time of which we are speaking it had in its new use its literal meaning of a group of ten. In the south, then, the duty of producing its members in court fell upon the township or manor, while in the centre it was borne by the group of ten men. In most of the northern counties, this system was never introduced.

Each tithing had a tithingman as its head and representative, who was present at the semiannual meetings of the hundred courts to report on the condition of his tithing. But when the tithing was a manor, an already existing system, by which the manor was represented at the local courts by reeve and four men when the lord or his steward could not be present, seems to have taken the place of representation by tithingman.[1] Holding groups of men responsible for the appearance in court of their members came to be known as frankpledge. This was apparently owing to a mistranslation by the Normans of the Anglo-Saxon *frithborg*, which they took to mean free-pledge instead of peace-pledge; it was the Anglo-Saxon name of the institution which they were continuing and developing. View of frankpledge was an examination of the pledges to see if they were full and properly organised. The special meetings of

[1] How these two systems of representing the tithing were related is not clear; there was much irregularity and overlapping.

the hundred courts held for this purpose and over which the sheriffs presided must be considered as essentially king's courts; their main purpose was the enforcement of a piece of police machinery devised by the king. Thus during Henry I.'s reign, both the shire courts and the hundred courts were, upon occasion, king's courts, and were always potentially such.

By the Assize of Clarendon, 1166, a new power was given the sheriff, the use of the accusing jury; and it has been suspected that Henry II.'s adoption of this procedure in his own courts, was suggested by the frankpledge system. "The machinery was apt for the purpose; the duty of producing one's neighbour to answer accusations could well be converted into the duty of telling tales against him."[1] The sheriff used the accusing jury in the semiannual meetings of the hundred court, where criminal cases were initiated that were to be concluded before the itinerant justices and where many minor criminal matters were disposed of. This court came to be known as the sheriff's *tourn*.[2] It was his semiannual visitation of the hundreds of his shire for the purpose of criminal jurisdiction. In such a court, where he was as distinctly a royal justice as the itinerant justice was in his court, the sheriff naturally assumed more and more of the judging function; he was not a mere presiding officer or one who looked out for the royal interests in a court that derived its authority from a

[1] Maitland, Introduction to vol. ii. of the *Selden Society Publications*, p. xxxvii.

[2] The word *tourn* or *turn* was not, until after the thirteenth century used as a sufficient description of the court; it was *Curia visus franciplegii domini regis apud B. coram vicecomiti in turno suo.*

source outside the king, as he had been in the old communal courts. This being the character of the *tourn*, it quite naturally became a court of record like the other king's courts. By this is meant that it kept a record of its proceedings and judgments, which could thus be used as precedents.[1]

The invasion of the old local court system by the king's jurisdiction has become sufficiently marked, as we reach this point, to make it appear certain that the former will finally disappear. The relations of the two were very complex during the next century and a half; and this makes it necessary here to distinguish and summarise the later history of the old system, as far as it is possible to do so, before continuing the discussion of the new system which the king was putting in its place. The last epoch in the history of the shire court, the hundred court, and the private courts will be considered, taking each separately and in the order named.[2]

By the end of Henry II.'s reign, the shire court seems to have met much oftener than twice a year, its custom in the Anglo-Saxon period. Henry I. had decreed semiannual meetings, but had in mind the occasional necessity of greater frequency.[3] The increase of

[1] The old local courts, both public and private, began to imitate the king's courts and keep records about the middle of the thirteenth century, a half century after the king's courts began the practice. These records, of course, had no public authority.

[2] No clear and detailed account of the steps by which this older jurisdiction waned is possible. The further it is traced, the more scanty and obscure does the information become, a proof in itself of the steadiness with which it declined.

[3] Stubbs's *Select Charters*, p. 104.

business, which resulted from a more rigid enforcement
of justice and more use of the local courts by the king,
made the exception the rule by the end of the twelfth
century.   By that time also, by the use of commissions,
the shire court, when summoned for certain specified
kinds of business, was completely transformed into
a king's court.[1]   Such a court had, of course, ceased
to be, in any proper sense, a shire court, and forms no
part of our present subject.   By the system of commissions, the old communal court was shorn of much
of its jurisdiction.   The itinerant justice and the
sheriff in his *tourn* were absorbing criminal justice,
and the old court's civil jurisdiction was being eaten
into by the possibility of evoking cases into the king's
court by writ.   The enormous popularity of the possessory actions, which could only be brought in a
royal court, made the work of the shire court seem
relatively small; and as these actions often gave rise
to corresponding proprietary actions, they constituted
a positive drain upon the old court.

In Henry III.'s second reissue of Magna Carta, 1217,
there was a regulation that the shire court be held
monthly, the language implying that it had been held
oftener.[2]   It was becoming distinctly a court for the
lesser civil cases, held at frequent intervals for the
accommodation of the people.[3]   In it, the old procedure survived; it did not adopt the jury as did the
private courts.   It only used jury trial when the king's

---

[1] See above pp. 167, 168.   [2] Stubbs, *Select Charters*, p. 346.
[3] "It entertains some of the initial proceedings in criminal cases,
but for the more part it is a civil, non-criminal court; it has an
original jurisdiction in personal actions; real actions come to it
when feudal courts make default in justice; cases are sent down
to it for trial by jury from the king's court."—P. and M. i., 530.

court sent some case into it in order that it might
be tried in the locality. The shire courts clung to
the old procedure because the dwindling number and
importance of their cases hardly made it worth while
to attempt anything new, but the result was undoubtedly an accelerated decline. No one was interested in their survival. They were the courts of the
people, and the people were finding it more to their
interest to get their cases tried in the king's courts.

A further weakening resulted from a decreasing
attendance. Suit of court had always been regarded
as a burden and attempts had been made to avoid
it; now there was no need of enforcing it so rigidly as
in times past. The Statute of Merton, 1236, made it
no longer necessary that all freeholders who owed
suit of court should attend in person; they might send
substitutes. Some of the greater landowners, who
had now very little concern with this court, were attempting to withdraw from it entirely, and during
the thirteenth century a great many of them, especially those who represented great religious houses,
purchased or were freely granted charters of exemption. Many simply stopped attending and, in course
of time, claimed and obtained exemption through
prescription. Thus by the late thirteenth century,
the shire court was for small cases and small people.

A clause of the Statute of Gloucester, 1278, was so
interpreted as to make the cases grow still smaller.
"The clause in question seems on its face to have quite
another object: it says that none is to have a writ of
trespass in the king's courts unless he will affirm that
the goods taken away were worth forty shillings at
the least. This seems to have been construed to

imply a very different rule, namely that no action for more than forty shall be brought in a local court."[1] By 1290, this had become law, and, as money decreased in purchasing power, the number of cases brought before a shire court grew steadily less. By the end of the fifteenth century, its judicial work was of no importance; but no statute brought this side of its activity to an end or changed the limitation set in 1278 until the erection of the new county courts in 1846. The shire court had always had some functions that were not judicial, and it lasted for the purpose of electing such local officials as the coroners and verderers and, a far more important matter, electing the knights to represent the shire in Parliament.

Much that has been said of the process by which the shire court ceased to be a judicial body applies to the hundred court, but there are some distinctive points in the latter's history. By Henry II.'s time, the hundred court was also meeting more frequently than it had before the Conquest or for some time after; it was probably meeting every two weeks. In 1234, Henry III. sent out orders to his sheriffs that it should be held every three weeks. This change was doubtless owing to a decrease in business which resulted from the same forces that were weakening the shire court. The hundred court came to be known as Curia Parva Hundredi, apparently in contrast with the sheriff's *tourn*. Its business, at the end of the twelfth century, was confined to petty civil cases.[2] The statutes of

[1] Maitland, Introduction to *Select Pleas in Manorial Courts*, p. lvi.

[2] The hundred court's "competence seems much the same as that of the county court, though its powers are confined within narrower geographical limits; but real actions do not come to it, nor do we

Merton and Gloucester had the same effect upon its make-up and competence as in the case of the shire court.

But another process greatly hastened the hundred court's extinction. Before the Conquest, the jurisdiction over many parts of hundreds and over some whole hundreds had passed into private hands, though there was little consciousness of this change.[1] After the Conquest, the process went on more rapidly, the country was covered with manors, and, by the end of the thirteenth century, little was left of the old hundredal jurisdiction. Petty civil cases for all classes could be taken care of by the private courts and the shire courts; and, moreover, the interpretation placed upon the Statute of Gloucester was carrying an increasing number of small suits straight to the king's courts. In fact, this went so far that, in course of time, it produced an unfortunate condition of things; while there came to be a satisfactory provision for local criminal jurisdiction, it was necessary in nearly all civil cases (for the slight civil jurisdiction which the Justices of the Peace acquired is negligible) to begin the action in one of the courts at Westminster; and the case was tried there unless before (*nisi prius*) it was reached in the regular succession of cases the justices of assize held their session in the county concerned.[2] Thus the old communal hundred court became a superfluity and soon had no work to

hear of actions being transmitted to it by the king's court."—P. and M. i, 530.

[1] See above, pp. 44, 45.

[2] See above, p. 161. It was not until the nineteenth century that any proper provision was made in the localities for minor civil jurisdiction.

do, but no formal act brought its existence to an end.[1]

Before speaking of the decline of the second great class of local courts, those in private hands, a word should be said in passing of the borough courts.[2] The boroughs had been steadily acquiring privileges during the twelfth century, and their courts were flourishing. These courts were destined, in the course of time, to become assimilated, in a general way, to the new royal, local system, and were to be permanent in all the more important boroughs. But until they had thus acquired some common characteristics, it is very hard to generalise concerning them.[3] They still corresponded somewhat loosely to the hundred courts, but, as has been shown,[4] boroughs had passed under lords, and the extent to which, in the thirteenth century, they were independent of their lords' jurisdiction varied infinitely. The boroughs were naturally suspicious of the newfangled methods of the king's courts, which seemed so potent in extending the royal jurisdiction, and were, at this time, holding firmly to the old forms. The more important sessions

[1] The provision in the County Courts Act of 1867 to the effect that no action, which can be brought in a county court (in the later sense), shall be brought in a hundred or other inferior court that is not a court of record may perhaps be said to mark in a very distant way the formal ending of hundredal jurisdiction.

[2] For a very full account of the borough courts and the law administered therein, see Miss Bateson's Introduction to *Borough Customs*, vol. ii. (Selden Society Publications).

[3] "The cities and boroughs—vills, that is, which have attained to a certain degree of organization and independence—have courts of their own. But of these municipal courts very little can be said in general terms; they are the outcome not of laws, but of privileges."—P. and M. i., 532.

[4] See above, p. 96.

of the borough courts were probably supposed to be attended by all the burgesses, who were to find the judgments after the fashion of the suitors in the shire and hundred courts. But, as in the shire courts, there was a tendency, from early times, to place this function in the hands of a selected group. Where such a group became identified with the body of borough officials, the government of the borough became very aristocratic. To some boroughs was granted, in the thirteenth century, their own view of frankpledge, and this very effectually drew them out from under the sheriff's jurisdiction.[1]

Like the old communal courts, the private courts also began to be straitened in their jurisdiction by the

[1] Miss Bateson's comment, suggested by the passing of the borough customs, can be appropriately quoted in connection with our consideration of the general decline of the old, local system of justice. "The 'dust on antique time would lie unswept' if all the objects of borough ambition had been attained and retained, but, provided the dead past be not restored to tyrannise over us, at a safe distance we may admire its picturesque ruins and half regret the cruel work of dissolution done by the common law in the name of reformation. For the sake of uniformity of worship, many quaint rites have been abandoned; in the great temple of the common law the side chapels are altarless and empty. The justice of the local courts has been ruthlessly condemned as incompetent, provincial, archaic, unprogressive, unable to adapt itself to a new state of society. The old local justice is 'antiquity forgot, custom not known,' because in the system of national justice the general destroyed the particular, no doubt for good reason. And yet for the true understanding of the 'jus et consuetudo regni,' founded upon a rock-bed of unwritten tradition, on general immemorial custom, it may be well to stoop to examine the unworthy particular. In borough custom we have a neglected series of rocks, not primary in antiquity, but full of the signs of life, and the extinct forms which it permits us to handle have a place in the history of the making of the common law."— *Borough Custom* ii., clvi. (Selden Society Publications).

great extension of royal justice in the reign of Henry
II.[1] But in their case, there was material for a struggle
against the growing power.   Justice was profitable,
and the lords who possessed it wanted to retain what
they had; there was little chance of their acquiring
more.   Grants to individuals of judicial authority,
as well as of various immunities, were still common
in the late twelfth and during the thirteenth century;
but the general terms, used in such grants at an earlier
time, were very carefully limited.   As the idea grew
that criminal justice was the king's business, and as
capital punishment took the place of fine, the amount
of such justice granted to individuals grew steadily
less.   And when the kings began to reflect upon the
amount of criminal jurisdiction which some individuals
already held, they did not scientifically study the past
in order to understand the matter; they came to the
conclusion that, while there might be a kind of civil
and petty criminal justice that went with the possession
of a manor, this higher kind could never have been
lawfully acquired except by definite royal grant.[2]

That no such distinction as this was made at the
time of the Conquest, nor for long after, it is hardly
necessary to state.   But it was this attitude of mind
which led directly to an act of Edward I. which had a
profound effect upon the later history of private courts.
In 1278, he issued the Writ Quo Warranto, which
demanded by "what warrant" those who were exercising what he was pleased to consider regalian

---

[1] The best account of private jurisdictions in the thirteenth
century (with many hints of their earlier history) is to be found
in Maitland's Introduction to *Select Pleas in Manorial Courts*
(Selden Society Publications).

[2] On the origin of private jurisdiction, see above, pp. 92–94.

rights were doing so. It was assumed that, if they could not show a written grant from the king, the only means of acquiring such rights in Edward's time, they were to be deprived of them. This roused such formidable protest that Edward abated his demand; he may possibly have foreseen the necessity of this from the first. Those who could show an unbroken exercise of these rights from the coronation of Richard I. were allowed to retain them. But two important things were accomplished. In the first place, any further acquisition of such rights was out of the question; and, mindful of the possibilities of forfeiture and deprivation which a powerful monarchy always possessed, it is easy to see that the exercise of high judicial power by private individuals would, at no distant time, pass away. In the second place, the theory that part of the jurisdiction was exercised by royal grant, and part by manorial right, was so emphasised that it soon became an established principle. This principle resulted in a distinction between courts that must next be examined.

Private courts had been quick to adopt the new royal procedure of jury presentment and trial, though the limited number of suitors on some manors interfered with this. For private courts in England were becoming, for the most part, manor courts. The courts of great honours, the true feudal courts composed of vassals, had always been less important in England than on the continent; and now they were becoming extinct, not only through the invasion of the royal courts and the limitations placed upon grants of justice, but through an important series of legislative acts of Edward I. which checked subinfeudation and tended to break down the feudal hierarchy.[1] A distinction began to be made in the judicial work which the lord did in his manor court. He might be doing work analogous to that of the sheriff in his *tourn*, if by grant or prescription it had come to him. But this was criminal jurisdiction and view of frank-pledge; it was, according to the view we have just seen develop, a strict regality and could only be carried on under royal commission. Hence a court which did this was a royal court, a court of record; it must be sharply distinguished from a court which the lord held as of his own right, which he held because he had tenants. A new and distinguishing name, that of Leet, was applied to it. This term, whose antecedent history is very obscure, was probably first used in this connection in the reign of Edward I. From that time, we hear of Leets, the adjective use of the word, as in Court Leet, not appearing until well into modern times. Here, then, was one part of the old, private jurisdiction, modified in its content and procedure by innovations from the king's courts, and finally taken up into, and made a part of, the royal judicial system; the lord's steward who conducted this court now conducted it as a royal officer. Thus it passes out of the field of our immediate consideration; but it may be remarked here that it survived the middle ages, still in a quite vigorous condition, and, though more and more limited by a new and better local machinery, the justice of the peace system, some traces of it are to be seen at the present day.

---

[1] A careful study should be made of documents 39, 40, 42, and 45 in A. and S. For a discussion of these acts, see Stubbs, *Constitutional History*, § 179, *passim;* also Medley, p. 291.

While the Leet was, in theory, a jurisdiction quite separate from that which the lord possessed in his own right, it was customary to exercise both in the same tribunal. It now remains to ask what was this residuum of truly private jurisdiction and what was its fate. It is heard of under the name of Court Baron,[1] a name that came into common use simultaneously with Leet. It follows from what has been said of the Leet that the Court Baron had a civil jurisdiction. Now the typical manor contained both freemen and villeins, the freemen usually being in a marked minority. Thus the Court Baron, as had always been the case with manor courts, was made up of these two classes. A distinction between them had appeared in the procedure; it seems to have done no violence to the idea of judgment by peers for inferior to be judged by superior, but superior could not be judged by inferior—villeins were judged by freemen and villeins, freemen only by freemen. But now something had arisen which farther distinguished the classes in these courts; it was the increasing use of the jury there. The lord could, by his own authority, make his villeins take oath as jurors; but the jury was a royal institution, and by the accepted theory of this period, no one could do the same by freemen without a royal commission.[2] This split in the per-

---

[1] The significance of the word *baron* in this connection is not at all clear. The terms by which private jurisdictions were ordinarily known in earlier times were Libera Curia and Halimote. The former usually indicated the higher judicial authority of a lord, but did not signify a court of freemen as opposed to unfree. The latter, lasting on from Anglo-Saxon times, probably meant hall-court, thus distinguishing the court held in the hall of the manor from the old open-air courts of hundred and shire.

[2] This was definitely laid down as law in article 18 of the

sonnel and procedure of the Court Baron was soon reflected in nomenclature; the Court Baron (in a narrower sense) was the lord's private court for his freemen, while the Court Customary, that which administered the custom of the manor, was his villein court.

The later history of these two courts was not at all the same. The Court Baron very soon became decadent. The fact that the king's courts were so desirable and possible a place for freemen to bring an increasing variety of actions was, of course, the main reason for this. But there were, besides, a number of specific causes which developed in the middle and latter part of the thirteenth century.[1] A change in the law of distraint, which made it possible for a lord to distrain his tenant for rents or services without judgment of a court, made his own court of much less value to him; for that had been the place where he could most readily obtain such judgments. In 1285, the lord was given an action in the king's court which made it possible for him to eject his freehold tenant for default of service. The forty-shilling clause in the Statute of Gloucester had, through its peculiar interpretation, the same effect in limiting the competence of the Court Baron that it had in the case of the communal courts.[2] But perhaps the most decisive matter was the threshing out, in the thirteenth century, of the question whether a lord's court should be a court of appeal from the courts of his vassals. Such appeal

---

Provisions of Westminster, 1259 (see A. and S., p. 66), and was embodied in the confirmation of these Provisions known as the Statute of Marlborough, 1267.

[1] Maitland fully discusses all these causes in his Introduction to *Select Pleas in Manorial Courts*, pp. lii.–lx.

[2] See above, pp. 173, 174.

had evidently been the practice in some countries,
and there was clearly a struggle. But the lesser
vassals were opposed to it and so was the king. Bracton argued somewhat uncertainly about it on the basis
of the wording of the writ of right,[1] which told the lord
to do right in his court and that if he did not the
sheriff would. This implied that, in default of justice,
the case had been taken immediately from the court
of first instance to the king's court. But the writ of
right had to do with only one class of cases, albeit
a very important class. In the Provisions of Westminster, however, is found a statement which covered
the matter broadly and conclusively: "None but the
king from henceforth shall hold plea in his court of a
false judgment given in the court of his tenants; because such pleas do especially belong to the king's
crown and dignity."[2] "We may regard this as a
turning point in the history of the feudal courts. If a
great baron had been able to make his court a court not
merely for his immediate tenants but also a court with
a supervisory jurisdiction over their courts, it would
have been worth his while to keep his court alive;
it might have become the fountain of justice for a
large district. But a court merely for the suits of his
great freehold tenants, some dozen or half-dozen
knights, was hardly worth having and became less
worth having as time went on."[3] There were, of

[1] For the origin of the writ of right, see above, p. 135.

[2] A. and S., p. 66. The words *false judgment* are important,
for it was by enforcing the principle here stated that great progress
was made towards building up the modern conception of appellate
jurisdiction. For an account of the origin of appeal from court
to court, see P. and M. ii., 664–669.

[3] Maitland, Introduction to *Select Pleas in Manorial Courts*, p. lix.

course, many lords, whose freeholders were not knights, who had manors and hence courts of their own; with them this matter of appeal had no concern. For the reasons enumerated, then, the Court Baron, the civil jurisdiction which lords, big or little, had over their freehold tenants, ceased to be operative long before the end of the middle ages. Something approaching it was perhaps occasionally used in connection with the jurisdiction over villeins.

The villein court, the Court Customary of the manor, lasted much longer. But forces were at work in the fourteenth and fifteenth centuries that were steadily undermining it. It has been seen that the outward mark of unfreedom in the case of the villein was that he could not bring an action in the king's courts, and that these courts came to their conclusion upon an individual's status by ascertaining the degree of uncertainty in his service.[1] Two changes,[2] which began in the thirteenth century, so fundamentally modified manorial conditions in the two following centuries as to do away with this uncertainty of service. The first was the commutation of payments in kind and labour to payments in money. The increasing use of money as a medium of exchange made it possible for the lord to give something for labour other than land, and for the tenant to give something for land other than labour. A man could leave the manor with some chance of placing himself more advantageously elsewhere; at least, he could sell his labour where he could

[1] See above, pp. 82–84.

[2] These changes were caused mainly by economic and social forces that cannot be considered here. See Cheney, *The Disappearance of English Serfdom*, The English Historical Review xv., 20–37, and Page, *The End of Villainage in England*.

get the most for it. This tended to break up the
manorial economy and to make labour free. Fugitives
from manors became more numerous; and such fugitives, if no proofs were brought to the contrary, were
always accounted free before the king's courts. This
rise of the servile classes was favoured by the Black
Death of 1348, which, for a time, placed the peasantry
upon the right side of the labour market, and possibly
to a slight extent by the peasant revolt of 1381. The
growth of copyhold tenure was a partial reflection of
this change.[1] This tenure certainly looked toward
that definiteness in the kind of service to be rendered
from day to day which was the touchstone of the
royal courts in determining the free status of him who
sought remedy in them. But the tenure still retained
some servile characteristics, as, for instance, in the
form of alienation; and when, a century or more
later, it came to a question of the lord's right to evict
his copyhold tenant, the king's courts usually upheld
that right.[2]

The second change was the lord's parcelling out of

---

[1] In copyhold tenure, instead of the service being based upon immemorial custom, a definite entry of the service was made upon
the manor roll, and ordinarily a copy of this, in the nature of an
indenture, was in the hands of the peasant.

[2] This was certainly a denial of the free character of the tenure
as such. The frequent divorce, in England, between tenure and
status has already been commented upon; see above, p. 84. The
occasion of these evictions, whose number has probably been
greatly exaggerated, was the enclosing of large tracts of land for
the purpose of raising sheep. This use of land was found increasingly profitable in the late fifteenth and early sixteenth
centuries. After this particular motive for seizing copyhold land
subsided, the nature of the tenure ceased to be a burning question,
and copyhold served, in all essentials, as a free tenure. During
the last century, this tenure has been rapidly disappearing.

his demesne into leases at a money rent. Where this was done, the lord ceased to be an immediate employer of labour. The labour service of his villeins and all the petty litigation and consequent fines connected therewith—an important part of the manor court's work—ceased to be a matter of consequence to the lord. He was becoming pure landlord. "That fundamental relation between the lord and the villein, that the former could force the latter to stay on his land and work for him, was now a relation without special interest or value." [1]

It should be constantly kept in mind in connection with these two changes that the royal courts always favoured liberty, that is, they sought to draw to themselves as much litigation as possible. When the question of villein status was raised, the burden of proof always rested upon the lord, and it was usually a considerable burden and hard to handle; the kind of proof to be accepted was limited and the court was strict. The Court Customary was thus being weakened along two lines. Fundamental economic changes in the manor were so modifying society and the relations of lord and peasant as to remove its *raison d'être*; as it became less and less a source of income to the lord, he would cease to strive to maintain it. Secondly, the all-absorbing royal courts were ready to take advantage of every change which might be construed as adding to the ranks of freemen, and thus of possible litigants. There were other ways in which individual villeins became free in the later middle ages which it is unnecessary to discuss here. Only a glance at the fundamental changes which

[1] Cheney in *English Historical Review* xv., 36.

affected the whole class has been attempted. The
Court Customary did not die suddenly; it was decadent
at the end of the middle ages, but had some importance
well into modern times. However, the forces which
were to bring it to an end have been seen in full operation in the fourteenth and fifteenth centuries. With
this court is completed the list of the older local
courts which fell before the royal judicial system.
It remains now to finish the consideration of the attempts of that system to put into the localities something that could work in harmony with itself, and
that could adequately furnish that local administration
of justice which, in some form, is always necessary.[1]

It is especially needful in any judicial system that
much criminal business be done quickly and on the
spot. Frequent and efficient as judicial iters might
become, the king would find it necessary to have
resident criminal justices. From what has been said
of the sheriff's *tourn*, it might seem that that was
destined to meet this need. But hardly had the
tourn come into existence before the king found that he
must have something more and something different.
The sheriff was too great a local, landed personage to
be entrusted with a power that would have to be
extended in many directions as the peace-keeping and
administrative activities of the central government
reached out and touched the localities. Henry II.'s
dissatisfaction with the sheriffs and the grounds for it
are shown in the famous Inquest of the Sheriffs.[2] The
situation called for the creation of a local official who

[1] See above, pp. 167–171.   [2] A. and S., document 15.

should be strictly under royal control and to whom part of the sheriff's work should be given. Such a creation we find in the regular establishment of coroners in the reign of Henry II.   There is evidence of something very like a coroner in Henry I.'s time, when occasional mention was made of justices who were to "keep the pleas of the crown." It was in the earlier reign that the conception of crown pleas first became at all clear.[1]   Like Henry I.'s other creations, coroners, if there were any, disappeared under Stephen. Henry II.'s coroner was a local justice, chosen probably by the shire court and from the class of knights. His being a justice implies that he tried cases and could empanel a jury to make presentments. If he had not actually tried cases, he could not, according to the ideas of the time, have used such a jury. But he also *kept* the pleas of the crown, and this came to be his special work; it meant that he held preliminary hearings and kept a record of local criminal matters for later use by sheriff or itinerant justice. This was his principal work in Richard's reign, as is evidenced by the well-known mention of him in the commission of the itinerant justices in 1194.[2] This has often been regarded as the order creating the office, but the coroner's previous existence has been clearly proved, and this order was undoubtedly for the purpose of making coroners general throughout the counties and fixing their number and functions. But that the coroner did not cease to be a justice at least until 1215 is proved by article 24 of Magna Carta, which prohibited the sheriff as well as the coroner from holding pleas of the crown.[3] The sheriff continued thereafter

[1] See above, p. 147, note 2.   [2] A. and S., p. 30.   [3] A. and S., p. 46.

to be a justice in the lesser criminal cases and in civil cases, but the coroner's judging functions became very slender and his duties largely those which he has since kept. But there were, for a time, a vagueness and an elasticity about them which allowed many exceptions and which are a reminder of the original motive in creating the office. During the thirteenth century, the coroner held inquests in cases of sudden death or injury, and preliminary hearings in criminal cases in which appeals had been made; his place in the county court was often much like that of the sheriff, and he might try civil cases there; he could even hold the sheriff's *tourn*. But aside from his judicial functions, and of more importance than some of them, was his work as a local administrative official of the king. In this, he supplemented or took the place of the sheriff. In fact, he was often so much like the sheriff that it is hard for the modern mind to see what the distinction was. One thing is certain: the kings intended that these locally elected knights, two or four to each shire, should check the power of the single aristocratic sheriff, under whom there might indeed be more than one shire. It was not long after the creation of the coroner that the choosing of certain juries was taken from the sheriff and given to the county court. It was another royal method of limiting the sheriff and guaranteeing good local service by allowing the people to participate in it.

But the coroner proved no complete solution of the local government problem. Before the end of the thirteenth century, local complaints were made about him as well as about the sheriff. Just why limitations were so early placed upon the coroner's judicial activities is hard to tell.[1]   Inasmuch as the final solution of the problem was found in groups of local magistrates appointed by the king, one is led to surmise that the trouble with the coroner lay in his elective character, but our imperfect knowledge of the conditions of the time prevents us from understanding why. But the coroner was the king's first experiment in building up a local government in harmony with the rapidly growing central government, and he hit upon knights as the class best fitted for this purpose.   These facts, together with the considerable local importance which the coroner continued to have, are reasons for noticing him in this connection.[2]

Besides the local use of knights just mentioned, we have noted their increasing importance on all sorts of juries and have seen them associated with justices in holding the assizes; and when gaol deliveries were entrusted to local commissions, knights might have to exercise criminal justice of the highest sort.   This last-mentioned use of knights was, as will presently appear, a very interesting foreshadowing.   But we have now to consider knights in a new capacity, as *conservatores pacis* or *custodes pacis*, or, without special designation, their use, on certain occasions, for purposes directly or indirectly connected with keeping the peace.   Here they were clearly supplementing the work of both sheriffs and coroners, and were often regarded as a check upon the sheriffs.   The king was

[1] It is interesting to note that the right to empanel a jury which the coroner still has is a survival of that transient twelfth-century phase of his existence when he was a *bona fide* justice.

[2] A most satisfactory account of the origin and activities of coroners is to be found in Gross's Introduction to *Coroners' Rolls* (Selden Society Publications, vol. ix.),

evidently still dissatisfied with the policing and general
administering of the localities. It is interesting to
note how early in the history of the coroners this new
use of knights began. In 1195, the justiciar, Archbishop Hubert Walter, issued an edict by which
knights were appointed to take oaths throughout the
kingdom from all over fifteen years old. By this
oath, men bound themselves not to be thieves, robbers,
or the receivers of such, to join in the hue and cry,
etc.; and malefactors taken as a result of the edict
were first to be delivered to the knights and the knights
were to deliver them to the sheriffs.[1] In the "writ
for enforcing watch and ward and the assize of arms"[2]
in 1252, the king assigned two knights to each sheriff,
the three to co-operate in taking oaths throughout
their shire that proper arms be borne, constables
appointed, and other matters looking to the preservation of the peace attended to. By the Provisions of
Oxford, 1258, four knights from each county were
chosen to keep the pleas of the crown[3]; but, in their
case, this function was to be interpreted very amply:
they were expected to do almost anything in the way
of detecting criminals and preparing cases for the
itinerant justices. Equally broad powers, but with
more detailed instructions on the use of the *posse
comitatus* and the pursuit of criminals, were given to
the custodians of the peace appointed in 1264.[4] Such
was the increasing need of knights that, in 1278,
the king issued a writ for what is known as "distraint
of knighthood"[5]: it was to compel all whose land

---

[1] Stubbs, *Select Charters*, p. 264.   [2] *Ibid.*, pp. 371–373.
[3] A. and S., p. 57.   [4] Stubbs, *Select Charters*, pp. 411, 412.
[5] A. and S., pp. 70, 71.

brought an income of twenty pounds a year, whether
they held from the king or others, who "ought to be
knights and are not," to receive the insignia of knighthood within a specified time. The evident disinclination to become knights is a striking testimony
to the many duties and burdens of the class. In the
early years of Edward I., knights were, upon several
occasions, put to uses similar to those just mentioned.
In the famous Statute of Winchester,[1] 1285, Edward
repeated, with some important additions, the previous
assizes of arms and watch and ward; and in the elaborate arrangements for keeping the peace, in the local
"constables chosen" and "justices assigned," there
was an important advance in the royal attempts to
devise an effective local government controlled by,
and in harmony with, the central.

The decline of the sheriff's power kept pace with
the increasing local use of knights. The Statute of
Marlborough, 1267, exempted from the sheriff's *tourn*
all above the degree of knights unless they were
specially summoned. Many boroughs were allowed
their own view of frankpledge, thus removing an important element from the *tourn*.

Edward II. continued the use of the new local
guardians of the peace, with some enlargement of
function on the administrative side. Year after year
commissions were issued appointing them until they
were regarded as an indispensable and regular part
of government; and at the beginning of Edward III.'s
reign, they were about to receive the powers and
organisation which gave their office its completed
form. They were appointed by the king, not locally

[1] A. and S., pp. 76–79.

elected. This point must receive some notice here.
The coroner failed to supply the *desideratum* in the
local government, perhaps because of his elective
character. It was natural that he should have been
locally elected, for he originated at just the time that
the king was learning the wisdom of taking from the
sheriff the appointment of the non-judicial juries; and,
like the knights on those juries, the coroners dealt
with matters connected with the sheriffs' work. But
in the thirteenth century a new method was tried; the
king himself, probably from locally furnished lists,
appointed the knights who were to be keepers of the
peace. And, as far as can be learned, this remained
the method, with the exception of a few occasions
early in Edward I.'s reign. On those occasions, local
election was used, and, it may be added, was often
used at other times to fill vacancies when death or
other cause suddenly terminated the service of those
appointed by the king. The system of royal appointment has been abundantly justified by all the later
history of the justice of the peace. He was a king's
official and his court a king's court, a court of record. His appointment by the king seems to have
been an indispensable element in securing the satisfactory correlation of central and local jurisdiction
and administration.

After some interruption late in Edward II.'s reign,
conservators of the peace were again appointed in
1327; and in 1328 is the first indication of their exercising a real judging function. But, for some time
after that, judging was not their ordinary work; they
were still "little more than constables on a large
scale." In 1330, some of their duties were defined

13

and enlarged and their relations to the justices of
assize made clear.   After speaking of the justices of
assize, the statute continues:

. . . also there shall be assigned good and lawful men
in every county to keep the peace; and in the said assign-
ments, mention shall be made that such as shall be indicted
or taken by the said keepers of the peace, shall not be let
to mainprise [bail] by the sheriffs, nor by none other
ministers, if they be not mainpernable by the law; nor
that such as shall be indicted, shall not be delivered but at
the common law . . . and that the said keepers shall
send their indictments before the justices, and they shall
have power to enquire of sheriffs, jailers, and others, in
whose ward such indicted persons shall be, if they make
deliverance, or let to mainprise any so indicted, which
be not mainpernable, and to punish the said sheriffs,
jailers, and others if they do anything against this act.[1]

It is easy to see how such an official would cut into
the parallel work of the sheriff's *tourn*, weakened as this
court already was.   From this time, this last judicial
stronghold of the sheriff steadily declined until its
practical extinction in the reign of Edward IV.   It
was in 1361 that the judicial work of the keepers of the
peace was made regular and important, and in the
same year they were first called justices of the peace.
An act of that year granted them the power to " hear
and determine at the king's suit all manner of felonies
and trespasses done in the same county according to
the laws and customs aforesaid"; and there was added
significantly: "And the king will, that all general inquiries before this time granted within any seignories,
for the mischiefs and oppressions which have been

[1] A. and S., p. 101.

done to the people by such inquiries, shall cease utterly
and be repealed."[1] From this time till the end of the
middle ages, there was no crime except treason that
could not be tried before the justices of the peace.
Thus they and the justices of assize were, on the criminal
side, doing the same work, and much that had formerly been done by the justices itinerant was now done
by these justices resident.[2] It was an anomalous and
awkward situation, and not until after the Tudor
period was a serious attempt made to clearly distinguish between the two jurisdictions.

As the new local courts encroached upon the *tourn's*
business of indicting and holding preliminary hearings, the sheriffs became more and more solicitous
about their declining jurisdiction and the profits which
accrued from it. They were tempted to many abuses,
especially the entertaining of accusations made for
purposes of extortion. There was an increasing outcry
against these misdeeds during the fifteenth century,
and in the first year of Edward IV. an act was passed
to the effect that in the future "the above persons"
(sheriffs and their various deputies) "should not have
power to arrest anyone, or levy fines by colour of indictments so taken; but they should deliver all such
indictments to the justices of the peace at their next

---

[1] A. and S., pp. 127, 128.

[2] This parallelism of jurisdiction and the early popularity of the
justices of the peace are illustrated in the petition of the commons,
in the oppressive and troublous early reign of Richard II., "that
during the war justices in eyre and of trailbaston shall not go on
circuit among the said poor commons, but that the justices of the
peace hold their courts according to the tenure of their commission."
—A. and S., p. 143. Justices of *trailbaston* were circuit justices
specially commissioned to deal with the organised bands of lawless
followers and desperadoes known by that name.

sessions of the peace, under the penalty of forty pounds."[1]   On the face of it, this would seem to take away from the *tourn* everything except view of frank-pledge, but in after years much uncertainty arose as to just what it had been the intention to include in this restriction.   It was finally interpreted as applying to felonies and all the more serious crimes, also to new matter made punishable or actionable by statute.   In this crippled condition, the *tourn* survived the middle ages, and the sheriff, who had been a dangerous local power for four centuries and against whom a long line of strong kings had waged relentless war, was fast becoming a minor executive officer in the county.

The justices of the peace, as judges acting under royal commission, of course used the jury procedure of the older royal courts; but they had to deal with many petty offences which demanded a more summary process.   The variety of their work led to a differentiation in the business and names of their sessions of court.   A single justice exercised many police functions and was empowered by statute to deal with a small number of petty offences.   His principal business was to conduct preliminary hearings. Two or more justices could act together in what came to be known as Petty Sessions; they sat usually, but not necessarily, at an accustomed time and place and for a definite part of the county, often the hundred. They dealt with many cases summarily and with some that required jury trial.   The chief court held by justices of the peace was, from the fourteenth century, and is still, known as Quarter Sessions.   It was, in theory, made up of all the justices of the county;

---

[1] Reeves, *History of the English Law* ii., 10.

but all seldom attended, even in the early days when there were few justices to the county. It finally became established that two might constitute a legal session. The origin of Quarter Sessions was in an act of 1362 "that in the commissions of justices of the peace, and of labourers, [1] express mention be made, that the same justices make their sessions four times by the year, that is to say, one session within the utas of Epiphany, the second within the second week of Mid-Lent, the third betwixt the feasts of Pentecost and Saint John Baptist, the fourth within the eight days of Saint Michael."[2] This court tried the great criminal cases that were outside the competence of the Petty Sessions, and also heard appeals from that court and from the court held by a single justice.

In studying his origin, it has been seen that the justice of the peace, or keeper of the peace as he was first called, was a police officer, a sort of head-constable, before he became a judge; this earlier character he never entirely lost. Another set of functions, the administrative, of which he had never been wholly devoid, became very important toward the end of the fourteenth century. Much effort was expended in futile attempts to enforce the labour legislation of that century; the justice became the chief medium of communication between the king and the localities,

---

[1] These were justices given a special commission to enforce the statutes of labourers of 1349 and 1351 (A. and S., pp. 114–117). They might or might not be identical with the justices of the peace. After 1368, no separate commission for enforcing the labour statutes was issued; that function was included in the commission of the justices of the peace. See Miss B. H. Putnam, *The Justices of Labourers in the Fourteenth Century*. English Historical Review xxi., 517–538.

[2] A. and S., p. 129.

all minor officials were made answerable to him, and Quarter Sessions became a veritable governing body for the shire.

Until 1439, there was no legislation which bore directly upon the qualifications for this office. Knights had been usually appointed; but there is evidence that men of smaller substance were occasionally justices, for the abuse of the office for purposes of extortion became serious enough to be taken account of by the government. An act of 1439 contained this clause: "the king willing against such inconveniences to provide remedy hath ordained and established, by authority aforesaid, that no justice of peace within the realm of England, in any county, shall be assigned or deputed, if he have not lands and tenements to the value of xx pounds by year."[1] This annual value was the old measure of the knight's fee. This inaugurated the policy of identifying the new office with a class of men above bribery and of consideration and authority in their neighbourhoods. In modern times, the office has become purely honorary; but from the reign of Richard II. until after the close of the middle ages, a fee of four shillings a day was allowed the justices. The number of justices for each county was limited by statute in 1388. This limitation was not strictly regarded, however, and the number became variable with a general tendency to increase.[2]

[1] A. and S., p. 194.

[2] "Towards the close of Elizabeth's reign no less than fifty-five are enumerated in Devonshire alone. The smallest counties now contain many more than six; while the most numerous magistracy—that of Lancashire—reaches to more than 800. The whole number must be little short of 20,000; but considerably less than half of these are 'active.' justices who have taken the requisite oaths and received from Chancery the necessary

Thus by the middle of the fifteenth century, England's local, aristocratic system of government had been created, and most of the features which conditioned its success and fame in modern times were clearly discernible. No such system was possible outside of England, for no other country in Europe possessed that peculiar middle class of country gentry out of which it was made. It might seem that the king's depriving the sheriffs of local power and bestowing it in augmented form upon the justices of the peace, was merely breaking down one feudalising and disintegrating element in order to set up another. But the gentry possessed just the degree of approach to the class below and of distinction from the higher nobility to be a perfect instrument for this local work. Knights were too self-respecting and substantial to become petty eye-servants, too small to make any setting up of local authority upon their own private account seem attainable. "It is such a form of subordinate government for the tranquillity of the realm as no part of the Christian world hath the like, if the same be duly exercised."[1]

writ of power."—Medley, *English Constitutional History*, p. 395.

[1] Cited from Coke's *Fourth Institute*, p. 170, in Maitland's *Justice and Police*, p. 93. Chapter viii. of the latter work is the best brief account of the county magistracy as it exists to-day. Jenks comments upon the uniqueness of England's local government in his *Law and Politics in the Middle Ages*, pp. 182–184: "The comparative success of England in the matter of local government has given her a unique place among Teutonic countries, if we except, perhaps, Scandinavia. With this possible exception, England, and England alone, has succeeded in reconciling the absolute supremacy of the State with the existence of local independence. While the State in France became a rapacious bureaucracy, tempered only by municipal and feudal disintegration; while

3. The Later Judicial History of the Curia Regis, Especially the Origin and Early History of the Court of Chancery.

—When that fertile parent stem, the Curia Regis, had put forth such mighty judicial branches as the common-law courts and the itinerant justice system,[1] it had not drained itself of judicial power or exhausted its ability to create. It has been shown how, in the reign of Henry I., there were two regular manifestations of the Curia Regis: the fuller meeting of tenants-in-chief, summoned at the three great yearly festivals and at other times as occasion re-

---

the State in Germany died of inanition, and gave place to a crowd of absolute principalities, whose rulers treated their subjects as food for the cannon, or as milch kine for the supply of taxes; the State in England developed into a strong unity, whose elements yet maintained that vivid consciousness of local life which is essential to the existence of a free and self-respecting nation. The State in England has not ruled through feudal proprietors; therefore there have been no hereditary local despots who have defied her mandates. She has not destroyed the old landmarks; therefore her subjects have not felt themselves to be helpless atoms under the heel of a bureaucracy. Her officials have not been a privileged caste of adventurers, speculating in their offices, and exempt from the ordinary rules of law; therefore they have respected the rights of the citizen, and are by him regarded neither with jealousy nor with fear. The State has boldly used the local units as the basis of its own organisation. . . . In England the State has fearlessly left to local control much that a timid State keeps in its own hands—police, road-making, sanitation, education. The result of the whole policy has been to foster, if not to produce, some of the best features of the Englishman's political character: his deep respect for law, his independence in the face of authority, his self-reliance, his practical good sense, his willingness to compromise, his sincere though silent patriotism." The lack in continental countries of almost everything which characterises England's local system has led many continental writers to pick out the local magistracy as the most distinctive and valuable feature of the English constitution.

[1] See Part III., § I., 1.

quired, and the small body of officials and barons in attendance on the king, which the increasing business of the central government kept quite continuously in session.[1] The larger body, after the regular dropping out of the minor barons and a partial change in the basis of attendance, was, in the early · fourteenth century, the embryonic House of Lords [2]; while what there was left of the smaller body, after it had thrown off the court system, was the early Council.[3] But in both of these, there remained much of the undifferentiated power that is characteristic of primitive government; in conjunction with the king, either might exercise what would now be distinguished as executive, legislative, or judicial functions. And even at the date named, any conscious distinction between the two bodies themselves must have been slight. One could quite imperceptibly become the other. The smaller had, perhaps, a more official character—certainly there was a large body of officials—but it was attended by such of the prelates and barons as the king wished at his court, and, by a quite arbitrary summons of more prelates and barons, it might become the larger body. While the bulk of judicial business had, of course, gone to the court system, these original bodies still retained the power to deal at first instance with any case, criminal or civil, which the king cared to bring before them. They entertained many cases of a special character, and had, as was natural, a kind of supervisory jurisdiction over the ordinary courts.

While finally ceasing to be an administrative body, the House of Lords carried over from its earlier history, and has always retained, certain judicial functions.

[1] See above, pp. 102, 103, 125. [2] See below, pp. 299–302. [3] *Ibid.*, pp. 285–290.

When it was the king's feudal court, the king's vassals were judged in it by their fellow-vassals, their peers; in it, as in any feudal court, was judgment of peers (*judicium parium*). In the House of Lords, any English peer has the right to be judged, in capital crimes, by his fellow peers. In the procedure, known as impeachment, which developed late in the fourteenth century, the House of Lords judges and the House of Commons prosecutes.[1] And in the same century it was established that the House of Lords was to be the highest court of appeal for all England. This it has continued to be except in a few classes of civil cases which are appealed to the Council.

When the House of Lords was engaged in this judicial work, it was known by the technical and curious name of "king in parliament"—curious, because it perpetuated an idea derived from the primitive relation of king and Curia Regis, long antedating anything that could be properly called Parliament.[2] But there was also a tribunal called "king in council," and this was the Council, the descendant of the smaller Curia Regis, acting in its judicial capacity.[3]   We have

[1] See below pp. 376, 377.   For a description of the modern, central judicial system, see Maitland, *Justice and Police*, chs. v. and vi.

[2] On the earliest use in England of the word *parliament*, see below, pp. 320, 321.

[3] Speaking of "the king in parliament" and "the king in council," Maitland says: "And the two are not so distinct as an historian, for his own sake and his readers', might wish them to be. On the one hand those of the king's council who are not peers of the realm, in particular the judges and the masters of the chancery, are summoned to the lords' house of parliament, and only by slow degrees is it made plain to them that, when they are in that house, they are mere 'assistants' of the peers and are only to speak when spoken to.   On the other hand there is a widespread, if not very practical, belief that all the peers are by rights the king's

seen that both bodies might, at the beginning of the fourteenth century, entertain any civil or criminal case. While the larger, which was becoming the House of Lords, specialised its judicial activity along the lines just mentioned, the smaller, the future Council, retained the earlier and broader competence. During the fourteenth and fifteenth centuries, there developed from it, in both the criminal and civil fields, something of great importance in English judicial history.

The criminal side can be dealt with briefly. The late fourteenth and the fifteenth centuries were, for England, a time of degeneration and lawlessness among the nobility. Starting in the factional strifes and personal hatreds of Edward II.'s time, the lawless tendencies were stimulated by the endless foreign war. It was the time of *livery and maintenance*. In suits to which the great and powerful were parties, juries were so bribed or intimidated that a fair trial in the ordinary courts was exceptional. Just when Englishmen first began to realise what a valuable and unique thing the jury was, it was being proved a failure in a certain class of cases. It had become established that cases involving capital punishment could only be tried by a jury, but there was still a very useful sphere of activity for a court not bound by established rules of procedure and which could not be bribed or intimidated. The Council became such a court acting on its own original judicial authority and on several statutes of the Lancastrian period which specially empowered it to deal with certain cases. It exercised a sort of supplementary criminal juris-

councillors, and that any one of them may sit at the council board if he pleases."—Traill, *Social England* ii., 483.

diction, and punished severely by fine or imprisonment.   Rioting, conspiracy, and bribery furnished it
much work; and of special importance was its activity
in bringing perjured jurors to justice.   Here was a
method of preventing the complete degeneration of
the criminal jury; when the juror accepted a bribe
or yielded to fear, he knew that he might be severely
dealt with for it.   The way of the fifteenth-century
juror was hard, the local terror on one side and fine
or imprisonment at the hands of the Council on the
other.   The procedure of the Council was summary,
and, in other respects, in sharp contrast to that of the
common-law courts.   It has been described as doing
justice in an "administrative way."   It utilised many
of the methods of the canon law.   It took short cuts
to justice, and exercised what may be termed a criminal
equity. [1]   It is evident that the Council in this capacity
might easily be a blessing or a menace to the nation;
much depended upon the character of its members,
more upon the character of the king and whether the
king controlled it or was controlled by it.   Its value
was very great throughout the middle ages and during
parts of the Tudor period.   Naturally the common-
law judges were jealous of it and there was much agitation against it in Parliament; but agitation was in
vain while this criminal justice was exercised moderately
and well. [2]

[1] "It sends for the accused; it compels him to answer upon oath
written interrogatories.   Affidavits, as we should call them, are
sworn upon both sides.   With written depositions before them the
lords of the council, without any jury, acquit or convict.   The
extraction of confessions by torture is no unheard of thing."—
Maitland in Traill's *Social England* ii., 484.

[2] In later history, the Council acting judicially was known as the

The civil jurisdiction of the Council, like its criminal jurisdiction and the appellate jurisdiction of the House of Lords, had its root in the idea that the king was the source of law, and in his administration of the law through his Curia. The Curia Regis gave birth to special courts, but they were all king's courts. The king was less closely identified with them, however, than with their parent, his Council, and there were no definite boundaries to the judicial powers remaining in it. Such boundaries would have been paradoxical, for the king was the source of law and the Council was the king in action. As such, it could exercise a concurrent, a supervisory, or a supplementary jurisdiction. We are next to examine the conditions in the fourteenth century which made it necessary for the Council to develop a new line of activity in civil cases.

Court of Star Chamber, and this name was of ancient origin: in Westminster, "a new pile of buildings, between the great hall and the palace, and next to the exchequer receipt, was begun at least as early as 1346. . . . It was expressly appointed for the use of the council, and was henceforth so used. It was called the 'star chamber' from the first, though it was quite as often referred to as 'the council chamber next to the receipt of the exchequer.'"— J. F. Baldwin, *Antiquities of the King's Council*, English Historical Review xxi., 16. Under the Stuarts, all the evil possibilities of the court were realised; controlled by a despotic sovereign, it invaded the liberty of the subject and did the exact opposite of its earlier service of protecting the people against oppression. Consequently the Long Parliament, in 1641, so regulated the Council's judicial capacity as to abolish this court. The idea, which obtained at this time, that the Star Chamber Court originated in the statute of Henry VII. (1487), which placed this criminal jurisdiction in the hands of certain specified men— most of them councillors—and which, for a time, practically took this work from the Council as a whole, was without historical foundation. See further J. S. Leadam, *Select Cases in the Star Chamber*, pp. ix–lxxi. (Selden Society, vol. xvi.)

The system of writs, by which the common-law courts gained their civil justice and which laid the foundation of the common law itself, has been described; as also the rapidity with which new writs were created and the general adaptability of the new civil jurisdiction.[1] This condition lasted till about the middle of the thirteenth century. From that time, new forces began to limit the creation of writs; that is, they limited the creation of new actions, and hence tended to fix and stereotype the common law. The writ-making power had been in the hands of the Chancellor, always a learned ecclesiastic of the king's Council. In his increasing business, he had gathered around him a staff of assistants, known as Masters, who were also ecclesiastics, and, like the Chancellor, learned in the Roman law. The first important objection to the issuing of new writs was when Henry III. made his unfortunate attempt to rule without ministers and writs were being issued without a Chancellor in an irresponsible and unusual way. The common-law courts had become established with their benches of judges. These judges were not always ecclesiastics, as formerly; and there had gradually formed a body of men, who might not very improperly be termed professional lawyers. There was already a body of law and a procedure that, in the eyes of such men, could not lightly be modified, and precedent was becoming very important in the administration of justice. The objection soon went beyond the matter of the irregular issue of writs: the Chancellor, on his sole authority, must not make new writs. To make new writs was to make new law,

[1] See above, pp. 138–140.

and the idea was growing that the law was nearly complete. By the Provisions of Oxford, 1258, the Chancellor was to swear "that he will seal no writ, excepting writs of course, without the commandment of the king and of his council who shall be present."[1] Moreover the judges took it upon themselves to decide whether writs issued by the Chancellor were innovations or not; they did this by refusing, if they saw fit, to allow the use of such novel writs in the actions for which they were issued. This was such an arbitrary and mischievous checking of the law's natural growth that a sort of compromise was attempted in 1285 in the Statutes of Westminster, the Second:

And whensoever from henceforth it shall fortune in the chancery, that in one case a writ is found, and in like case falling under the law, and requiring like remedy, is found none, the clerks of the chancery shall agree in making the writ, or shall adjourn the plaintiffs until the next parliament and write the cases in which they cannot agree, and refer them to the next parliament, and by consent of men learned in the law, a writ shall be made, lest it might happen hereafter that the court should long time fail to minister justice unto complainants.[2]

But even this slight power to innovate, merely creating writs for actions which were similar to those already having writs of course, was opposed by the judges and soon became inoperative. "Henceforth the common law was dammed and forced to flow in unnatural artificial channels. Thus was closed the cycle of original writs, the catalogue of forms of

[1] A. and S., p. 58.　　　　[2] A. and S., p. 76.

action to which nought but Statute could make addition."[1]

The mention, in the Statute of Westminster, of Parliament as a place of legislative authority and the use of the word statute suggest that Parliament was about to solve the difficulty by making new laws for new cases. But there was no Parliament in 1285 in the sense in which the word is now understood. In this act, it probably meant nothing more than the king's Council. But there was a Parliament with a recognised statute-making power by the middle of the fourteenth century, and the principle was being asserted that no new law of a permanent character could emanate from any other source. Had Parliament then proceeded to legislate in a copious and intelligent manner, the need felt at that time would have been met in substantially the same way as at present. But this early Parliament played a dog-in-the-manger part. It stoutly opposed the making of new writs, but did not itself produce their equivalent. After an extraordinary outburst of legislation under Edward I., when Parliament, if we may speak of one at all, was in its primordial fragments, there ceased, with a few noteworthy exceptions in the fourteenth century, to be any important law-making until the Tudor period.[2] This brings the situation

[1] Maitland, *Bracton's Note Book*, cited in Medley, *English Constitutional History*, p. 352.

[2] "Parliament seems to have abandoned the idea of controlling the development of the common law. Occasionally and spasmodically it would interfere, devise some new remedy, fill a gap in the register of writs, or circumvent the circumventors of a statute. But in general it left the ordinary law of the land to the judges and the lawyers. In its eyes the common law was complete or very nearly complete. And then as we read the statute-

squarely before us. Where are the new cases to go
that the "dammed-up" common law and its courts
did not provide for?

It cannot be denied that, as time passed, a good
many small leaks began to show in the dam. While
fearfully afraid of avowed innovation in the law, the
common-law judges were not unmindful of changed
conditions or of the value of gaining new kinds of
cases. But they must be gained through such juggling
with the old law as would make it appear that there
was nothing new.[1] There was much, however, for
which the common law did not provide, or for which
it provided inadequately. Plaintiffs began to seek
relief, in such matters, at the higher and more ancient
tribunal from which the common-law courts themselves had sprung, the king in his Council. There
might be grounds for this action other than the inadequacy of the common law to cover their cases:
they were poor and unable to bear the expense of
ordinary litigation, or their poverty rendered the law's
delay disastrous; they were labouring under some
local prejudice and distrusted jury trial, or they were

---

roll of the fifteenth century we seem for a while to be watching
the decline and fall of a mighty institution. Parliament seems
to have nothing better to do than to regulate the manufacture
of cloth."—Maitland in Traill's *Social England* ii., 477.

[1] "In the fifteenth century there were great judges who performed
what may seem to us some daring feats in the accomodation of
law to new times. Out of unpromising elements they developed
a comprehensive law of contract; they loosened the bonds of those
family settlements by which land had been tied up; they converted
the precarious villein tenure of the middle ages into the secure
copyhold tenure of modern times. But all this had to be done
evasively and by means of circumventive fictions. Novel principles could not be admitted until they were disguised in some
antique garb."—*Ibid.*, 480.

14

contending with a wealthy and powerful lord who could buy or intimidate the jury and to whom delay was indifferent. On the same plenary conception of his judicial power, which authorised the king to pardon the criminal condemned by the common-law courts, he could entertain in his Council the cases of these poor petitioners.[1] Thus, in the fourteenth century, the Council exercised more and more, what it had never fully ceased to exercise, a justice concurrent with, and supplementary to, that of the common-law courts.

But the Council was a large, inchoate body, and if this line of activity were to increase and become regular, some specialisation must take place within it. The king could not attend to it personally, and the whole Council could not. For two main reasons, the Chancellor was the member of the Council to whom it was increasingly intrusted. He had become the king's chief minister by the end of the thirteenth century, and presided over the Council in the king's absence.[2] If petitions were not brought directly to the king, they naturally went to the man who most

[1] "Odd though this may seem to us, that court which was to become a byword for costly delay started business as an expeditious and a poor man's court."—Maitland in Traill's *Social England* ii., 486.

[2] The Chancellor was taking the place of the Justiciar, who, from the Norman Conquest, had been the greatest official and had represented the king in the latter's frequent and long absences on the continent. "The Chancellor first appears in England under Edward the Confessor. He was the chief secretary, head of the king's chaplains, and keeper of the royal seal. The name was derived from the *cancelli* or screen behind which he worked. Owing to the literary qualifications of the office, in the early days it was always in the hands of an ecclesiastic."—Medley, *English Constitutional History*, pp. 378, 379.

regularly represented him. And the Chancellor was a learned man with a corps of learned assistants, who knew the civil, that is, Roman, and canon laws. The common-law judges had many a time borrowed the principles of Roman law in dealing with new problems; an official specially versed in that law could most appropriately entertain unusual cases. On general principles, trained men were needed to deal with civil cases, the most important of which had to do with the increasingly intricate land law. Criminal cases brought before the Council, might be handled summarily by the king and the whole body; civil cases must be examined in the Chancery. It may be remarked further that the Chancellor was more at leisure than he had for long been; the writ business was declining—the chief reason, as has been shown, for the Council's growing judicial activity.

The first evidence that the Council's civil jurisdiction was being turned over to the Chancellor is found in an ordinance of 1290. By the end of Edward II.'s reign, it had become a regular, perhaps the most important, part of his work. Moreover, suits to which the king was a party, suits which, before this, the king had apportioned quite evenly between the common-law courts and the Council, he now preferred to have tried before the Chancellor. Nevertheless, Chancery emerged as a court separate from the Council gradually, almost imperceptibly. For a long time, civil cases, like criminal, were brought to the "king in Council," and were heard directly by him and his Council or were turned over to the Council's chief official as the royal convenience or the nature of the individual case dictated. As time passed, an increasing number actually went to the Chancellor. But in either case, the work was done in the Council, and no one was conscious that anything new was being created. Finally it was an accomplished fact; by the end of Edward III.'s reign, it could no longer escape notice that out of the Council a new court had grown, and men began to speak of it as such. But even at that time, it was hardly a separate jurisdiction; it was rather a permanent and recognised judicial committee of the Council, constantly drawing its authority from that body.

While Chancery grew, it used new principles and developed a new procedure. Indeed, its growth depended upon its ability to do this. As, at an earlier time, the Curia Regis and its first offspring, the common-law courts, were plastic, and developed a law and procedure vastly different from the antique formalism of the Anglo-Saxon court system,[1] so now Chancery was measurably in the same relation to these common-law courts, now themselves growing old and formal. But history was not to repeat itself to the extent of Chancery's assimilating or exterminating these courts. The common law was virile, but needed supplementing at a time when it refused to grow fast enough and was not being helped by statute. It was Chancery's use of new principles and procedure that was mainly responsible for its recognition as a distinct court. The procedure seems to have been borrowed directly from the canon law; it was the same as that of an ecclesiastical court. "In flagrant contrast to the common law, it forced the defendant to answer on oath the charges that were brought against him; it

[1] See above, p. 129 and note 2.

made no use of the jury; the evidence consisted of written affidavits." [1]

On the other hand, the Chancellors' training in Roman and canon law did not lead to a wholesale borrowing of that law for their court, as has often been taken for granted. They did not abandon the common law and adopt a new system. While they knew of the equitable jurisdiction of the Roman Prætor, they did not attempt to adopt the results of that jurisdiction. Rather, both Roman Prætor and English Chancellor, *mutatis mutandis*, acted under the same fundamental authority, the authority of the sovereign as source of law, to deal with the law as occasion required. [2] When Chancery is spoken of as a court of *equity* or

---

[1] Maitland, in Traill's *Social England* ii., 488.

[2] This principle, as far as the nations of western Europe are concerned, originated in Rome. Of its ultimate source there and its disposition during the Republic, Sir Henry Maine says: "At the crisis of primitive Roman history which is marked by the expulsion of the Tarquins, a change occurred which has its parallel in the early annals of many ancient states, but which had little in common with those passages of political affairs which we now term revolutions. It may be best described by saying that the monarchy was put into commission. The powers heretofore accumulated in the hands of a single person were parcelled out among a number of elective functionaries, the very name of the kingly office being retained and imposed upon a personage known subsequently as the Rex Sacrorum or Rex Sacrificulus. As part of the change, the settled duties of the supreme judicial office devolved on the Prætor, at the time the first functionary in the commonwealth, and together with these duties was transferred the undefined supremacy over law and legislation which always attached to ancient sovereigns, and which is not obscurely related to the patriarchal and heroic authority they had once enjoyed."—*Ancient Law*, pp. 61, 62. Since the Norman Conquest, the English kings had been more and more putting their judicial authority into commission. The analogy between the fourteenth- and fifteenth-century Chancellor and the Roman Prætor is in many respects striking.

the Chancellor as exercising an *equitable* jurisdiction, the meaning is that, while the common law was used as far as possible, when it was found that its use resulted in what was not equitable or in conformity to the dictates of conscience, then it was modified or supplemented as the ends of natural justice seemed to require. In doing this, the Chancellor might utilise his Roman or canonical learning, but he more often preferred to extend or modify some already existing principle of the common law.[1] He was, as it has been aptly expressed, making an appendix to the common law. He was in no way concerned with making a new body of law; he dealt with each case singly as it arose. Generalisation was not his function, and, in the early days, past decisions were not much used as precedents. "Sufficient for the day are the cases in that day's cause-list."

The common-law judges were not friendly to this upstart jurisdiction, and protest against it often found voice in Parliament. In the early days, before Chancery attempted much supervisory jurisdiction, the chief objection was against its purely common-law practice. When the common law had a sufficient remedy, the fact that a party to a suit was poor or feared his powerful opponent was not regarded a

[1] "To restrain an unconscionable or inequitable use of legal rights is not (such seems the theory) to override the law, it really is to do what the law means to do, but is prevented from doing by causes not to be foreseen. . . . But we may perhaps mark the character of equity by calling it supplemental law. From the first the theory had been that equity had come not to destroy but to fulfil, and the success of the Chancery, which was jealously watched by Parliament, had depended on at least an outward observance of this theory."—Maitland, *Justice and Police*, pp. 36, 38.

sufficient reason for drawing such suit from the court where it naturally belonged. This side of Chancery's business never became important, and in time tended to decrease. To its supplementary or equitable juris-diction, Parliament was never able to urge very valid objections, and the common-law courts tacitly, though grudgingly, conceded that here the new court had a reason for existence. But though Chancery's work in this line was soon considerable, it was desultory, the field of activity was vague. No important, de-finable class of cases had been appropriated. Had this condition continued, Chancery could hardly have become a separate jurisdiction, and its later his-tory would have been radically different and far less important.

About the end of the fourteenth century, a special kind of business, growing out of the inadequacy of the land law, was brought into Chancery in such quantity that it was soon regarded as the peculiar jurisdiction of that court. Under the common law, it was impossible to will land, and the feudal accom-paniments of tenure were often felt to be burdensome and antiquated. Was there no possibility of enjoying the use and profit of land while escaping the respon-sibilities of ownership? Was there no way in which a man could determine who should have the use of his land after him? Necessity was the mother of invention, or rather of extension and adaptation. For the required method existed already, but had been confined to a narrow sphere. In the thirteenth century, a device had been often used by which the Franciscan friars, who by the rule of their order could own no property, enjoyed the use of real estate while

not technically owning it.   A man disposed of lands
and houses to a party who was to be its legal owner,
but who, by the terms of the transaction, was to hold
them to the use of a certain body of friars.   This device
had been occasionally used from very ancient times,
but it never became prominent until the peculiar
need of the friars led to its rapid extension after their
coming to England.   In its early use, its success depended entirely upon the good faith of the legal owner
of the property; when the contract was made between
him and the grantor, he was bound in honour to hold
the land to the use stipulated.[1]   Because the device
had been so seldom used before the thirteenth century,
it had obtained no recognition in the common law;
for when it came into frequent use that law had passed
its receptive period.   So if the owner chose to disregard his honourable understanding, there was no
legal remedy for the party to whose use the property
had been given.   However, the beneficiaries being
for the most part clergy, it is probable that the church
courts sometimes took account of such breach of contract.   At any rate, the friars could always invoke the
terrors of excommunication and interdict against un-
faithful legal owners.

The king took little account of this method of
benefiting the friars, but he was becoming greatly
alarmed at the amount of land passing into the ownership of the church in general.   Hence the Statute
of Mortmain, 1279, which prohibited further alienation
of land to the clergy.[2]   The problem of dodging this

[1] When friars were the beneficiaries, the legal owner was very
often a borough.

[2] A. and S., pp. 71, 72.

statute immediately arose. The method was at hand. Friars could not own land because of their rule; by the Statute of Mortmain, the rest of the clergy [1] could own no more land than they already had. To meet the second case, as the first, legal ownership might be vested in a person or persons, who, for substantial reasons, entered into a private understanding to allow the use of the land to the church. Thus the practice of *uses* was greatly extended as the fourteenth century progressed. An act of 1392 very effectually put a stop to it as far as the church was concerned[2]; but before that time, it had occurred to laymen that here was a neat way to accomplish for themselves certain things not provided for by the common law.

Assuming the feoffees to uses [3] to be willing and faithful instruments of the beneficial owner, his advantages were great. Though he were involved in the civil strife of York and Lancaster, and dealt with as a traitor by victorious enemies, the land would be secured for his children; for it legally belonged not to him but to the feoffees to uses, and therefore was not forfeited by his attainder. For the same reason nothing was payable to the overlord on his death; there could be no legal succession while any of the feoffees remained alive, and herein was the convenience of naming several in the first instance. The numbers might be kept up from time to time by new conveyances, as is the common practice to this day with

---

[1] The language of the statute limited its application to the monastic clergy, but in its later interpretations this limitation was not observed. See Gross, *Mortmain in Medieval Boroughs*, American Historical Review xii., 741.

[2] A. and S., p. 155.

[3] This was the technical term for legal owners.

bodies of trustees established for charitable and public purposes. [1]

It will be seen from this how the beneficiary could virtually will the land. While the legal ownership could not be regulated by will, the extra-legal use could be disposed of in a purely informal way; the beneficiary could declare to the legal owners where the use should go after his death. With outgrown land laws and much to make ownership burdensome and hampering, the idea of uses just fitted the situation and became so popular that a large part of the land of England was affected by it in the early fifteenth century. [2]

But uses were not recognised by the law, and the crucial question was where an authority could be found to force the legal owner to keep his honourable agreement. For when the practice became general, trusting to personal honour proved an inadequate guarantee. The same resource was found as in other cases in which the common law failed to provide a remedy; the distressed beneficiary, who was being defrauded of his equitable rights, appealed to the Chancellor as the special depository of the king's all-powerful and overriding justice. The Chancellor interfered and, by fine or imprisonment, forced the legal owners to keep faith. It was not long before this work, developing subdivisions and minutiæ that cannot be examined here, was the chief and char-

[1] Pollock, *The Land Laws*, p. 93.

[2] At the beginning of the fourteenth century, nearly all free tenures in England were subject to the law of primogeniture. By the system of uses, provision could be made for younger sons and daughters. This furnished a powerful motive for extending the system.

acteristic business of the Court of Chancery. Thus
during the last two centuries of the middle ages, a
transformation of the land laws was well under way,[1]
and a new court with a special jurisdiction had come
into existence. For Chancery's monopoly of this
new field completed its separation from the parent
stem; by the reign of Edward IV., the Chancellor,
in his judicial capacity, no longer acted for the Council.
His court had already created considerable supplementary law, and, with the evolution of the common-
law courts in mind, it is not hard to understand that
there would come a time when the Chancellor's conscience had become "a technical conscience" and his
court as much bound by precedent as its predecessors.[2]

[1] On this strange method of changing a body of law, Maitland
comments: "It is an exceedingly curious episode. The whole
nation seems to enter into one large conspiracy to evade its own
laws, to evade laws which it has not the courage to reform. The
Chancellor, the judges, and the parliament seem all to be in the
conspiracy. And yet there is really no conspiracy: men are but
living from hand to mouth, arguing from one case to the next case,
and they do not see what is going to happen."—*Social England* ii.,
487. It is apparent that, as this way of manipulating legal ownership grew more common, the number of occasions upon which
the great landholders could collect reliefs, and the king reliefs and
primer seisins, would decrease. There is some evidence that king
and lords were becoming aware of this during the fifteenth century;
but Henry VIII. was the first king who was fully aroused to the
situation. He attempted to cope with it by forcing through Parliament the famous Statute of Uses in 1536. For a discussion of the
failure and the peculiar legal results of this statute, see Pollock,
The Land Laws, pp. 97–106. For further discussion of the Chancellor's jurisdiction, see W. P. Baildon, Introduction to *Select Cases
in Chancery* (Selden Society, vol. x.).

[2] For a brief summary of the later history of Chancery, see Medley,
English Constitutional History, pp. 381–383. Maitland has very
perfectly summed up the constitutional significance of the two late
judicial developments with which this section has been mainly con-

4. **The Common Law.**—The exceptional character of English legal history has been an important element in determining the final character of the English government. In the period covered by this book, the main features of the law were established. It is therefore proper here, without touching the content of the law, to examine briefly these distinguishing features; especially is it the purpose to note their constitutional bearing. The term *common law*, with which it seems necessary to head this division, is at present used in more than one sense and often vaguely. It has been thus defined:

(a) In its most general sense, the system of law in force among English-speaking peoples, and derived from England, in contradistinction to the civil or Roman law and the canon or ecclesiastical law. (b) More appropriately, the parts of the former system which do not rest for their authority on any subsisting express legislative act; the unwritten law. In this sense common law consists in

cerned: "Somehow or another England, after a fashion all her own, had stumbled into a scheme for the reconciliation of permanence with progress. The old medieval criminal law could be preserved because a Court of Star Chamber would supply its deficiences; the old private law could be preserved, developed, transfigured, because other modes of trial were limiting it to an appropriate sphere. And so our old law maintained its continuity. . . . The Star Chamber and the Chancery were dangerous to our political liberties. Bacon could tell King James that the Chancery was the court of his absolute power. But if we look abroad we shall find good reason for thinking that but for these institutions our old-fashioned national law, unable out of its own resources to meet the requirements of a new age, would have utterly broken down, and the 'ungodly jumble' would have made way for Roman jurisprudence and for despotism. Were we to say that equity saved the common law, and that the Court of Star Chamber saved the constitution, even in this paradox there would be some truth."—*Social England* ii., 489.

those principles and rules which are gathered from the reports of adjudged cases, from the opinions of text writers and commentators, and from popular usage and custom, in contradistinction to statute law. (c) More narrowly that part of the system just defined which was recognised and administered by the king's justices in contradistinction to the modifications introduced by the chancellors as rules of equity in restraint or enlargement of the customary and statutory law.[1]

Beside this, may be placed the history of the term. Common law first meant a law that was common to all England, a law not for this or that county or borough. It was thus used in the twelfth and thirteenth centuries. It was next used in opposition to statute law, as the latter developed during the fourteenth century; then in opposition to equity when the Court of Chancery became important in the fifteenth century. By that time, the conception of it as a body of law older than, and in important ways distinguished from, two other bodies of law had crowded the original meaning out of the word *common*. The first of the present usages, cited above, seems to have arisen from applying to the whole of England's law the name of its most characteristic and historically important part. It is an untechnical use, but serves to distinguish England's law and legal history from those of other European countries.

Had no system of king's courts grown after the Norman Conquest, the Anglo-Saxon law, administered in the local courts, would, of course, have continued to

---

[1] The Century Dictionary. This definition has been quoted in full to make clear the present, accepted usages, and to avoid the necessity of explanations in the course of the discussion.

develop.   It seems certain from what is known of continental history that from such a law, administered in courts so isolated from one another, no law common to the whole country could have grown.   Without the common courts, there could not have been the common law.   Rather, the differences, which existed among the localities when the population was primitive and homogeneous, would have become ever more numerous and inveterate.   The kind of law used in the twelfth-century king's courts has already been noticed—it's adaptability, the multiplicity of its sources.[1]   What needs insistence here is that these courts were common courts.   The Curia Regis was opening wider to all litigants; ever more regularly did it send out judges to travel through the country and administer law.   The same judges went on various iters and gave the people the same law the country over.   The reign of Henry II. was most distinctly the period when the foundation of the common law was laid, both as to its content and its characteristic of commonness; it was the most creative period that English law has known.   But legislation was informal and largely unconscious:

. . . a few written or even spoken words communicated to his justices, whom he was constantly sending to perambulate the country, might do great things, might institute new methods of procedure, might bring new classes of men and things within the cognisance of the royal court.   Some of his ordinances—or "assizes," as they were called—have come down to us; others we have lost.   No one was at any great pains to preserve their text, because they were regarded, not as new laws, but as mere temporary instructions which might be easily altered. They soon sink into the mass of unenacted " common law."

[1] See above, p. 129 and note 2.

Even in the next, the thirteenth, century some of Henry's rules were regarded as traditional rules which had come down from a remote time, and which might be ascribed to the Conqueror, the Confessor, or any other king around whom a mist of fable had gathered.[1]

From the middle of the twelfth to the middle of the thirteenth century was the time when the common law, as opposed to statute law or equity, was made.[2] Those who then had most to do with the common law were trained in the Roman and canon laws; and it was considerably influenced from Roman sources, not by much actual borrowing, but by the unconscious influences of spirit and method. It has been well said that, at that early time, the common law was sufficiently inoculated with the Roman law to make it unlikely to fall under the latter's completer sway at a later period.[3] In the last half of the thirteenth century, there was a radical change of attitude in the guardians of the law. Law was no longer in the hands of ecclesiastics; a class of professional lawyers was forming. As the common law became more fixed and circumscribed,[4] any attempt to modify or enlarge it, especially from what was doubtless regarded as a rival system, was looked upon with disfavour.

The significance in legal history of the two great treatises of Glanville and Bracton, the one coming at the beginning and the other at the end of the common law's creative century, must be touched upon here.

---

[1] Maitland, in Traill's *Social England* ii., 408, 409.

[2] Its growth, at that time, through the making of writs has been dealt with above, pp. 138–140.

[3] See the citation from Brunner in Maitland, *English Law and the Renaissance*, note 55.

[4] See above, pp. 206–209.

Late in Henry II.'s reign was written a *Treatise on the Laws and Customs of England*, ascribed to Ranulf Glanville and always passing under his name, but more probably the work of Hubert Walter.[1] The impulse to write such a treatise, a very remarkable performance for the time, probably came from the revived interest in Roman law characteristic of the twelfth century. But there is little Roman law in the work, and the author shows no desire to adopt it; it is not Roman even in the matter of arrangement. Though the Treatise was unofficial, it had a great influence upon the law and procedure with which it dealt. It was an able attempt to formulate and arrange a very vague and elusive material, and put into durable condition many valuable things that might otherwise have been lost. Its coming at the end of Henry II.'s reign was extremely opportune.

Equally timely was the more colossal work of Bracton, *Concerning the Laws and Customs of England*. It was written about the middle of the thirteenth century, and is by far the most important law-book which appeared in England in the middle ages. It owes much more to Roman law than Glanville's work, about one fifteenth of it being borrowed from the *Summa* of Azo, "a legist who stood at the head of the Bolognese school of law early in the thirteenth century." There was also much that was Roman in Bracton's arrangement and method of systematising. But with the exception stated, the law that Bracton gives is thoroughly English. It is not theoretical, an ideal system; but emphatically the law of his time, the law that had been made by

[1] See Maitland's article on Glanville in the *Dictionary of National Biography*.

adjudged cases, and the specific cases that he cites are many. Just as this work appeared, the forces tending to fix the common law were beginning to make themselves felt. Although, like. Glanville's, this was a purely private undertaking, it is hardly necessary to state that such a comprehensive and sympathetic statement of English law coming at such a time became an authority of the highest influence.

An epoch in legal history was closing with Bracton. A new system of courts, with appropriate law and procedure, had been made; borrowing from the Roman law, at least for a long time to come, was at an end; the making of new writs, that is, new forms of action, was no longer easy; a system of legal forms had been created.[1] One is, at first, surprised that a law and procedure so young and mobile under Henry II. should have grown old and rigid in his grandson's reign. The truth seems to be that the time was too early to obtain, by any process, a permanent and rational system of equity. England passed rather rapidly from "the old oral and traditional formalism" of the Anglo-Saxon period to this "new written and authoritative formalism" which "in part supplanted and in part reinforced it." But the advance of the new over the old was very great. That there was any break from the old system and a time when new courts exercised an equitable jurisdiction for all England, a time of legal

---

[1] This system greatly resembles the Roman formulary system, especially in its manner of growth, but was not derived from it. It could not have been, for the lawyers of this time were interested, if at all, in the finished product of Roman law, the Justinian Code, not in the history of that law; they were probably not aware that it had passed through an evolution analogous to that through which English law was passing.

15

creation on a splendid scale, was owing to the Norman Conquest. And the new formalism was a *common* formalism, while the old was not.

The development of the new formalism was not an unmixed evil. When a man chose an action in the late thirteenth century, he embarked on a sure course, all was marked out for him; in an unspeakable mass of rules, an attempt was made to provide for every contingency. This meant that the discretionary power of the judges was small. With the judges of the three common-law courts so fully under royal control as they were for four centuries after this, the formulary system must be regarded as having been an important safe-guard of the subject's liberty. The modern develop-ment has been to give the judge more freedom, to allow him, in many particulars, to suit the action to the peculiarities of the case; "but discretionary powers can only be safely entrusted to judges whose impartiality is above suspicion and whose every act is exposed to public and professional criticism."[1] It must not be conceived, however, that the judges of the later middle ages were entirely powerless to initiate; they were always making some new law when they made their judgments. But their judgments of law were based upon the verdicts of jurors drawn from the people, and these verdicts were increasingly judgments of fact; the judges applied the law to facts judged by the people. This kept the law from any theoretical flights which might have borne it away from the

---

[1] P. and M. ii., 563. For a full discussion of the forms of action, see *ibid*. ii., 558–573. "Die Form ist die geschworene Feindin der Willkür, die Zwillingschwester der Freiheit."—Ihering, *Geist des römischen Rechts* ii. (2), § 45, quoted in P. and M. ii., 563, note 2.

domain of the practical and the serviceable. The law never escaped from the people; they were actually making their law or keeping it from being made. No absolutism was running the people into the mould of a foreign, or theoretically perfect, law. On the contrary, the law has reflected all the peculiarities, incongruities, and conservatisms of the English people at any specific time. This went far to make it ineradicable; the people could not get along without it because it was a part of them.

Another agency that helped make the English common law permanent had its origin at just the time the law was completing its period of rapid growth. The great English law schools, the Inns of Court, are first dimly seen about the end of the thirteenth century. They became thoroughly established in the reigns of Edward III. and Richard II. It is an interesting fact that the common law did not find its home in the universities. There the ground had been taken by the civil and canon laws, and the teaching of these had become so identified with the university work that when there was an English law to teach it seemed an unnatural thing to give it a place beside them.[1] No one consciously founded the law schools; they grew out of the needs and conditions of the time, which

[1] " The voice of John Wyclif pleading that English law was the law that should be taught in English universities was a voice that for centuries cried in the wilderness. . . . It was 1758 before Blackstone began his ever famous course at Oxford. The chair that I cannot fill was not established until the trans-Atlantic Cambridge was setting an example to her elderly mother."—Maitland, *English Law and the Renaissance*, pp. 25, 26.—Maitland was Downing Professor of the Laws of England in the University of Cambridge.

determined their location and most else about them.

In the first half of the thirteenth century, it was becoming evident that English justices would soon cease to be drawn from the clergy. The spirit of this period of papal power and church unity was to keep the clergy from participating in lay affairs. If they touched such things, it should be as masters, not participants. It was especially unseemly for bishops to sit on the bench and dispense a layman's law, which dealt with much that was a contamination to an ecclesiastic. A series of canons, forbidding the clergy to deal with secular law, began to appear, and were not without effect. The clergy became more careful to withdraw when the death sentence was pronounced or a matter considered to which they might not listen without scandal; and many were the devices of elision and abbreviation in wording by which their share in such affairs was concealed and their consciences saved. But it was harder to conceal a breach of the new rules in the case of the higher clergy, and bishops were found less and less among the justices; their places were taken by laymen who had come to a knowledge of the law by filling subordinate positions in the courts. At the end of Henry III.'s reign there were more laymen than clerks connected with the courts, and, though there were clerical justices throughout the reign of Edward I., the end was well in sight. A well-defined body of lawyers, practising in the king's courts, had formed and many justices came to the bench who had already served as advocates. To speak of a class of professional lawyers and lay justices, who had been lawyers, seems very modern, and, in truth, Edward I.'s reign, in many ways, marked the beginning of the modern period in the legal history of England.

When English law severed its connection with ecclesiastics, it was separated from the Roman law and also from the learning and literature of the time. The danger that absolutism might be fostered by the absorption of too much Roman law was past, and there was also little possibility that the law of the future would be blessed with any great legal treatise similar to that of Bracton. The divorce of law and learning produced bad results. Edward I. was conscious of the fact and, in 1290 and 1292, instituted commissions of inquiry. By the second commission, it was suggested that promising students be gathered from the various parts of England and placed in proximity to the courts at Westminster, with the evident intention of having them trained for service in those courts. The origin and early history of the Inns of Court are not known in detail, but here was the situation out of which they grew. A common law was recognised; some sense of its national character was dawning, of its distinction from Roman or canon law; it was in the hands of laymen and it could not be taken for granted that these men had received any training, legal or other, at the universities—as a matter of fact, they got their knowledge of the law and entered its higher service through training in its courts. And these courts were at Westminster; this was the home of the common law, not Oxford or Cambridge. Young men looking to a legal career gathered in the vicinity, and the four great law schools were born: Lincoln's Inn, the Inner Temple, the Middle Temple, and Gray's Inn. It is not the place here to say anything of the organisation or work of these schools. Let it merely be noted that their character was unique; in origin essentially fraternities of lawyers, and always remaining such, they undertook the training of students, devised a system of instruction, government, and discipline entirely their own, had their own preparatory schools, and conferred "what in effect were degrees, and degrees which admitted to practice in the courts."[1]

The importance of the law schools in this connection was their decisive influence in making the common law enduring; they were thus largely responsible for that law's share in England's governmental destiny. This achievement of theirs is summed up in Maitland's saying that "taught law is tough law." It would "be difficult to conceive any scheme better suited to harden and toughen a traditional body of law than one which, while books were still uncommon, compelled every lawyer to take part in legal education and every distinguished lawyer to read public lectures."[2] In the law schools, were used the Year Books, also a unique product of the English court system and a further proof that at the end of the thirteenth century a new era in English law had begun.[3] In 1292, just when Edward was

[1] Maitland, *English Law and the Renaissance*, note 60; see this note also for literature upon the subject. "What is distinctive of medieval England is not parliament, for we may everywhere see assemblies of estates, not trial by jury, for this was but slowly suppressed in France. But the Inns of Court and the Year Books that were read therein, we shall hardly find their like elsewhere."— *Ibid.*, p. 27.

[2] *Ibid.*, pp. 27, 28.

[3] A valuable account of the Year Books in general is given in Maitland, *Year Books of Edward II.*, vol. i., pp. ix–xx. (Selden Society, vol. xvii.).

investigating the decline in legal learning which resulted
from the withdrawal of the clergy, the Year Books
began. They continued, with almost no interruption,
until 1535. They were "so called because there was
one for each regnal year. They are anonymous law
reports, written in French, containing the discussions
of the judges and counsel on the points of law, and the
grounds of judgment in important cases tried before
the royal justices either at Westminster or in Eyre.
According to an old legal tradition, these reports had
official sanction and were drawn up by reporters in
the employ of the crown."[1] These reports, continued
with such regularity and fulness, are a proof of the
persistence of the spirit of conservatism and respect for
precedent which marked the time of their birth, and
they aided greatly in its preservation. Since no more
law was to be created, the matter of chief interest was
to know how successive judges had used the already
existing principles and procedure. During the fourteenth and fifteenth centuries, precedent was built
upon precedent and the mass of recorded rules was
reasoned upon and refined to the last extremity of
logic in the academic atmosphere of the Inns of Court,
until the common law had become a marvel and a
terror to every one outside the legal fraternity. Since
Edward I., the law of England has undergone no such
fundamental change as it experienced in his time.
The modern lawyer may trace back his legal traditions
quite easily through more than six centuries, but the
attempt to follow them into the wonderful, creative century before Edward I., in many cases, proves fruitless.[2]

[1] Gross, *Sources and Literature of English History*, p. 353.
[2] But the number of such cases has been greatly lessened by the

It has been shown how the law of England was made
a common law to all freemen and all localities; how it
was created by the people, their legal garment made
bit by bit and fitting into all the sinuosities of the
national character; how it was "toughened" by teaching and the unbroken yearly record of its application.
In the middle of the sixteenth century, when England
was passing into the full tide of Renaissance influence
and the worship of the Roman law was supreme in
Europe and *receptions*[1] were the order of the day, the
vitality of the English law was put to a severe test.
From the middle of Henry VIII.'s reign to the early
part of Elizabeth's, there were many evidences of its
decline.   Other European countries received the Roman law because their old law was not a *common* law,
was not a vital, growing law with a hold upon the
people, in short, because it was an impossible law for
states advancing rapidly in unity and civilisation.
As far as can be judged, England narrowly escaped a
reception, for all the surface forces—and many of them
were powerful—were working for it.   But she escaped
for the simple reason that she had a law that measurably
sufficed her, a law with such deep and tough roots in
the national life that to tear it away would have been
a sort of national suicide.   When England passed from
the medieval into the modern, she did not, like some of
her sister countries, leave the medieval law behind.[2]

---

work of Pollock and Maitland which deals mainly with that
century.

[1] The technical term for the adoption of the Roman law by a
nation.

[2] Maitland's brilliant lecture, *The English Law and the Renaissance*, should be read in this connection.   It is with a sort of con-
gratulatory enthusiasm, possible only to one who had entered so

The constitutional importance of this preservation of the old law can hardly be overstated.

The English common law was tough, one of the toughest things ever made. And well for England was it in the days of Tudors and Stuarts that this was so. A simpler, a more rational, a more elegant system would have been an apt instrument of despotic rule. At times the judges were subservient enough: the king could dismiss them from their offices at a moment's notice; but the clumsy, cumbrous system, though it might bend, would never break. It was ever awkwardly rebounding and confounding the statecraft which had tried to control it. The strongest king, the ablest minister, the rudest lord-protector could make little of this "ungodly jumble."[1]

deeply into the life of the crochety but salutary old system, that he speaks of its safe passage of the crisis and of its recovering strength. "When the middle of the century is past the signs that English law has a new lease of life become many. The medieval books poured from the press, new books were written, the decisions of the courts were more diligently reported, the lawyers were boasting of the independence and extreme antiquity of their system. We were having a little Renaissance of our own: or a gothic revival if you please. . . . That wonderful Edward Coke was loose. The medieval tradition was more than safe in his hands."—P. 29. "Sir Edward Coke, the incarnate common law," he calls him in another place, who "shovels out his enormous learning in vast disorderly heaps. Carlyle's felicity has for ever stamped upon Coke the adjective 'tough'—'tough old Coke upon Littleton, one of the toughest men ever made.' We may well transfer the word from the man to the law that was personified in him."—Traill, *Social England* ii., 481.

[1] *Ibid.* Roman law had these same characteristics "during the ages of its growth, and it is well to remember that, as Roman law took on a more scientific form, and was reduced to an organised system, its life and power of growth ceased. History does not show any necessary connection between these two events; but certainly, if the formation of a scientific system on the basis of the English common law is to mean that our law and institution-making power is past, then every Anglo-Saxon may most heartily pray that

A final struggle between king and people would probably have occurred in the seventeenth century even if the old law had been replaced by the Roman, "but it would hardly have been that struggle for the medieval, the Lancastrian, constitution in which Coke and Selden and Prynne and other ardent searchers of mouldering records won their right to be known to schoolboys,"[1] and one can hardly feel much hope for the people in such hypothetical conflict, the Stuart kings having the Roman law for their ally.

But to say nothing of the political side of the matter, of the absolute monarchy which the Roman law has been apt to bring in its train, it is probably well for us and for the world at large that we have stumbled forward in our empirical fashion, blundering into wisdom. The moral glow known to the virtuous school-boy who has not used the "crib" that was ready to his hand, we may allow ourselves to feel; and we may hope for the blessing which awaits all those who have taught themselves anything.[2]

In conclusion, a word needs to be said about the equity of the Court of Chancery and about statute law. Of the former it is only necessary to remark, by way of reminder, that English equity was, in essence, a supplement or appendix to the common law, and that because of it that law was much better fitted to meet the requirements of the sixteenth century and pass successfully the crisis which it then encountered.[3]

Statute law began nominally in the thirteenth

---

our law may long remain unscientific."—Adams, *Civilisation during the Middle Ages*, p. 102, note 1.

[1] Maitland, *English Law and the Renaissance*, p. 30.

[2] Maitland in Traill's *Social England* i., 280.

[3] See above, pp. 213, 214, 219, note 2.

century. But there had always been law made by
the central government, by the king in his Council;
and king and Council have continued, upon occasion,
to make it. In the fourteenth century, a new law-
making element, the House of Commons, came into
existence, and statutes, in the proper sense of the
word, were made by king and Parliament. Some
acts of the thirteenth century are traditionally termed
statutes which are really ordinances, made by king
and Council; and some had an anomalous origin and
are, strictly speaking, neither ordinances nor statutes.[1]
For several reasons Magna Carta has been regarded
as the beginning of England's written law and holds
first place in the statute book.[2] The informality of
earlier legislation led to its rapid absorption in the
mass of unwritten tradition; the events leading to
Magna Carta and the document itself were extraordinary; by the frequency of its confirmation, it was
kept before men's minds and its greatness seemingly
enhanced; and under Edward I., a class of secular

[1] On the origin of statutes and their early relations to ordinances,
see below, pp. 365–372.

[2] The text in the Statutes of the Realm is that of the confirmation
of 1225. "The text of the Great Charter issued the eleventh of
February, 1225 (ninth year of Henry III.), is of exceptional importance. In the first place it is definitive and has never been
modified (save in a single point of detail) in any of the official confirmations and copies which have been published since. It is the one
text that has always been appealed to either in the courts or in the
houses of Parliament, or in law books. In its form it approaches
closely the redactions of 1216 and 1217, and therefore differs much
from the act of 1215. The Charter of the Forest was renewed and
confirmed at the same time. They are now the first statutes of
the kingdom of England, the corner-stone of its written constitution."—Translated from Bémont, *Chartes des Libertés Anglaises*,
pp. xxix., xxx.

lawyers began to be interested in England's legal history. Yet the Great Charter is not a statute. It is largely a written amplification of the king's feudal contract with his tenants-in-chief; this is its fundamental element. It contains also sundry semi-feudal or non-feudal grants to other classes of people, and there are elements of compromise and bargain. It had immediate ends in view and aimed at restoring the customary law. It did not create new law, but in later years many of its clauses, often misunderstood, had a profound influence upon legislation.

Two acts of Henry III.'s reign have been called statutes: the Statute of Merton, 1236, and the Statute of Marlborough, 1268; both of these were products of king and Council. There was still no system of keeping rolls and it was largely a matter of chance which acts were preserved and, of these, which were known as statutes. The term has been quite generally applied to the important acts of Edward I.'s reign. In making some of these, there was concerned one or other of the new elements which, with the evolving House of Lords, later formed Parliament. It was a transition period, and it is hard to say whether or not there was a new form of legislation. Be this as it may, the statutes of Edward I., the written laws made by the central government, have borne a most important and special relation to the common law. Coming just at the end of that law's rapid extension through new writs, they formed a new starting point and laid down principles, upon which, with but little conscious creation, much new law was based and elaborated. Especially was this the case with land law. Such statutes as Mortmain, De Donis Conditionalibus, and Quia Emptores[1] were fundamental.[2] But this great legislative reign was exceptional; in the two following centuries, the common law was left to elaborate itself, little important supplemental material being furnished it by Parliament. In the Tudor period, important legislation began again and it has since steadily increased in quantity. Hence it might seem that all law-making power would ultimately pass to Parliament and that the independence of the judicial system, with its self-developing body of law, would cease. But this has not proved to be the case.

That the common law has been radically revolutionised by statute on some subjects in very recent times, as, for example, in real estate law, is not an evidence of the decline of this self-developing power. It is rather due to the rapid and revolutionary change in society itself, which demands equally rapid and revolutionary change in the law to accompany it. The statutes themselves are subjected at once to the ordinary process of common-law development in the interpretation and application of them made by the courts.[3]

[1] These are also known as De Religiosis, Westminster the Second, and Westminster the Third. See A. and S., documents 40, 42, 45.

[2] "Blackstone, in order that he might expound the working of the law in his own day in an intelligible fashion, was forced at every turn to take back his readers to the middle ages, and even now, after all our reforms, our courts are still from time to time compelled to construe statutes of Edward I.'s day, and were Parliament to repeal some of those statutes and provide no substitute, the whole edifice of our land law would fall down with a crash."—P. and M. i., xxxiv.

[3] Adams, *Civilisation during the Middle Ages*, p. 101, note 1. "In the United States the existence of a written constitution as fundamental law has led to a most important and valuable extension of this principle in the power which the courts have assumed, without

Thus has England's common law—common law (in the narrower sense), equity, and statutes—remained incomplete and unscientific, but alive and growing; not a ready-made system brought in from outside and imposed upon the people, but made by the people and administered by them. The common law has been a potent ally of constitutional government.

5. **Relations of the State Courts and the Church Courts.**—In the later middle ages in all the countries of western Europe, lay jurisdiction was more or less invaded by that of the church. [1] The discussion of the English court system cannot be concluded without notice of the causes and extent of this invasion in England and its bearing upon the effectiveness of the judiciary. In the Anglo-Saxon period, there had been no such invasion; this was because England was not touched by the increased church unity and influence

---

express sanction, to declare a law regularly passed by the national legislature unconstitutional and therefore null and void."—*Ibid.*, p. 102.

[1] "Starting from the words of the apostle against going to law before unbelievers, growing at first as a process of voluntary arbitration within the Church, adding a criminal side with the growth of disciplinary powers over clergy and members, and greatly stimulated and widened by the legislation of the early Christian emperors, a body of law and a judicial organisation had been developed by the Church which rivalled that of the State in its own field and surpassed it in scientific form and content."—Adams, *The History of England* (1066–1216), pp. 278, 279. It will be useful, in this discussion, to keep in mind that the church drew cases to its courts upon two general grounds: something clerical about the parties to a suit, or something clerical about the suit itself. Now clerical persons might do very unclerical deeds and unclerical persons could litigate few causes in which ingenuity might not discover some trace of the clerical. With this double hold, there was opened up before the church a jurisdictional vista practically without end.

resulting from the Carolingian patronage and the pretensions of the forged Decretals. Criminous clerks were tried in the popular courts; litigation between clerks and between clerks and laymen and the enforcement of many of the laymen's ecclesiastical obligations found place there also. Only for holding clerks to their clerical duties, did anything in the nature of an ecclesiastical court exist, although there seems to have been an occasional attempt to close civil differences between clerks by a kind of extra-judicial arbitration.

It has been seen how, by the Conquest, England was brought into the current of continental influence, and how this immediately showed itself in the church, checked only by the Conqueror's will.[1] The most striking of the early manifestations of that influence was the so-called separation of the lay and ecclesiastical courts. At some time between 1070 and 1076, William ordained:

. . . that no bishop nor archdeacon do hereafter hold pleas of episcopal laws in the Hundred, nor bring a cause to the judgment of secular men which concerns the rule of souls. But whoever shall be impleaded by the episcopal laws for any cause or crime, let him come to the place which the bishop shall choose and name for this purpose, and there answer for his cause or crime, and not according to the Hundred, but according to the canons and episcopal laws, and let him do right to God and his bishop. But if anyone, being lifted up with pride, refuse to come to the bishop's court, let him be summoned three several times, and if by this means, even, he come not to obedience, let the authority of the king or sheriff be exerted; and he who refuses to come to the bishop's judgment shall make good

[1] See Part II., § II., 6.

the bishop's law for every summons.   This too I absolutely
forbid that any sheriff, reeve or king's minister, or any
other layman, do in any wise concern himself with the
laws which belong to the bishop, or bring another man to
judgment save in the bishop's court.   And let judgment
nowhere be undergone but in the bishop's see or in that
place which the bishop appoints for this purpose.[1]

This shows, first, that laymen, as well as clergy,
were now to be tried before church courts for breaches
of church law; second, that laymen were forbidden to
concern themselves with the administration of church
law or, for an offence against it, to bring any one to a
court other than the bishop's; but that, third, the
authority of the king might be exerted to enforce the
bishop's summons.   William assumed that it was
clear to every one what breaches of church law were.
There is certainly no intimation from his reign of "any
immunity of clerks from secular jurisdiction or temporal punishment."   Simply, the old local courts no
longer dealt with laymen's failures to meet their
church obligations.

Between the time of this ordinance and the famous
controversy between Henry II. and Becket, the jurisdictional claims of the church made a great advance.
It was then that there took place in England what has
been aptly termed the "reception of Gregorianism."
This might easily be taken to mean too much, but the
English church did become deeply and lastingly affected by the principles of the great pope; and such
a change in so large and important an element of the
population necessarily touched the government, and
that most markedly in the judiciary.   The unknown

[1] A. and S., document 1.

author of the *Leges Henrici Primi*, writing under Henry I., said that all ordained clergy "are to be accused before their prelates for all crimes, both the greatest and the lesser." This writer borrowed so much from continental principle and practice that it is difficult to tell how far this reflects the English custom of his time. But there is reason to believe that it is not entirely contrary to fact, and it may safely be concluded that there was some attempt, in Henry I.'s reign, to accuse and try criminous clerks in the bishop's court. William's ordinance said nothing about criminous clerks, and he unquestionably intended, at the time of its issue, that they should be dealt with as they always had been in England; for it was manifestly concerned with changing the Anglo-Saxon and not the Norman practice. But here it must be noticed that there were three distinguishable parts in the criminal procedure: the accusation, the trial, and the punishment. William had come from the continent and dealt with prelates who, for the most part, had had a continental training; and, apart from what this particular ordinance said or did not say, Maitland thinks "it very possible that Lanfranc would have demanded and the Conqueror conceded the general principle that the *trial* of the accused clerk must take place before the spiritual forum"; but doubts "whether more than this would have been conceded or even demanded, whether as much as this could always be obtained." [1] If the accusation were in a lay court, a sort of possession of the case was thus obtained which made possible a share in the punishment. The church could not pronounce a judgment

[1] P. and M. i., 454.

which involved loss of life or limb; hence it was vitally important to the peace of the country that the civil authority be able to supplement, in the case of heinous crimes, the church's degradation of the clerk. It is significant that no one ever denied Henry II.'s claim that the procedure he advocated was the actual practice in the time of his grandfather.[1] We may venture, then, to sum up the competence of the church courts during the first three Norman reigns. They had jurisdiction over all clergy and laymen in matters falling within the domain of the canon law, and, by their interpretation, that domain increased constantly and many civil cases were being drawn from the lay courts. They had the trial of ordained clergy who had been accused of crimes in the lay courts, and, in cases where a blood judgment would have been rendered in a lay court, they turned the degraded clerk over to the secular arm for further punishment. But there must have been many exceptions to this rule, if one may venture to call it such; there were probably instances in which criminous clerks had accusation, trial, and sole punishment in the church court, and it is certain that in some cases the church did not even get the trial.

In the reign of Stephen, the church courts made their highest pretensions and attained their widest jurisdiction. Stephen's temperament and the circumstances of his succession led him, early in his reign, to make broad and unwise promises to various individuals and classes. His second charter, which he felt under the necessity of granting the spring after his coronation, was largely occupied with concessions

[1] See below, pp. 245, 247.

to the clergy. He gave them everything they wanted, and along a variety of lines. "The English Church would have reached at a stroke a nearer realisation of the full programme of the Hildebrandine reform than all the struggles of nearly a century had yet secured in any other land, if the king had kept his promises."[1] In the matter of ecclesiastical jurisdiction, he said: "I permit and confirm justice and power over ecclesiastical persons and all clerks and their effects, and the distribution of ecclesiastical goods to be in the hands of the bishops."[2] This certainly brought the accusation of the clerk, as well as the trial, within the church court and was a grant of civil jurisdiction in all that pertained to church property.

But Stephen did not keep his promises. He struggled very stoutly against the concession concerning criminous clerks, and it is known that there were instances in his reign in which criminous clerks were accused, tried, and punished in the king's court. On the whole, however, the church was far more successful in the contest than the king. In civil jurisdiction, the church went far beyond what was contemplated in the charter, for such jurisdiction was gained "not only in the purely spiritual causes, as for example matters relating to matrimony and contentions over land held in frankalmoin, but also the investigation as to whether a piece of land pertained to frankalmoin, cases concerning wills, tithes, *advowson* or presentation to churches, and contracts secured by an oath."[3]

---

[1] Adams, *The History of England* (1066–1216), p. 201.
[2] A. and S., p. 8.
[3] Translated from Böhmer, *Kirche und Staat*, pp. 399, 400.

The great work of Gratian, known as the Decretum, appeared about 1142. This was a fruit of the twelfth-century revival in the study of Roman and canon law. Gratian was a monk of Bologna, the centre of the revival, and was a teacher in the law school there. Church law had been very disorderly and complex, and his was the first important attempt to codify it. Such codification and clarifying as Gratian gave it could not but increase its availability, heighten its authority, and stimulate the already expanding church courts. The Decretum came at a time when England was especially susceptible to its influence. So many things were working to the same end that England, long exceptional in the nationality of her church and her independence of the pope, was no whit behind France or Italy in her progress towards the Gregorian ideal.

When the great ruler and lawyer, Henry II., came to the throne, he had to face the results of nineteen years of weak rule, many of them years of sheer anarchy. It is only to be noticed here how he dealt with the advancing jurisdictional claims of the church, which Stephen's reign had so favoured. Four considerations go far to account for Henry's action when, in 1163, he was at last free to look into England's internal abuses. First, he found criminous clerks no small element in the horde of unpunished criminals who were making governmental progress impossible; "it was said that a hundred murders had been perpetrated by clerks during Henry's reign before the king took action." [1] Secondly, he was conscious of the serious crippling of government that must ensue if men belonging to an

[1] P. and M. i, 454, note 1.

organisation so independent of, and out of harmony
with, the state could control such a vast civil jurisdiction. Thirdly, he genuinely appreciated the good government of his grandfather's time, and had a settled
purpose to make it his model in his work of restoration. Fourthly, the ideas of his time were not without
their influence upon him and he had a great respect for
established law; he probably respected Gratian's
Decretum; at any rate, as his struggle with the church
drew on, he may have seen the strategic advantage
of being able to claim harmony with it.

Some flagrant miscarriages of justice with respect
to criminous clerks were the immediate cause of
Henry's action. His preliminary negotiations with
Archbishop Thomas and the bishops indicate that the
practice of inflicting lay punishment upon the convicted and degraded clerk had largely lapsed under
Stephen, for he received very unsatisfactory replies
when he demanded the attitude of the clergy upon
this point. Becket took an extreme position, and
must have seemed to Henry to be distinctly heading
a state within the state. Late in 1163, Henry instructed some of the elder barons of his Curia, who
supposedly knew the customs of his grandfather's
time, to draw up a statement of such customs as bore
upon his controversy with the church. The result
was a document of sixteen articles, presented at a
meeting of the Curia Regis at Clarendon in January,
1164. It is known as the Constitutions of Clarendon.[1]
While not strictly confined to the points of judicial
controversy between church and state, those points
are the most prominent in the document. In the

[1] A. and S., document 13.

third article, is a statement of the most crucial matter, the procedure in the case of criminous clerks. The language is brief and somewhat dubious, but Maitland's interpretation is now generally accepted and seems conclusive:

A clerk who is suspected of a crime is to be brought before the temporal court and accused there; unless he will admit the truth of the charge, he must in formal terms plead his innocence; this done, he will be sent to the ecclesiastical court for trial; if found guilty he is to be deposed from his orders and brought back to the temporal court; royal officers will have been present at his trial and will see that he does not make his escape; when they have brought him back to the temporal court, he will then—perhaps without any further trial, but this is not clear—be sentenced to the layman's punishment, to death or mutilation.[1]

Becket objected to three parts of this procedure: the preliminary hearing in the lay court, the sending of the royal officer into the church court, the infliction of the layman's punishment upon the deposed clerk. The first two of these were clearly contrary to the Decretum; but Henry felt that he had conceded all that he could when he allowed the canonical trial, and seemed disposed to emphasise the fact that he was not contradicting the canon law. These were all important points, but the question of punishment was vital. Becket rested his objection upon the principle that a man should not be punished twice for the same offence. But the Decretum does not seem to con-

---

[1] P. and M. i., 448. For a full discussion, see Maitland, *Roman Canon Law in the Church of England*, essay iv.

template the case under consideration in connection with that principle, and Becket was quite original in his application of it and in the prominence which he gave it. He argued that degradation was the extreme punishment of the church and was sufficient for the first offence; if the man committed a second crime, he did it as a layman and would receive the layman's punishment. Henry regarded it as subversive of law and order to allow every clerk to commit one crime for which there was no punishment adequately deterrent. There was small chance of their coming to a satisfactory understanding. Henry's position was substantially correct historically; it represented the practice of his grandfather's time. Becket's position was correct canonically, with the probable exception of the matter of punishment. Henry's position was certainly in harmony with the fundamental requirements of effective government.

In the Constitutions of Clarendon, Henry not only attacked the church's claim to exclusive jurisdiction over clerks, but also its claim to some important civil actions. In the first article, he demanded all advowson cases. In the ninth article he drew into his court a preliminary procedure in cases where there was litigation over land between clergy and laymen, and this procedure later grew into an independent assize. [1] In article fifteen, he declared that "pleas of debt due under pledge of faith or without pledge of faith are to be in the king's justice."

Henry was put in the wrong by the murder of Becket and was obliged to renounce, or seem to renounce, what he had claimed in the Constitutions. A chronicler

[1] See above, p. 132.

thus recorded this abjuration: "He also swore that those customs inimical to the churches of his land which had been brought in in his time he would utterly do away with."[1]   Considering his former claim that these customs were all those of his grandfather's time, this does not appear to have been a very thorough renunciation.

From Henry's time, there was a decline from the Constitutions of Clarendon in the royal control over the trial and punishment of criminous clerks; while in civil jurisdiction, the kings not only kept in their courts what was then claimed, but continued to draw business away from the church courts. On the latter subject, nothing further needs to be said here, for at an early date the civil jurisdiction of the church ceased to seriously hamper that of the state.[2] But notice must be taken of the immunity of the clergy from lay jurisdiction, for it proved a serious breach in the efficiency of the English government until the Reformation. Becket was murdered in 1170 and Henry was reconciled to the church, through the renunciation noted above and other engagements into which he entered, in 1172. After the murder, it was impossible

---

[1] *Gesta Regis Henrici Secundi Benedicti Abbatis* i., 33.

[2] " .   .   .   still the sphere that was left to the canonists will seem to our eyes very ample. It comprehended not only the enforcement of ecclesiastical discipline, and the punishment—by spiritual censure, and, in the last resort, by excommunication—of sins left unpunished by temporal law, but also the whole topic of marriage and divorce, those last dying wills and testaments which were closely connected with dying confessions, and the administration of the goods of intestates.   Why to this day do we couple 'Probate' with 'Divorce'?   Because in the Middle Ages both of these matters belonged to 'the courts Christian.'"—Maitland, in Traill's *Social England* i., 283.

for him to enforce his claims over criminous clerks; the matter was passed over in silence. In the years that followed, however, the clergy got into some logical difficulty by having it pressed home to them that if the clerical murderer of a layman could escape punishment by death, there ought to be reciprocation and the lay murderer of a clerk enjoy the same immunity. The fact that Becket's murderers escaped punishment lent some point and weight to this argument. The clergy began to feel uncomfortable, doubting whether their own lives were to be properly protected. This situation made it possible for Henry, in 1176, to gain a concession; but in doing this he was forced to a more formal allowance of their claims over criminous clerks than he had yet made. A papal legate was in England at the beginning of the year, and he conceded that Henry could try clerks in his own court for forest offences; on the other hand, he received a letter from Henry to the pope in which the king agreed that murderers of clerks should not be exempt from punishment, and that, except for forest offences and cases which grew out of a clerk's holding a lay fee with a lay service attached, no clerks should be brought in person before his courts.[1] This concession may be regarded as formally inaugurating the "benefit of clergy."

The precise terms upon which the clergy enjoyed their immunity varied from age to age, but, in general, they became more lax. The core of "benefit of clergy" was this: when an accusation was brought against a clerk in a lay court, his bishop might appear and demand that he be turned over to the church court for trial; bishops regularly made this demand, and there

---

[1] Adams, *The History of England* (1066–1216), p. 319.

could be no further punishment than the church courts were competent to inflict.[1] In the thirteenth century, the clerk who had been arrested by the sheriff was imprisoned by the bishop until the coming of the itinerant justices, when he actually appeared before them and was accused. Late in the century, after accusation and transmission to the bishop's court, the justices submitted his case to a jury and obtained a verdict. This was not his trial, but if the verdict were guilty his property with its income was held for the king until his fortune in the bishop's court were known. But the ecclesiastical trial became a farce. Compurgation was still used, an antiquated form of proof that, under the changed conditions, had lost what little virtue it had ever possessed as a method of ascertaining the truth.[2] It was especially inept when a clerk selected the compurgators from his own order. The church might inflict severe punishments, as life imprisonment; but such seem to have been seldom used.

There were still, in the thirteenth century, some valuable limitations to benefit of clergy: the privilege had not been extended to the lower orders of the clergy,

[1] The strangest factor in the survival of this practice in England is that it was out of harmony with the best authority in the church itself. Maitland says: " . . . that opinion, though owing to his (Becket's) martyrdom it was suffered to do immeasurable mischief in England by fostering crime and crippling justice, was never consistently maintained by the canonists; had it been maintained, no deposed or degraded clerk would ever have been handed over to the lay power as a heretic or a forger of papal bulls. As a general principle of law, Becket's theory about double punishment was condemned by Innocent III.; the decree which condemns it is to this day part of the statute law of the Catholic church."—P. and M. i., 455.

[2] Compurgation was not prohibited by statute until 1833.— Traill, Social England i., 289.

where most clerical crime lay, but was confined to ordained clergy, monks, and nuns; the worst forms of treason were not within its operation; and, in the lighter offences, the misdemeanours, clerks were dealt with as laymen. But before the end of Edward III.'s reign, benefit of clergy had acquired most of the well-known characteristics which have made it opprobrious: its extension to the lower orders of clergy, the right of the clerk to prove his clergy even if his bishop refused to demand him, and the farcical method of proof by reading.[1]

One of the worst evils of the later Middle Ages was this "benefit of clergy." The king's justices, who never loved it, at length reduced it to an illogical absurdity. They would not be at pains to require any real proof of a prisoner's sacred character. If he could read a line in a book this would do; indeed, it is even said that the same verse of the Psalms was set before the eyes of every prisoner, so that even the illiterate might escape if he could repeat by heart those saving words. Criminal law had been rough and rude, and sometimes cruel; it had used the gallows too readily; it had punished with death thefts which, owing to a great fall in the value of money, were becoming petty thefts. Still cruelty in such matters is better than caprice, and the "benefit of clergy" had made the law capricious without making it less cruel.[2]

The state did occasionally break through the privilege in specially flagrant cases, and was even assisted by the church in so doing; but with slight exception the abuse remained as described until two acts, one in the reign of Henry VII. and the other in the reign of

[1] Reeves, *History of the English Law* ii., 324–326; 428–430.
[2] Maitland, in Traill's *Social England* i., 298.

Henry VIII., did much to abolish it. It was long after these acts before it entirely ceased.[1]

[1] "But it lingered on until comparatively recent times, and even in cases where it was withdrawn from all others who had hitherto claimed it, an Act of Edward VI. saved it for 'a Lord or Peer of the Realm though he cannot read.' Readers of *Esmond* will remember the escape of Lord Mohun by this means from the penalties of his successful duel with Lord Castlewood."—Medley, *English Constitutional History*, pp. 567, 568.

1. **The Genesis of Limited Monarchy.**—After William I. had conquered England and the early attempts of the English to throw off the yoke had been put down and enough time had passed to bring out the nature of his government, certain of his subjects began to show much resentment and disappointment. In one sense, they were not his subjects; they were his vassals. They were bound to him by the private tie, the feudal contract, rather than the public tie which relates the subject to the state. Indeed, at that time there was little of this public relation in its purity. The men of the great servile class were under various obligations to their lords which made it impossible for them to hold any full and free relation of subject to a sovereign state; the vassals of the king's vassals had private contracts with their lords which made their relations to the king only mediate. The object of the Salisbury oath was to bring all freemen under immediate and supreme obligation to the sovereign, but it could only accomplish its purpose slowly and partially. The non-noble freemen were the only people who approximated to our conception of subjects. But they were not the ones to resent William's government. Free as they were, they were more concerned with the rule

of their own. Norman or Saxon overlords, who, not-withstanding the definite terms of their service, might oppress them in many ways.

It was not, however, because the classes other than tenants-in-chief were less closely related to the king that they did not resent his severity; it was because there was, for them, no source in law or precedent whence the idea of resistance could come. The German barbarians had found no such thing in the Roman empire; there power was all on the side of the state and obligation all on the side of the individual. It was essentially the same in the empire of Charlemagne; and that empire had fallen to pieces, not because of any constitutional attack upon it, but because the primitive emperors and subjects alike had been unable to maintain their Roman imitation. In the ruins of this empire, there grew among the upper classes a set of relations, termed feudal, in which lord and vassal were bound to each other by a contract freely entered into and entailing mutual obligations. If one of the parties to the contract broke it, the other might attempt to force him to keep it or might regard the relation as entirely dissolved.[1]

William the Conqueror did not turn out to be the kind of king that his vassals had expected; he did not treat them as the French kings treated their vassals. He did not consciously modify feudalism when he came into England or deliberately undertake to weaken his vassals. But he was as strict and stern a king in England as he had been duke in Normandy. His great followers seem not to have expected this; they

[1] The institutional source of the contract element in feudalism was the Roman *patrocinium*. See above, pp. 75, 85.

thought he would be like other kings and they like other kings' vassals. He found in the English sheriff a means to accomplish things in the localities and he instructed him to hold pleas involving royal interests even within the holdings of great lords. The profits of this jurisdiction went to the king and lessened the judicial income of the vassal. Peace was maintained, and the rights of private warfare, which surely, it was thought, belonged to a king's vassals even if not to a duke's, were rigidly suppressed. Many of William's vassals felt that what he was doing amounted to a breach of his contract. They rose against him, and, dispairing of making him recognise their rights, they purposed to break all relations with him and drive him from the land. Thus occurred, in 1075, the first true feudal revolt in England. It was a revolt not against William as king, but as suzerain.

When William II. came to the throne, he not unnaturally had a revolt of these barons on his hands at the very outset. It is interesting that he began to make verbal promises of good laws, especially a mitigation of the forest laws. He did this in order to gain the support of the English and of as many Normans as possible. But during his reign, with the help of Flambard, he broke his feudal contract in more specific and exasperating ways than his father. Feudal dues and the rights of overlords with respect to marriage, wardship, and other feudal incidents were becoming fixed by custom, and hence were covered by the feudal contract without specific mention. These he abused beyond measure. When, in 1093, William believed that he was about to die, he made general, oral promises of reform; and it is of special significance that he cancelled some debts due him and released prisoners by written orders. The act approached a written acknowledgment that others had rights as against him.

Henry I., in his famous coronation charter, made very definite promises to correct specifically mentioned feudal abuses of his brother. In the reaction bound to follow his brother's reign, he thus emphasised, either through necessity or policy, his contractual relation to his tenants-in-chief. But throughout his reign, he was strong enough to break his promises very freely. But the very regularity of his tyranny, while rather extending the powers of the crown, tended also to strengthen the contract idea; he was not capricious; with respect to a portion of his population, he was acting upon a recognised set of principles.[1]

When Stephen came to the throne, he felt it necessary to strengthen his doubtful claim by confirming his uncle's charter. He merely confirmed " the liberties and good laws," with no mention of their having been abused and with no specific points of correction.[2] A few months later, he found it necessary to gain the support of the church by a charter which made very sweeping concessions.[3] The church included a class necessarily in close, but often ill-defined, relations with the king. Stephen limited his power by allowing the church a greater independence than it had ever had before. Throughout his weak reign, both barons and clergy steadily gained power from the crown.

[1] Much more was this the case if we accept the statement of Stubbs that the coronation charter was "probably reissued from time to time as he found it necessary to appeal to the sympathies of the people against their common enemies."—*Select Charters*, p. 99.

[2] A. and S., document 10.　　　　　[3] *Ibid.*, document 11.

Henry II., at his coronation, ignoring what had happened in the intervening reign, confirmed the laws and liberties of his grandfather in a general but emphatic charter, and mentioned Henry I.'s having granted these in charter form. The rapid progress of centralisation under this king, especially in the foundation of the king's court system, has been noted.[1] In 1173, began the last purely feudal revolt in England, almost a hundred years after the first one. An important cause was the king's invasion of what had been regarded as the jurisdictional rights of his vassals. Again the understood contract between lord and vassal —whose content varied from age to age, but was always a reality—had been broken, and the barons made an unsuccessful attempt to hold the king to its terms.

By the end of Richard I.'s reign, one party to the contract, namely, the king, appears to have been so uniformly successful that all contract element was likely to pass away, and the king be limited with respect to no portion of his population. From 1066 to 1199, there had been but one weak reign; taking into account also the tremendous fact of the Conquest itself, one sees how absolute monarchy was being attained in England almost at a stride. Richard I. issued no coronation charter. The memory of past events was short in the middle ages. Would Henry I.'s charter be forgotten, and would English kings grow so all-powerful as to destroy their character as suzerains by continued, successful violation of much that that character implied? The fact that feudalism in many of its aspects was then waning in England looked towards an affirmative answer.

[1] See above, pp. 125–131.

17

The issue was to be settled in John's reign, but an event late in the reign of Richard first demands attention. At the end of 1197, Richard commanded his English vassals to unite in providing a force of three hundred knights to serve him on the continent. This was substantially an application of the principle of scutage which was then coming into common use. Scutage was the commutation into a money payment of a part at least of a vassal's military service in cases where the length or location of the military undertaking rendered the individual service of all the vassals impossible. "The union of the military tenants to equip a smaller force than the whole service due to the lord, but for a longer time than the period of required feudal service, was not uncommon."[1] The constant necessity which the English kings were under of fighting upon the continent, while there was little need of fighting in England, extended and made regular the use of the scutage principle. This particular demand of Richard's received a decided refusal from the bishop of Lincoln, a man of the highest character. His example was followed not only by many clergy, but by laymen. It was stated that the military tenants of England were not bound to render service outside the country. There was no good feudal precedent for this in England or elsewhere; the letter of the law or custom was on the side of the king. Yet it is not surprising that such a protest should have at length arisen. The English Channel lay between the king's English and French possessions; England was a natural unit. To use the feudal contract for a forty-day personal service as the basis for making English vassals

---

[1] Adams, *History of England* (1066–1216), p. 383.

regularly pay for soldiers to fight in Normandy or Aquitaine seemed a breach of the spirit of that contract—and that, too, whether the soldiers were mercenaries hired on the continent or equipped knights sent from England. It was evidently not a constitutional resistance to taxation, as has often been represented. There was, properly speaking, no taxation and no idea of constitutionality concerned in the case. Its significance lies in the fact that, upon the eve of John's reign, the contract idea in the English feudal population still had considerable vitality.

If the authenticity of the reported speech of the archbishop at John's coronation could be trusted, rather sweeping conclusions might be drawn concerning the constitutional importance then attaching to the election of a king. But the speech is almost certainly the fabrication of a later time, and the conception of limited monarchy was not reached through the development of any early ideas of election.[1] John did much

---

[1] How slender was the conception of elective monarchy in the Anglo-Saxon period has been noted above (pp. 51, 52). For more than a century after the Conquest, there were scarcely any specific principles of royal succession. There was an ill-defined but inclusive idea of heredity, with the addition of certain vague criteria of designation, age, general availability, recognition by the great men of the realm, etc. But each succession had its exceptional elements. William I. was king by conquest, but he did not venture to assume the crown offered him by Edgar and the great men until he had consulted, and received the assent of, his own Norman vassals. With the establishment of the Norman house, it seems to have been taken for granted that the crown was hereditary; it was often so spoken of. William II. was designated by his father, and made good his position by promptly seizing the treasury and gaining the support of Lanfranc. Henry I. gained the crown by prompt action upon the death of his brother, securing the treasury at Winchester and gaining the approval of the magnates and others who happened to be present. His coronation charter and his masterful personality

to transform scutage into a true tax; he was constantly doing violence to its feudal character. He levied it every year until late in his reign. This element of regularity, which disconnected it with specific military undertakings, made it no longer a payment to a suzerain, but to a sovereign. Moreover when, as a suzerain, he assembled his feudal forces to follow him to France, he would give up the expedition and take money instead of service. This he did repeatedly, and spent the money as he pleased. John's abuses were manifold, but this is not the place for an enumeration of the causes of Magna Carta. It is true that there was hardly an element among his people that did not have a grievance, but some were only oppressed indirectly. Those who bore the brunt of his oppression were his vassals. All the feudal abuses of William II. were repeated in an aggravated form. John broke

---

secured his position. Stephen got the throne instead of the designated and direct heiress, Matilda, by promptly going to England, while she remained on the continent. London supported him at the outset, and he gained one influential element after another through lavish promises. Much is heard of "election" in connection with his succession, but an examination of what actually took place shows that it meant a formal assent after a *quid pro quo*—not anything which we would regard as a constitutional election. Henry II. was looked upon as Stephen's successor before the latter's death because of the strong claims derived from his mother, a powerful ecclesiastical backing, his own manifest ability, the weakness of Stephen, and the death of Stephen's oldest son. Richard I. became king because, as Henry II.'s elder and abler son, there was no reason why he should not. Probably primogeniture, a principle which originated in feudalism in the inheritance of fiefs, had begun to influence succession to the crown. John came to the throne, however, instead of the primogenitary claimant, Arthur, under Richard's designation, but mainly because the old fear of a minority was still stronger than the new principle. The nine-year-old Henry III. was made king because he was John's oldest son

every provision which a feudal contract of his time could possibly have contained. Finally, most of his vassals refused to follow him to the continent, basing their refusal on the same grounds offered by the bishops in Richard's reign. The uprising which resulted in Magna Carta was not a purely feudal revolt, of which we saw the last instance in 1173. The church was here concerned, and not simply in its baronial character; the barons also had a substantial backing in the discontent of the lower classes. There was in it the hint of a national revolt.

Whence came the possibility in England of anything even verging upon a national revolt at a time when such a thing was impossible elsewhere in Europe? The regular arrangement of the important elements in previous conflicts had been king, church, and lower classes against feudal nobility. Throughout the middle ages in Europe, the lay nobles stood alone; their interests could not be identified with those of any other

---

and the English people preferred a minority to the rule of the foreigner, Louis of France. Beginning with this succession, primogeniture prevailed in all normal times; violent misrule, with resulting usurpation and action by Parliament, might interfere with it. It became subject to the principle that the king was under the law.

A reflection of the growth of a determinate, hereditary succession is found in the disappearance of the interregnum. Until the succession of Edward I., between the death of a king and his successor's coronation, there was no king; the king's peace was dead and confusion and lawlessness sometimes resulted. Edward I.'s succession was a transition in this matter. He was on crusade when his father died; but four days later, upon his father's burial, a considerable number of prelates and barons took the oath of allegiance to him notwithstanding his absence. From that time, he was regarded as king, and was the first so regarded before coronation. With the succession of Edward II., the change was complete; he became king by the fact of his father's death.

class. While people and church saw a lesser danger
in the growing power of the king than in the power of
numerous local tyrants, there was no possibility of a
constitutional winning of power from the king on the
part of the nation. In England, from the Conquest
to the end of the twelfth century, the feudal nobility
had received such a succession of staggering blows that
royalty reached at a stride a position which it took
centuries to attain in France or Spain. The simple but
fundamental causes of this divergence in England's history were the Norman Conquest itself and the remarkable line of sovereigns which it brought to the throne.

The atrocious character of John's reign was suited
in every detail to rouse the opposition of every element
that could make itself felt. The situation is significant
beyond exaggeration, not so much in making national
opposition possible at an early date, for opposition
without a guiding principle would have wasted itself;
but in making it possible just early enough to rescue
from decadent feudalism the principle upon which
constitutional monarchy was to be built.[1] The Norman Conquest was responsible for the English constitution, first in bringing feudalism into the country, and,
secondly, in making possible a national appropriation
of feudalism's most important idea. But not to antici-
pate by further generalisation, let it be emphasised
that the national character of the rising of 1215 is very
easily exaggerated; there was enough of nationality in
it to hint of possibilities in the near future, but it was

---

[1] See below, pp. 264–267. In decadent continental feudalism,
the nobility retained a character which made co-operation with the
other elements of the population impossible long after the contract
idea had become obscured.

substantially a feudal revolt. How John would have
been dealt with had Henry I.'s charter not been discovered it is hard to conjecture. It had been a long
interval since 1154, and the idea of making the suzerain
bind himself by a written contract had evidently
passed out of mind. But this fact did not in the least
affect the fundamental character of the rising; the
suzerain had broken his contract, and his vassals
proposed to compel him in some way to keep it, or else
sever their relations with him and take to themselves
a new overlord.

In connection with the present subject, only a few
articles of the Great Charter [1] need be considered, but
those the most critical and characteristic. The early
articles are predominantly feudal and show the use that
was being made of Henry's charter. Like William II.,
John had abused the feudal *incidents*, and here was the
correction, enunciated with care and detail. But on
reaching article twelve, something is found not contained in the earlier document. The meaning of the
article is perfectly clear when viewed in the light of the
king's relations with his vassals in the matter of scutage
and service abroad.

No scutage or aid shall be imposed in our kingdom except
by common counsel of our kingdom, except for the ransoming of our body, for the making of our eldest son a knight,
and for once marrying our oldest daughter, and for these
purposes it shall be only a reasonable aid; in the same way
it shall be done concerning the aids of the city of London. [2]

This is a statement of the regular feudal principle that

---

[1] A. and S., document 29

[2] For the reason for mentioning London in this feudal connection,
see Adams in *English Historical Review* xix., 702–706.

no payments beyond those implied in the contract could be levied without the consent of the vassals concerned. That the "common counsel" referred to was simply that which the king found in his feudal court is made certain by the detailed description, in article fourteen, of how such counsel was to be taken. The purpose of article twelve was to bring back to strict feudal observance a king who had been turning scutage into a regular tax. But in the period following the Charter, feudal ideas and practices were rapidly disappearing; taxation developed along several lines; the Charter, though, with this, among other articles, omitted, was frequently confirmed, and the contract idea running throughout it was thus kept alive—and that in a period when people were not scientific in their use of history and hence did not enquire carefully what the contract covered or meant at an earlier time. The result was that, whereas in 1215 the king's vassals held him to the feudal law that there could be no unusual aids without their consent, at the end of the century the king's subjects said that he should not tax them without their consent.

A completer illustration of the same matter is found in article sixty-one. This is the most important article, for it is the clearest exposition of the principle upon which the whole Charter rested. It says, in effect, that there were recognised customs and laws, such as those just set down, which the king was bound to keep, and that if he did not his people could compel him to keep them; and it provided the clumsy machinery of the twenty-five barons to this end. The feudal system was clearly the source whence this principle came. The feudal contract was the formal ground for this whole baronial movement, that which saved it from being a mere unformulated protest against oppression. The feudal character of Magna Carta, as far as the objective contents of the articles is concerned, might be easily overstated; other than feudal abuses were corrected, and non-feudal classes were to some extent concerned. But a study of either the remote or immediate causes leaves one in no doubt as to where the animus of the movement lay; the initiative was taken by the barons and the bulk of the work was done by them. Magna Carta powerfully emphasised the contract between the suzerain and his tenants-in-chief, and between the tenants-in-chief and their vassals. To understand the origin of limited monarchy in England one has mainly to watch the perpetuation of the contract principle and how it came to relate the sovereign to his subjects, while most else in feudalism passed away.

This is saying that the English constitution rests finally upon the feudal system. Without that system the constitution as it existed in the fifteenth century or as it exists to-day would not have been possible. The English limited monarchy of later times could never have been regarded as a direct outgrowth of the Saxon, non-feudal state, as it existed under Canute, except by a preconceived and strained interpretation of the facts of history. The whole drift of that state was towards a monarchy of the Carolingian type in which the crude checks upon the sovereign's will or equally crude machinery for operating the nation's will, belonging to the primitive German public law, had either entirely disappeared or been dwarfed into insignificance. The accomplishment of this result was made impossible in England by the Norman Conquest. It was the thorough feudalisation of England which resulted from the Conquest that made the constitution possible, not by establishing a strong monarchy against which primitive Teutonic liberty reacted later, but by introducing with the strong monarchy a new conception of the relation of the king to those of his subjects who in that age constituted the nation, and who alone could constitute it, by introducing the definite contract-idea of the feudal system.[1]

The conditions in England which made the contract idea survive feudalism and take the important form and place that it did have next to be examined. The reign of John was followed by a long minority, practically a new thing in English history. In order to get every possible backing for the new king, the Charter was immediately reissued, but with the omission of the clauses just considered. The change was in the interest of the central power, but the Charter was still a compact. Three times during the minority was it reissued, and in 1217 the forest articles appeared in an enlarged form as a separate charter; hence the constant reference after this to "the Charters."[2] The edition of 1225 may be considered the final form of the Charter, that which was used so frequently during Henry III.'s reign and in the specially important confirmation of Edward I. Henry's minority, when Louis of France was forced to leave England and John's foreign mercenary leaders were driven from their fat holdings and from the country, was a time when English national feeling was becoming a prominent factor in events.

[1] Adams, *The Critical Period of English Constitutional History*, American Historical Review v., 651, 652.

[2] Bémont's *Chartes des Libertés Anglaises*, with its valuable introduction and notes, serves best for a study of the various editions of the Charter. See also Stubbs, *Select Charters*, pp. 296–354, *passim*.

Englishmen were proud that they were Englishmen and distinguished themselves sharply from Frenchmen. It was a time favourable to new ideas or new applications of old ones. The contract idea had been emphasised by three reissues of the Charter and the government was in the hands of ministers chosen by, and responsible to, the feudal council. There was a favourable soil for a conception of limited monarchy to take root in.

But the time was critical and very much depended upon the character of Henry III. Had he been a strong and intelligent ruler, the contract idea would have died with the rest of feudalism. But his weakness, meanness, extravagance, and love of foreigners did just the work that was necessary. Never has a country been so fortunate as England in having good sovereigns and bad sovereigns mingled in just the right proportions. There was no possibility of forgetting the Charters in Henry III.'s reign; to make the king confirm them gave his exasperated subjects something to do that seemed rational; for many years there was a dawn of hope each time he solemnly swore to observe them. But finally men began to realise with how mean and petty an individual they were dealing. Since the Norman Conquest, with one possible exception, Henry was the first king who had not been feared, and it is interesting to note the increasing freedom with which his shortcomings were denounced to his face.[1] It would have been dangerous to stable government to have had such a condition last very long; but something of this sort was needed to break

[1] For a good example, see the conversation quoted in Taswell-Langmead, *English Constitutional History*, p. 251.

down the tremendous prestige of the Angevin monarchy, and it lasted just long enough.

Sometime between 1235 and 1259, Bracton wrote his great work, *De Legibus et Consuetudinibus Angliæ*. In the first book, in treating of the "dignities" of divers persons and classes, he set forth the dignity of a king in words which clearly embody the principle of limited monarchy. They are worthy of remembrance as the first formulation of the principle and for their precision and force: "For the king ought not to be under man but under God and under the law, because the law makes the king. Let the king therefore bestow upon the law what the law bestows upon him, namely dominion and power, for there is no king where will rules and not law." [1] When one reflects that this was written only a half-century after Richard's reign, some conception is gained of what the first half of the thirteenth century meant in constitutional foundation laying.[2]

As Henry III.'s reign progressed, there was an increasing tendency to enforce the principle contained in article sixty-one of Magna Carta, that the king could be compelled to keep the law. In 1244 there was an attempt to place extraordinary authority in the hands

[1] " Ipse autem rex, non debet esse sub homine, sed sub Deo et sub lege, quia lex facit regem. Attribuat igitur rex legi, quod lex attribuit ei, videlicet dominationem et potestatem, non est enim rex, ubi dominatur voluntas et non lex."—Bracton, *De Legibus* (edited by Twiss in the Rolls Series) i., 38.

[2] In France, till the reign of Philip Augustus, the power of the kings had been very far behind that of the post-Conquest kings of England; but at the very time that Bracton was writing, the principle was being enunciated there that the will of the king is the highest law. Up to this point and even afterwards, the French and English governments were in many respects analogous, but the parting of the ways had been reached and the divergence was very rapid.

of four counsellors, and one is struck with the fact that the Curia Regis was not so wholly feudal in its action and in its relations to the king as formerly; there was a germ of constitutionality in its behaviour. Feudalism was passing, but feudalism's leading idea was, thanks to the character of the reign, living and expanding. The crisis of the reign came in 1258, resulting in the rise of Simon de Montfort, the civil war, and the last seven peaceful years, when the good results of the conflict appeared in the administration of Prince Edward. The rising of 1258 was, in essential features, like that of 1215, very much of a barons' affair. Its immediate result was the attempted form of government outlined in the Provisions of Oxford.[1] Here was a repetition of the device, originated in article sixty-one of the Charter, to put the government into the hands of an aristocratic group, but with much variation and elaboration of detail. It is no matter of regret that the device was unsuccessful, for an aristocracy, once firmly established, would have been more difficult to deal with than the king. But the Provisions of Oxford served to continue and emphasise the idea that, under sufficient provocation, the king might be deprived of his power.

In the spring of 1265, shortly before the tide turned against the triumphant Simon, Henry III. confirmed the peace made the preceding year and at the same time the Charters. Perhaps the most striking clause in the famous sixty-first article of the Great Charter was that in which John was made to admonish his people to rise against him, in case he broke the law, and by the use of force bring him again to the lawful way. This

[1] A. and S., document 34.

was repeated with peculiar distinctness in this confirmation by Henry III. After premising unlawful acts of the king or Prince Edward, the language concludes:

. . . it shall be lawful for every one in our realm to rise against us and to use all the ways and means they can to hinder us; to which we will that each and every one shall henceforth be bound by our command, notwithstanding the fealty and homage which he has sworn to us; so that they shall in no way give attention to us, but that they shall do everything which aims at our injury and shall in no way be bound to us, until that in which we have transgressed and offenced shall have been by a fitting satisfaction brought again into due state, according to the form of the ordinance of the aforesaid, and of our provision or oath; this having done let them be obedient to us as they were before. . . . [1]

Such a legalising of rebellion was full of possibilities; it leads one to question what would happen if a king refused to be thus limited and so repeatedly broke his laws and agreements that there was no possibility of his people's again being obedient as they were before. The answer is suggested by what the barons attempted to do with the incorrigible John—depose him and put another in his place.

Henry's surrender of the administration, during the last seven years of his reign, to the able and law-abiding Edward was in itself a confirmation of these constitutional beginnings. The bad reigns of John and Henry had done a great work; for three quarters of a century, the idea of compelling a contumacious king to keep

[1] A. and S., document 36.

the law had been driven again and again into men's minds. Perhaps it would not be rash to say that limited monarchy was an accomplished fact. But still the men who had felt the situation most keenly had been the barons, those who had always been in contractual relations with their suzerain. We must get further out of the feudal period than 1272 before we should pause for congratulation.

In the reign of Edward I., many things contributed to the passing of feudalism. Little can be done here except to name some of the more important of them. Before his accession, Edward seems to have purposed some direct limitation of private jurisdiction, for almost immediately upon his arrival in England he sent commissioners throughout the country to enquire into the nature and extent of the franchises. Their report was embodied in the "Hundred Rolls," which contain much valuable information upon some aspects of local government. This enquiry resulted in the Statute of Gloucester, 1278, whose main purpose was to limit and regulate the private courts. The assumption seems to have been made—perhaps not seriously even at first—that every holder of important franchises must produce some written royal warrant for them or else surrender them. At any rate, itinerant justices, armed with the Writ Quo Warranto, were sent to investigate each case. It was soon found impossible, without causing a barons' rebellion, to carry out such a procedure in a thorough fashion. Notwithstanding the dictum of Bracton that no prescription held against the king, those who could prove an uninterrupted exercise of their rights back to the coronation of Richard I. (the limit of legal memory) were allowed to retain them.   But the great thing that was accomplished was the establishment of a definite policy of the crown to make no further grants of judicial powers or immunities.   As the franchises were always liable to escheat to the crown through such causes as failure of heirs or forfeiture, under the policy inaugurated by Edward the jurisdictional side of feudalism was bound eventually to disappear. [1]

Edward's land legislation had the same general animus as his proceedings against the franchises.   The Statute of Mortmain, [2] while not a direct blow to feudalism, was calculated to strengthen the state by stopping a kind of land alienation that was depriving the state of its proper resources.   The Statutes De Donis Conditionalibus and Quia Emptores [1] were, especially the latter, decided limitations upon the normal feudal right to alienate land.   De Donis made possible a strict entail of estates which greatly increased the chances of escheat to the original grantor or his heirs, while Quia Emptores prevented subinfeudation, a process essential to live feudalism.   Edward had the great feudal lords on his side, for the more land and vassals a lord had the more benefit would he derive from these measures, and the king himself as the greatest

[1] "Speaking roughly we may say that there is one century (1066–1166) in which the military tenures are really military, though as yet there is little law about them; that there is another century (1166–1266) during which these tenures still supply an army though chiefly by supplying its pay; and that when Edward I. is on the throne the military organisation which we call feudal has already broken down and will no longer provide either soldiers or money save in very inadequate amounts."—P. and M. i., 252, 253.

[2] A. and S., document 40.

[3] *Ibid.*, documents 42 and 45.   A careful study of this legislation should here be made from the documents.

landholder and highest suzerain would profit most of all. If the principle of Quia Emptores were to be rigidly enforced, then, through the natural operation of escheat, all freemen would finally come to be tenants in-chief of the king—or rather his subjects, for then all proper meaning of tenancy-in-chief would have passed away.

The great conflict of 1297, although led by two earls and outwardly as much an affair of the nobility as the risings of 1215 and 1258, clearly contained elements of conscious constitutionality. The king was attempting to lead into the foreign service not only his feudal levy, but every one in the country whose lands furnished a yearly income of £20 or over; and his taxation (there is now no hesitation in calling it such) affected all classes. Thus the resistance, however prominent a part in it was played by the nobility, was not a resistance to feudal abuses primarily, but to national abuses; it was not merely holding the king to his feudal contract, but preventing his oppression of the people. Of course in the thought of the moment, the baronage and the prelates were acting on purely selfish motives and were not putting themselves forward as champions of the nation; but such had been the changes in society and such the development of taxation that when they were standing for themselves they were standing for the nation and had to recognise the fact. But they could not have done what they did had not the feudal principle of holding a suzerain to his contract been teaching men to limit a sovereign's unlawful assumption of power. The men of 1297 were unconscious of any change, and believed that the difficulty lay in the fact that the Great Charter had not been properly enforced.

The protest which was drawn up in July, 1297, under the leadership of the Marshall and Constable, earls of Norfolk and Hereford respectively, purported to be in behalf of archbishops, bishops, abbots, priors, earls, and the whole community of the land (*tota terre communitas*); in its articles great prominence was given to the word *communitas;* and in article four there is mention of the omission or neglect of the articles of Magna Carta, the king being besought to correct this abuse.[1] The great constitutional enactment, *Confirmatio Cartarum,*[2] sealed by the king in November, will be considered in some detail in connection with the origin of Parliament.[3] It is sufficient to note here that in it was laid down the principle of no taxation without the consent of the taxed. It was not a restoration of the long omitted article twelve of Magna Carta; but the principle there enunciated that the suzerain could not arbitrarily levy unusual exactions upon his vassals had become a national principle determining the relation of sovereign to subjects.

There was an unfortunate sequel to this seemingly grand conclusion of the great struggle of Edward's reign. The barons seem never to have quite believed that Edward fully and with no mental reservations had granted what Confirmatio stated. Edward, on his part, was piqued and hurt at this lack of confidence, and seems to have exercised, in dodging the spirit of the charter, much of that "legal captiousness" with which Stubbs has credited him. Certainly in obtaining from Pope Clement V., in 1305, a release from the oaths taken in 1297, he almost justified

[1] Bémont, *Chartes des Libertés Anglaises*, pp. 76–78.
[2] A. and S., pp. 86–88.   [3] See below, pp. 361–363.

the barons' suspicions. Bémont has well stated the situation:

. . . at the Parliament of Lincoln (January, 1301), the first article of the petition addressed to the king was "that the two charters of liberty and of the forest be entirely observed in all their articles from this time forward." This precedent was fortunate: henceforth, and during the entire fourteenth century at least, most of the Parliaments began thus and the express consent of the king (*Placet; il plet au roy*) was carefully entered upon the rolls.[1] The precaution was not unnecessary: this is seen when Edward, finally at peace with France and Scotland, asked and obtained from Pope Clement V. absolution from all his oaths and the annulling of the charters (1305, 29 Dec. . . .). The best king of the thirteenth century had done then as the worst; like John Lackland, Edward I. had avowed that he had granted the Great Charter "voluntarily and spontaneously"; at heart neither the one nor the other ever believed that he had abdicated the least particle of his authority. This unfortunate attitude lasted as long as the old order of kingship, that is to say to the end of the seventeenth century.[2]

One may hesitate to judge quite so harshly a king who gave so many examples of fidelity to trust, but

[1] Bémont cites Sir Edward Coke's reckoning that **Magna Carta** was confirmed "15 times under Edward III., 8 times under Richard II., 6 times under Henry IV., once under Henry V.; and that, to sum up, the Great Charter and that of the forest have been expressly established, confirmed, or promulgated by 32 acts of Parliament." He adds: "These figures can be taken as exact; they show the value that the nation attached to these repeated confirmations; but also of what little importance the king made them." Translated from *Chartes des Libertés Anglaises*, pp. xlix., l. The people were certainly hammering in Bracton's principle that the king was under the law.

[2] *Ibid.*, pp. xlvii., xlviii.

there is here a valuable caution against overestimating the voluntary constitutionality of Edward and his successors.

In passing from a reign in which the vigour and wisdom of the king had accomplished so much of permanent value into the miserable reign following, the first feeling is one of overwhelming loss and misfortune; and in looking forward through the whole list of reigns between Edward I. and the first Tudor, one is conscious of a distinct stepping down from thirteenth century standards of thought and achievement. The fourteenth and fifteenth centuries were upon lower moral and intellectual plane. But with reference to the establishment of limited monarchy, it was hardly an unmixed evil that Edward I. was not followed by kings as great as himself. With Parliament not yet effective, it is to be doubted whether the principle of resisting a king who broke the law had become so engrained in the people that it could not have been eradicated. It was a long time, however, before there was an opportunity to forget the principle or before there was a king able to defy it with much chance of success. It was only the third year of Edward II. when the king's inability and wrongheadedness resulted in the third experiment of putting the government into the hands of a commission of nobles. The commission was known in this instance as the Lords Ordainers. The Ordainers forthwith decreed that the Charters be observed, issued orders against the most pressing grievances, and then proceeded to draw up a document of forty-one articles which was presented to the king and became law in 1311. These articles were called the New Ordin-

ances.[1] They dealt with the governmental abuses
of the time, some of which had originated in the
preceding reign. Taxation, the appointment of the
king's ministers, and annual meetings of Parliament
were the matters of chief constitutional importance.
The act which repealed the New Ordinances in 1322,
when Edward was under the control of the Despensers,
had a significant clause defining the competence of
Parliament in terms which anticipated the future.[2]

But the great fact looking towards limited monarchy
in Edward II.'s reign was his deposition. It might
seem that such an event would have been almost the
attainment and final guarantee of constitutionality;
but it is necessary, in weighing its value, to consider
carefully its cause. Edward was not deposed because
he had made a deliberate attack upon the constitution;
he had not the vigour of mind or will for such an undertaking. He was deposed because he was supremely
lazy and incompetent, one whose qualifications, such
as they were, fitted him for anything but kingship.
He is a striking example of a man born into the wrong
station in life. The articles of accusation,[3] which have
a deeply tragic interest, say, among other things, that
"throughout his reign he has not been willing to listen
to good counsel nor to adopt it nor to give himself to
the good government of his realm, but he has always
given himself up to unseemly works and occupations,
neglecting to satisfy the needs of his realm." In the
fourteenth century, the machinery of government was
not so perfected that it could run itself and allow the

[1] A. and S., document 51.
[2] Ibid., p. 97.   See below, pp. 356, 367.
[3] A. and S., document 55.

king to be a figurehead. Medieval kings, good and bad, were laborious; there was a personal element in their government that it is difficult for moderns to understand. A king that would not work was an impossible king. This is not quite the whole story regarding Edward II.; he did some positive things that aroused enmity, and his reign would have dragged on somewhat longer had it not been for the individual action of his wife and Mortimer. But the chief trouble was that the country was drifting into misrule through lack of governance, and it was felt that a change was absolutely necessary. But whatever the cause, there was nevertheless a deposition, and, in an uncritical age, it would be likely to serve powerfully as a precedent.

In the discussion of Parliament's acquisition of power, it will appear how, throughout Edward III.'s reign, the arbitrary action of the king was limited by his dependence upon the country for the great sums of money necessitated by the war with France.[1] The bare fact of fifty years of such limitation is all that need be noted concerning this reign in the present connection. The constitutional significance of Richard II.'s reign culminates in his deposition, a deposition much more important than that of Edward II. Leading up to it, are some matters of interest. Richard early showed himself extravagant, improvident, and addicted to favourites. The Parliament of 1386 proposed to impeach his Chancellor and appoint a commission of reform. The king's reply showed his lofty conception of the royal prerogative. Then the fate of Edward II. was recalled, and the king was reminded of it in words that show clearly the constitutional use that was being

[1] See below, pp. 356–357.

made of the early precedent.[1] The king yielded, the Chancellor, the Earl of Suffolk, was impeached,[2] and a commission of reform, consisting of eleven members, was appointed. It was given very broad powers and was to continue for one year. It can not be considered a commission of regency, for Richard was nineteen years old and Parliament's act was the result of his misgovernment rather than of his incapacity. It was a late instance of the device, used with John, Henry III., and Edward II., of placing the government under the control of an aristocratic group in time of crisis. Its use after Parliament was well established shows its tenacity of life and also how slowly the possibilities of parliamentary government were realized. But there can also be seen in it some attempt by Parliament to control a governing group within the Council; that it was created by, and in some sort held responsible to, Parliament somewhat diminished its oligarchic character.

A few months after the dissolution of the 1386 Parliament, Richard summoned the judges of his central courts and presented to them a set of questions bearing upon the legality of the recent acts of Parliament. The judges, through natural subservience or fear, answered unanimously in the king's favour.[3] Mindful of the origin of the royal courts, it is easy to understand that the judges, created by the king, felt closely identified with his interests. But now new conditions were arising; the differentiation of government into executive, legislative, and judicial divisions and the possibility

---

[1] A. and S., document 94. [2] *Ibid.*, document 93.

[3] For further detail, see Taswell-Langmead, *English Constitutional History*, pp. 233–234.

of much constitutional history growing out of the relations of these were foreshadowed. Richard II.'s use of the judges was the first notable instance in which the executive used the judiciary in a quarrel with the legislature. It was a prophecy of much future history, for the subservience of the judges to the king was the last serious fault in the English constitution to be corrected.

In 1389, Richard declared himself of age. The last two periods of his reign, that of constitutional government from 1389 to 1397 and that of attempted absolutism from 1397 to 1399, have long remained a puzzle. The absolutist tendencies at the beginning and end of his reign lead one to think of the middle period as a long dissimulation, while the extravagance of his later claims and the freakishness and recklessness with which he let slip the substance of power suggest madness. Mad or sane, however, his measures in the Shrewsbury Parliament[1] to secure his own unlimited authority were a methodical attack upon the limitations which Parliament had already imposed upon the sovereign. In his deposition, therefore, amidst the various motives which actuated it, there was a distinctly constitutional element. An attack had been made upon the laws and customs under which a king ought to rule, the precedent of Edward II. was in mind, Richard II. was rejected, and a king who would rule under the law was put in his place. Richard was made to declare himself "wholly insufficient and useless," and the act of Parliament which confirmed his deposition was based upon his "crimes and shortcomings," his "very many perjuries" and the "default of governance

[1] A. and S., documents 100, 101.

and undoing of the good laws."[1] When Edward II.
was deposed, he was succeeded by his son; Richard
II. was succeeded by his cousin who had no primogenitary claim. Primogeniture had been adopted as
the principle regulating royal succession; hence Henry
of Lancaster could have no legitimate claim to the
throne while there was a descendant of his uncle
Lionel, duke of Clarence.[2] He was king by conquest and consent of Parliament. This extension
of "the right of deposition into a right of breaking
the order of succession" was a very important advance in Parliament's control of the monarchy.[3]
This special dependence upon Parliament gave
Henry IV.'s reign its prematurely constitutional
character.

He kept the throne only because he proved a statesman
of sufficient ability to conciliate a majority of his subjects.
He had to perform miracles of tact, energy, and discretion,
in order to keep that sufficient majority of the nation at
his back. He succeeded in the task and ultimately won
through all his troubles to a period of comparative safety
and tranquillity. It was a weary and often a humiliating
game, for Henry had to coax and wheedle his parliaments
where a monarch with a strictly legitimate title would have
stood upon his dignity and appealed to his divine right to
govern. But the story is intensely interesting, as being

[1] Documents 102–104 in A. and S. illustrate the deposition of
Richard II.

[2] The foolish claim which may have been hinted at in the words,
"as I that am descended by right line of blood coming from the
good lord king Henry III." (A. and S., p. 164), which were used by
Henry when he made his oral challenge of the crown, had no foundation in fact and probably gained little credence at the time. See
Oman, *History of England* (1377–1485), p. 153.

[3] Adams, in *American Historical Review* v., 658.

the first episode of what we may call constitutional government in the modern sense.[1]

When the Yorkist line came to the throne in 1461,[2] there was, as might be expected from legitimists, a greater manifestation of independence and security. But the Yorkist sovereigns knew their limitations and never attempted such high-handed dealings with Parliament as are to be found in some parts of the Tudor period.   However, civil wars and weak or bad kings had, by 1485, so hurt the central power that England's greatest need was a strong and able royal line.   The overthrow of Richard III. and the succession of Henry of Richmond as a distinctly parliamentary sovereign, with a most slender hereditary title and to the prejudice of many more legitimate claimants, would seem likely to result in an extreme and, under the circumstances, dangerous limitation of monarchy.   That this was not the result was due to the extraordinary ability and tact of the Tudors.

Limited monarchy was an accomplished fact in England at the end of the middle ages.   If its evolution has been correctly traced, its origin is found in the introduction of continental feudalism through the Conquest.   The most important feature of that feudalism was the contract, voluntarily entered into by free men, a contract which entailed mutual rights and

[1] Oman, *History of England* (1377–1485), p. 154.   In a later connection (see below, pp. 387, 388), there will be occasion to note the relations of Parliament and Council to the king and to each other in this reign.

[2] The language of the parliamentary recognition of the Duke of York as heir to the throne and of the act validating the acts of the Lancastrian sovereigns brings out clearly the legitimacy of their claim.   A. and S., documents 128, 129.

duties. The Norman kings had many tenants-in-chief, and were thus, from the first, in this contractual relation with many of their subjects. A long succession of fortunate events and circumstances caused the contract principle to survive feudalism, its original habitat, and to form the basis of the relations between the king and all of his subjects The private relation of feudalism had become, in England, a public relation, and, perhaps, the most precious acquisition of the state.[1]

Under the Tudors and the Stuarts, especially the latter, the royal *prerogative* was a subject of much controversy, and the constitutionalists of the Stuart period often cited Lancastrian precedents and even harked back to the royal limitations, real or supposed, of Edward I.'s time. What was, then, the royal prerogative of the later middle ages? Substantially what Prothero has described it as being in the sixteenth century:

The prerogative of the crown consists in the peculiar rights, immunities, and powers enjoyed by the sovereign alone, including the precedence of all persons in the realm. These privileges rest partly on statute, partly on custom and precedent. But they are not vague and indefinite: they are known and capable of description. They do not amount to an emancipation from law; on the contrary, they

[1] "The thing which was peculiar to England and decisive in its constitutional history was not the creation of Parliament nor the invention of the representative system, however important and interesting some peculiarities of detail may be in both particulars. The peculiar and determining fact was that Parliament, at the moment when it came into existence as a distinct institution, found ready to its hands, as a result of a line of development independent of its own, a traditional policy of opposition and of the control of the sovereign, based upon definite principles and rights."—Adams, in *American Historical Review* v., 655, 656.

are limited by it.   This is the view of Bracton; . . . But these recognized and definite powers do not exhaust the rights of the crown, because circumstances may occur which are provided for neither by law nor custom.   . . . Thus beyond the definite prerogative and outside the area occupied by the law, there is, and must be, a vague and undefined power to act for the good of the State. . . . On this lawless province, law and custom gradually encroach, either in the interest of the sovereign or of the subject, . . .   The less advanced the State, or, in other words, the less complete the control of law and custom, the larger will be the area over which the sovereign is free to act.   It was still very large in the days of the Tudors.[1]

There was little attempt to define the royal prerogative in the fourteenth and fifteenth centuries.[2] There was clearly a recognition of those definite functions and rights of the crown which constitute the prerogative in the first sense; and there are indications that most of the sovereigns ascribed to themselves extensive powers beyond and were not so much impressed by the limitations implied in confirmations of the Charters and similar acts as were the people.[3] When it has been shown to what conscious power Parliament had attained by the end of the fifteenth century, a collision between crown and House of Commons in the "lawless province" will seem quite inevitable.   Not until the conflict was consciously on, would men concern themselves with

[1] Prothero, *Statutes and Constitutional Documents*, pp. cxxii.-cxxiv., *passim*.

[2] The first definitions of treason, 1352 and 1397, however, looked in this direction.   See A. and S., documents 72 and 99.

[3] See above, pp. 274-276.

"forming clear notions of sovereignty and defining its abode."[1]

2. **The Council.**—The executive division of the English government did not, at any time, consist of the king alone. The king always acted with or through some body of men, who counselled him with varying degrees of influence and authority. Before the end of the middle ages, there existed a very definable Council that kept its own records, had its traditions, and exercised important and distinctive administrative functions. The institutional source of this Council has been described.[2] We have called it the smaller Curia Regis. It was that Curia Regis which was left when, after the fuller meeting, the majority of the tenants-in-chief went home. What determined who should remain? The officials remained and some others, but there are no distinctive marks by which it can be told just who the others were. The king's will, their own will and convenience, the special business on hand, the part of the country where the king happened to be— such things as these probably determined. Thus the

---

[1] Prothero, *Statutes and Constitutional Documents*, p. cxxiv. Cowell, in his famous *Interpreter*, misquoted Bracton where he cited him as saying that the king " is above the law by his absolute power."—*Ibid.*, p. 409, and above, p. 268. Prothero comments upon Cowell's account of the prerogative: "Cowell describes the prerogative as 'that especial power, pre-eminence, or privilege that the king hath *above* the ordinary course of the common law,' and this was the watchword of the royalists. It required only an alteration of one word to enable Blackstone to adopt Cowell's definition, but in substituting the phrase, '*out of* the ordinary course of the common law,' for that which Cowell uses, he substituted a constitutional doctrine for one destructive of the constitution. The whole quarrel between the Stewarts and their Parliaments lies there."—*Statutes and Constitutional Documents*, p. cxxv.

[2] See above, pp. 102–104.

personnel of the smaller Curia Regis was very subject
to change. All that can be said is that, during the
twelfth and first half of the thirteenth centuries, the
officials were in practically continuous discharge of
their duties, and that the king had with them at frequent intervals, if not in permanent session, others who
for the time being were regarded as his counsellors.
And it should be added that during this time this body
was becoming less feudal both in make-up and business.

The work done in the early thirteenth century by
the smaller Curia Regis was manifold and hard to
define, for it rested upon no theory and there were no
constitutional limitations. During the minority of
Henry III., this body was specially active, as was
natural, and some writers have ascribed the origin
of the Council to that period. Beyond the fact that
the conditions of a minority hastened a natural evolution, little can be said for this theory; the counsellors
certainly acquired none of their technical distinctions
at that time. Some mention of what they did shows
their advance towards administrative work of a high
order. They shared the king's diplomatic work, ad-
vising with him upon peace and war, and they counselled him in his dealings with rebellious subjects.
The king might at any time consult them about routine
administrative work; many of the public and private
orders that he issued bear evidence that he had done
so. They were quite regularly concerned with forest
matters, the surveys being carried out under their
oversight; also with church matters, the filling of vacancies and points upon which royal and ecclesiastical
interests clashed; and with the government of Ireland, Poitou, and Gascony. During the minority, the

counsellors had much to do with straightening out the
Exchequer, which had broken down late in John's
reign; and since regulating taxation was one of their
special functions and many financial obligations to
the crown were then in an uncertain state, they sat as
a sort of board of equalisation. Their judicial province was large, but of a distinctly supervisory character. They sent mandates to the courts telling them
what to do under exceptional circumstances, as when
Innocent III.'s bull interfered with the ordeal; they
told into what courts unusual cases should go, and
judges often asked them for instruction upon points
of law; they were a court of first instance for many
cases touching barons, sheriffs, or judges; they were
often appealed to by litigants who claimed that the
judges had been unjust or the law wrongly construed.

But there could be no Council, in the later sense,
until there was some approach to a distinctive and
continuous membership. This was quite sure to come
owing to the increase of executive business and to the
maturing and defining influences with which time
touches all inchoate institutions which are exempt
from active sources of disintegration. It is important
to note at this point, while the attention is fixed upon
the Council's origin, that it drew its authority solely
from the king; Curia Regis was king in action, and the
Council, which grew from Curia Regis, was created by
no statute or other act outside the royal will. Till
about the middle of the thirteenth century, it lacked
the "two essential features" that were to give it a
"definite and complete organic character." These
were "the councillor's oath and its own council records.
The one was necessary to define its membership, the

other was necessary to give it independent standing."[1]
During the fourteenth century, the precise form of the
oath was often fixed by Parliament at times when new
counsellors were appointed. In 1425, the oath was
given its final form. The defining of the Council's
membership through the use of the oath had an important effect upon its composition: till the early
fourteenth century, the common-law judges were in
the nature of *ex officio* members, and in the reign of
Edward I. the King's Bench had scarcely differentiated
from it; but late in the century the judges had ceased
to be members.

The Council kept no regular roll till 1421; but we
are not without records of its earlier proceedings.
These early records were incidental to its work and
were for present use; there was no idea of keeping a
record for its own sake or for future reference. The
general character of its early work can be learned
through these original memoranda: writs issued under
the privy seal by its order, the king's open and private
letters that bear evidence of its participation, and
entries upon Exchequer or Chancery rolls that show
its dealings with or through those departments. It
entertained a great number of petitions from individuals or small groups, and the replies to these, which
would fall under the categories just mentioned, occupied
much of its time. Records of formal resolutions upon
more general matters are sometimes found. These
were its *ordinances*, its legislation.[2] In the very early
days, the records do not clearly distinguish what was

[1] Baldwin, *Beginnings of the King's Council*, Transactions of
the Royal Historical Society xix., 56, 57.
[2] See above, p. 103, and below, pp. 365-367.

done by the Council from what was done by the Council plus the estates, the primitive Parliament. It seems safe to conclude in doubtful cases that the Council was the acting body, and there was then a single and fairly definable body of men to which the name Council may be fairly ascribed.[1] Maitland has said:

. . .   it seemed necessary to remind readers who are conversant with the " parliaments " of later days, that about the parliaments of Edward I.'s time there is still much to be discovered, and that should they come to the decision that a session of the king's council is the core and essence

---

[1] From certain descriptive terms, applied loosely by the chroniclers to bodies of men of whose technical character they had little knowledge, it has sometimes been supposed that there was more than one kind of king's council at this time. Maitland, in his Introduction to *Memoranda de Parliamento*, p. lxxxviii., note 1, says: "The one point about which I venture to differ from what seems to be the general opinion of modern historians (and I am uncertain as to whether the difference is real) is that I cannot find in the official language of Edward I.'s time any warrant for holding that the king has more than one *concilium*, or rather *consilium;* any warrant, that is, for holding that this term is applied to two or three different bodies of persons, which are conceived as permanently existing bodies, or any warrant for holding that the term should be qualified by some adjective, such as *commune*, or *magnum*, or *ordinarium*. . . . The Latin language knows no article definite or indefinite; the language of the time knows no difference between counsel and council. One thing is clear: an order sending to their homes the prelates, earls, barons, knights, and other commoners, ' sauve les Evesques, Contes et Barouns, Justices et autres, qui sount du Counseil nostre seigneur le Roy,' is an intelligible order." This conclusion has been borne out by the detailed investigations of Baldwin. Later in the fourteenth century, these descriptive terms did receive some official recognition; but their use reflects no multiplication of councils. As the Council assumed a distinctive character in the thirteenth and fourteenth centuries, it very commonly bore the French name, Conseil.

19

of every *parliamentum*, that the documents usually called
"parliamentary petitions" are petitions to the king and
his council, that the auditors of petitions are committees of
the council, that the rolls of parliament are records of the
business done by the council,—sometimes with, but more
often without, the concurrence of the estates of the realm,—
that the highest tribunal in England is not a general assembly of barons and prelates, but the king's council, they will
not be departing very far from the path marked out by
books that are already classical.[1]

Because it has happened that many more of the Council
records have been preserved beginning with the tenth
year of Richard II., it has generally been concluded
that there was an organic change in the institution at
that time. But it has recently been shown that this
apparent beginning of the records is "a mere accident
of collection" and that before Richard's time the
Council had attained considerable maturity.[2] In
1421, a more purposeful record began; the minutes of
the proceedings were copied upon a regular roll, known
as the Book of the Council. It seems, however, never
to have been the intention to thus record all the business that was done.[3]

There were other evidences that the Council was
becoming a political entity. Payments to the coun-

---

[1] Introduction to *Memoranda de Parliamento*, p. lxxxviii.

[2] Baldwin, *Early Records of the King's Council*, American Historical Review xi., 14, 15.

[3] "Only fragments of the Book are extant, but it is evident that
it was a very imperfectly kept register. There is very good reason
to believe that there are other records of the council still un-
discovered, which may be hidden in one library or another."—
Baldwin, *Early Records of the King's Council*, American Historical
Review xi., 14.

cillors for their services became frequent early in the fourteenth century; these were sometimes annual salaries, sometimes annuities, and, for minor members, clerks, etc., day wages. The payments were liberal, and careful schedules were drawn up, which show the salaries graduated according to the rank of the councillors. The amount and regularity of the salaries show that the Council was a very busy governing body during the fourteenth and fifteenth centuries. In the reign of Edward III., it was deemed necessary that it have a more permanent and commodious meeting place, and in 1346 work was begun upon a building between Westminster Hall and the palace, destined for its especial use. From about the same time, it employed a clerk intermittently until Henry IV.'s accession, after which it had one constantly.

In Edward III.'s time, the Council was still very large and its membership vague and heterogeneous. It might include foreigners, favourites, minor officials, or honorary members, besides those who more regularly and properly composed it.[1] But these elements did not share equally the arduous routine work. That was doubtless done by a rather small group of men; an evidence of this is that only part of the members received a salary. But the sum-total of its administrative and legislative work was considerable and its relations with the king very intimate. During this same reign, Parliament was becoming a conscious and enthusiastic legislative body and saw no reason

[1] On the make-up and functions of the Council of this period, see Baldwin, *The King's Council from Edward I. to Edward III.*, English Historical Review xxiii., 1–14.

why it should not also try its hand at administration.[1]
There were signs of a clash towards the end of the reign
and the circumstance of Richard's minority made the
clash certain. As when Henry III. was a minor the
unformed body of counsellors undertook new duties
and responsibilities, so in Richard's minority the
Council saw occasion to extend its work and authority.
From the Good Parliament, 1376, to the end of Henry
VI.'s minority, 1437, was a distinct period in the Council's history. It was the time when Parliament made
vigorous attempts to curb and manipulate it. It
emerged without having succumbed to Parliament's
attacks, but it had undergone some important changes.
The history of the Council during this period can be
approached by noting what were Parliament's purposes regarding it. The most important attempt
of Parliament was to gain control over its personnel.
The formal appointing power lay with the king, under
the advice of the lords and prelates; but the House of
Commons tried to specify the qualifications of councillors, wished to be informed of names in advance of
appointment, and tried to make sure that its expressed
preferences should be regarded after the dissolution of
Parliament. There was also an attempt to make the
Council a smaller and more definite body than it had
been under Edward III. Parliament's idea seems to
have been that it should consist of the Chancellor, the
Treasurer, the Keeper of the Privy Seal, a few prelates,
earls, and barons, and a sprinkling of knights or even
burgesses. Under this influence, the Council, in
Richard II.'s reign, usually had a membership of from

[1] For an account of Parliament's administrative attempts and
the conflict between ordinances and statutes, see below, pp. 370–378.

twelve to fifteen. It was believed, moreover, that
frequent changes were salutary, and there were some
rather unsuccessful attempts to have yearly Councils.
In the second place, Parliament attempted various
regulative measures. With a small and certain membership and all the members sharing in the work with
substantial equality, it seemed proper that all should
be placed upon a definite salary basis, that salaries
be paid by the year or the day, and that annuities be
done away with. Parliament also undertook to dictate
what business the Council should do and how it should
do it; and in this connection came those attempts,
already noticed,[1] to limit the Council's judicial pretensions. Finally, Parliament, through its high judicial power of impeachment, set itself to supervise the
conduct of councillors and keep them from the many
kinds of corruption incident to their position.[2]

Most of this parliamentary control was lost during
Richard's last two years of personal and despotic rule,
but the same kind of pressure was resumed in the
Lancastrian period. Parliament, however, probably
exerted more real authority over the Council in the
early years of Richard's reign than ever before or after.
That this did not become permanent bears witness to
the fact "that the most important features which the
privy council of later times is known to have possessed
were well established before the reign of Richard II.
The organic changes through which it passed were
for the most part not those of statutory regulation,

[1] See above, pp. 214, 215.
[2] The articles of impeachment drawn in 1386 against the earl of
Suffolk, who had been Chancellor, excellently illustrate the nature
of fourteenth-century "graft."—A. and S., document 93.

but of gradual growth in an institution already mature."[1] But the period of parliamentary pressure produced some salutary changes that were stamped indelibly upon the Council: it was never again so large and vague as it had been under Edward III.; its membership was of a higher order and under a greater sense of responsibility; and, though it never wholly lost its legislative and judicial functions, it was at this time that it became established as a distinctively administrative body.

During the prematurely constitutional reign of Henry IV., king, Council, and Parliament worked together in remarkable harmony. The control of Parliament was such that there is a suggestion of the modern Cabinet system; in the notable governmental scheme of 1406, which received the king's assent, is seen a small administrative group working with the king and yet bound to reflect the sentiment of Parliament.[2] There was a decided change in the Council after Henry VI. came of age; parliamentary control was thrown off, especially under the influence of Henry's arrogant wife, Margaret of Anjou, who had no understanding of the English constitution. Instead of naming councillors for short periods, it now became the custom to appoint them for the king's life, and that, too, men who

[1] Baldwin, *Antiquities of the King's Council*, English Historical Review xxi., 20.

[2] For a further account of the constitutionality of this period, see Pt. III., § III., 8. "When in 1406 the house of commons told the king that they were induced to make their grants, not only by the fear of God and love for the king, but by the great confidence which they had in the lords then chosen and ordained to be of the king's continual council, they seem to have caught the spirit and anticipated the language of a much later period."—Stubbs, *Constitutional History*, § 367.

were often unacceptable to Parliament and the country
in general. This did not result in a greater royal
control over them; they often took matters entirely
into their own hands and ruled the king more arbitrarily than when Parliament was acting through them.
In 1444, an ordinance was enacted which did much to
secure this power. "Under the modest appearance
of a series of formal rules about the presentation of
petitions, it practically ensures that every grant of the
Crown should, from the moment of its presentation as
a petition to the time when it is formally issued as a
royal writ, be under the notice of the King's Ministers."[1]
From 1437 to the accession of the first Tudor, was the
time of the Council's greatest power. The kings seem
to have conjured up a spirit which they could not
control. Of the Council's remote ancestor, the Curia
Regis, it has been said that it was the king in action;
in the middle fifteenth century, the king was often the
Council in action. The Council had become by 1485
the great executive power of the nation [2]; but it wielded
a dangerous power, for it largely represented a class
that was dangerous to the constitution. But a line
of sovereigns very different from the Yorkists was to
succeed to the throne; a Council of masterful prelates
and lords might overshadow Edward IV. or Richard
III., but it would be hard to imagine a Council that

[1] Dicey, *The Privy Council*, p. 39.
[2] The Council's judicial work reached a very low ebb during the
fifteenth century; the Court of Chancery had separated from it,
leaving it almost no civil jurisdiction, while its criminal jurisdiction was often very slight; but this latter was to receive an extraordinary extension under the Tudors and Stuarts. As a criminal
court, whether acting through a committee or as a whole, it was
the famous Court of Star Chamber.

could do the same by Henry VII., Henry VIII., or
Elizabeth.   The Tudors seized the Council and made
it the most serviceable instrument of their despotism.
When the royal despotism was ended in the seventeenth
century, the old Lancastrian parliamentary control
came back, but was soon perfected and adapted
through the wonderfully successful device of the
Cabinet.

The Cabinet has been the only great creation in the
English constitution since 1485, and even that was
hinted at in the fifteenth century.   One hint of it
has been noted in connection with Henry IV.'s reign;
perhaps there was one even under Richard II.[1]   There
was certainly a second in the reign of Henry VI.   The
term council had always been loosely used; even when
there had come to be a recognised body of sworn councillors, a larger and vaguer group, containing men, as
for instance the common-law judges, whom the king
occasionally called in for advice, was sometimes referred to as a council.   To the smaller body, a descriptive name, such as *secret* or *private*, was at times
applied in the late fourteenth and early fifteenth
centuries.   This tendency to distinguish between the
Council proper and any larger body increased during
the minority of Henry VI., and meetings of the Council
were more often held in private.   It was a time when
much responsibility rested upon the councillors, and
they had been much annoyed on certain occasions at
having state secrets leak out, owing to the presence at
Council meetings of others than the sworn members.
As the civil war approached and the factions in the
nobility grew more partisan and bitter in their politics,

[1] See above, p. 279.

secrecy and exclusiveness were carried a step farther. The real administrative power did not lie with the Council as a whole, but with the leaders of the party for the moment in power, who formed a sort of inner clique or ring, a secret or *privy* council. Further, it was during Henry VI.'s reign that the term Privy Council came into general use, and unquestionably as a result of these conditions. "It is, therefore, sufficiently apparent that under Henry VI. a select Council was gradually arising from the midst of the general Council, that a change was taking place precisely analogous to the process by which, in a later age, the Privy Council itself gave birth to the Cabinet." [1] Under the Tudor sovereigns, when the Council was entirely under royal control, this tendency to form rings and much of the exclusiveness and secrecy were bound to pass away. But the term Privy Council clung, and has since been applied to whatever manner of king's council has existed in England. And when, after the Restoration, important political rings formed within the Privy Council, another term to signify clique or junto was sought, and *cabal* came into use; and when such inner administrative ring had outlived its early invidious character and was becoming a necessary part of the constitution, the name of the small private room in which it met was transferred to the body itself, and there was a Cabinet.

[1] Dicey, *The Privy Council*, p. 45.

SECTION III

1. **Origin of the House of Lords.**—In the thirteenth century a very fundamental change was taking place in the larger Curia Regis. When the change was completed, that body had become the House of Lords. At the same time there were bèing added to it certain new elements which were finally to form the House of Commons. These were the two great processes in the making of Parliament, with the first of which we are here concerned. In dealing with this subject, it is especially necessary to rid the mind of modern preconceptions; the very word Parliament produces involuntary mental images of the fully developed institution that are certain to interfere with the understanding of its beginnings. One must be willing to take one step at a time and to be mindful that the great institutional creations of medieval England were not the products of grand, purposeful building for the future, but that they grew very slowly through the skilful adaptation of means to immediate ends, that there was a careful preservation of the valuable things of the past and a spirit of caution and compromise which allowed to each of several contending interests its due consideration, and that physical environment and very many things which can be ascribed to nothing but pure chance played important parts.

It has been shown that the larger Curia Regis was the king's feudal court [1]; but unlike the feudal courts of other lords it might at times contain men who were not tenants-in-chief, for the king was always more than pure suzerain. From the beginning, the will of the king was an element in determining its make-up. The class of king's vassals in England was always very diverse within itself; while it contained all of the very great landholders, there was also within it a large number of small holders. Probably from the time of the Conqueror, there was some recognised cleavage between those who held much land of the king and those who held little. In the reign of Henry I., the great tenants-in-chief, who led their own vassals to the feudal host, received a special form of summons to the host, and there was a corresponding difference in the form of summons to court service. Hence arose the distinction between the *major barons* and the *minor barons*, of whom we begin to hear in the twelfth century.[2]

Attendance in the Curia Regis was not regarded as a privilege, but as a burden to be avoided if possible. This was especially true of the minor barons who were less able to bear the expense of attendance and who found little at the court to profit or attract them. They were coming to regard military and court service, their strictly feudal duties, as burdensome, and were giving more personal attention to their lands with a view to making them financially profitable; their

[1] See above, pp. 102–104.

[2] *Baron* was not a title of dignity, but a term applying to all who held land of the king on the basis of military service. In Henry II.'s reign, the major barons dealt directly with the Exchequer in discharging their financial obligations to the king, while the minor barons dealt first with the sheriff.

interests were becoming localised.[1] The different methods of summoning major and minor barons to the Curia Regis received formal recognition in article fourteen of Magna Carta, which was undoubtedly the work of the barons whose interests it favoured. An individual summons was to be sent to the greater barons, while to all the lesser tenants-in-chief was sent a general summons through the sheriffs. This latter was generally regarded as a permission to stay away, which was what the minor barons wanted. The make-up of the Curia Regis came thus to be more dependent upon the will of the sovereign and tenancy-in-chief less a basis for attendance, though it did not entirely disappear for centuries; in other words, peerage by writ of summons was taking the place of the feudal principle in determining the composition of the king's court.

The question naturally arises at this point whether there was in the thirteenth century a distinct class of major barons who might always claim the special summons or whether receipt of the summons wholly determined membership in the class. As in most medieval institutions, one finds here vagueness and irregularity, where he might expect adherence to a fixed principle. In Henry III.'s reign, there were certainly many barons so great and powerful that they would always expect or demand a summons. In the meeting of 1255, for instance, complaint was made that all had not been summoned who, by the provision of the Charter, should have been. On the other hand, the special summons made its recipient a major baron if he had not been one before. But attendance was

---

[1] See below, pp. 307, 308.

still felt to be a burden except in cases of special interest, as when an unusual aid was demanded. It was
doubtless for this reason that article fourteen of the
Charter provided for a statement in the summons of
the business to be transacted, that the time and place
of meeting be clearly indicated, and that the summons
be sent at least forty days in advance. The personnel
of successive meetings varied much; for the distinction
between major and minor barons was not sharply
drawn, and there was a wide province between the
very large and the very small holders in which the
king's will acted freely. This remained the condition
until well into the reign of Edward III.; there could
be no change until attendance upon a central assembly had become a thing to be desired.[1] The capri-

---

[1] Maitland has commented instructively upon the barons' "right"
to attend the "parliament" of 1305: "We must put duty in the first
line, right in the second. We have learnt to do this when discussing
the constitution of those county courts which send knights to the
house of commons; must we not also do it when we are discussing
the constitution of the house of lords and of the council? In 1305
the baron who had come from Yorkshire or Devonshire, had been
compelled to stay three weeks in London at his own cost, for he was
paid no wages. Did he very much want to spend another three
weeks there hearing dreary petitions concerning the woes of the
Scots and Gascons? At a later time a desire for political power or
social pre-eminence will make the English baron eager to insist on
his right to a writ of summons, eager to take a part, however
subordinate, in all that is done by the house of lords. But in
Edward I.'s day the baronage is hardly as yet a well-defined
body, and it may be that there are many men who, unable to fore-
see that their 'blood' is being 'ennobled' for ever and ever, are not
best pleased when they receive a writ which tells them that, leaving
their homes and affairs, they must journey and labour in the king's
service, and all this at their own cost. Thus for many years one
great constitutional question can remain in suspense. It is not
raised, no one wishes to raise it. So long as the king does not impose taxes or issue statutes without the consent of the baronage,

ciousness of the king's summonses shows that no new principle that would make a regular and self-conscious assembly was being introduced.

The change came as a result of Edward III.'s continuous demands for money and the increasing business brought before the barons; they were vitally concerned in the money grants and in some of the other business, and the growing activity and responsibility of the assembly gradually begot ideas of political power and honour. Late in Edward II.'s reign, the barons had first spoken of themselves as *peers of the realm* and this is perhaps the first indication that honour was being attached to the old burden of suit of court.[1] If a baron received one summons, he began to expect another at the next meeting. He by no means always got it, but the tendency of the fourteenth century was away from capricious summonses. And if he continued to receive summonses throughout his life, it raised the presumption that, after his death, his heir would receive them, for it was an age when all valuable rights were likely to become hereditary. Thus the fuller meeting of the old Curia Regis was being metamorphosed into a House of Lords, which peers attended on the basis of a strictly hereditary dignity without reference to tenure. The change was not complete in the reign of Richard II., for relics of the old feudal, tenurial basis lasted a surprisingly long time; but a comparatively small and quite compact body of hereditary peers had taken shape.

---

the baron hopes that the king will mind his own business (and it is his business to govern the realm) and allow other folk to mind theirs."—Introduction to *Memoranda de Parliamento*, pp. lxxxvi., lxxxvii.

[1] Pike, *Constitutional History of the House of Lords*, p. 109.

While it is true that fourteenth-century peers attended what we may venture to call the House of Lords because they received writs of summons from the king, it should be remembered that they were barons by tenure already. The writs did not make them barons; to use the old terminology, they made them major barons, or, in language more suited to the time, the writs did not determine who should be barons—which was still a matter of tenure—but which of the barons should be Peers of the Realm. As all the peers were barons, it was natural that the inheritance of the dignity of a peer should be regulated by the rules which applied to the inheritance of fiefs. Hence in default of male heirs, the dignity might pass, like the barony, to an heiress. No peeress was ever summoned to the House of Lords, but she might confer upon her husband a presumptive right to the king's writ of summons. In the later middle ages, there were many instances in which the husbands of such heiresses were summoned to Parliament as peers.

A change took place in the fifteenth century which eventually brought to an end this method of transmitting a peer's dignity and which was the last important step in the creation of the modern House of Lords. It had become the practice, by the end of the fourteenth century, to create titles of dignity by letters patent; these were open letters which differed from charters only in their less formal attestation. The title of earl had been conferred in this way since Stephen's reign, and the new titles of duke and marquess were so conferred in the late fourteenth century, and viscount in the fifteenth. In the letter creating the title, it was possible to regulate the succession of the title.   In 1387, was the first and, for a long time, the only instance of the creation of a baron by letter patent; this baron was also declared by the letter—and it was the object of his being created baron—an hereditary lord of Parliament.   Such creations became common in the reign of Henry VI.   It was a time of bitter strife among the nobility, and it was often found useful for the party for the moment in power to be able to raise men to the peerage who did not happen to be barons.   By the end of the century, it had become the normal method of creating peers.   The king could, in the letters patent, regulate the succession in any way he chose; but in practice, the title was made to pass to male heirs only, and that under the principle of primogeniture.   The advantages of the new system were obvious: heiresses could no longer confer the dignity of a peer upon their husbands and thus carry it into new families which might not be agreeable to the king or the existing peerage, and the king was now able not only to make a baron a peer, but any one whom he chose.   It seems clear however that these advantages were not fully recognised at first; immediate objects seem to have furnished the motives for the change, especially during Henry VI.'s reign when the letters patent were, so to speak, becoming the fashion. A gradual recognition of the broader advantages kept them in fashion.   It is obvious that through the use of letters patent the term baron would gradually lose all of its old feudal meaning.[1]

Here a query necessarily arises concerning the spirit-. ual lords.   No principles of inheritance could apply

[1] On the subject of the new titles of dignity and the letters patent, see Stubbs, *Constitutional History*, § 428.

to them. How were they faring during these changes?
Bishops and abbots had been summoned to the king's
feudal court, the larger Curia Regis, by virtue of the
baronies they held, that is, because they were tenants-
in-chief. They were major barons in the twelfth-
century sense; and they were wise and influential, and
hence important as counsellors. As the king's will
became a greater and greater factor in determining
who were to be major barons, the bishops still received
the writs of summons with practically unbroken uniformity; their greatness, tenurially and otherwise,
placed them beyond question. But with the abbots
and priors who were barons, the king exercised the same
capriciousness as with the lay barons of corresponding
importance. Also, as with the lay barons, the capriciousness decreased under Edward III.; certain abbots
and priors were known as scarcely ever summoned.
The abbots as a class were rather disinclined to attend.

When the barons began to call themselves peers,
the prelates were considered as fully peers as the lay
barons, for the technical basis of their attendance was
precisely the same. This continued to be the case
until well along in the fifteenth century. But a
different conception finally arose as a result of the
clergy's inability to share fully the judicial work of the
House of Lords.[1] They could not be present when
judgment was passed involving loss of life or limb, for
the canons forbade it; and they held aloof from their
right to be tried by their peers through their strict
adherence to the principle that no lay court could try
them. Hence the idea gradually took shape that they
could not be regarded as peers, while they were certainly

---

[1] See above, pp. 201–203.

20

lords of Parliament. In 1692, when, because of the
dissolution of the monasteries, the bishops had for
long been the only prelates in the House of Lords,
a formal declaration was made by that House to the
effect that bishops were not peers, but only lords of
Parliament. The fifteenth-century change from writs
of summons to letters patent could have no effect upon
the prelates, for no letters patent could create them;
their right to attend the House of Lords always drew its
sanction from their ancient baronies.

The number of lay lords summoned during the fourteenth and fifteenth centuries averaged from forty to
fifty or a little over; the spiritual lords numbered about
fifty. But often, especially during the Wars of the
Roses, the number of lay members fell considerably
below this, leaving the prelates in a majority. The
dissolution of the monasteries in the next century
gave a permanent majority to the lay members.

2. **Why there was a Middle Class in England. Origin
of Popular Election and its Connection with Representation.**—Having seen the structural transformation
of the Curia Regis into the House of Lords, we
begin here the study of the House of Commons by
enquiring into the conditions which made possible the
adding of new elements to the changing central assembly. The addition was made in the thirteenth century and the new elements represented a great middle
class. What was this middle class? It will be remembered that at the time of the Norman Conquest English
society was in a peculiarly unsettled condition. Many
freemen were being depressed in status and were
taking on characteristics of servility. With some, the
change had gone so far that they might well be ranked

with the servile classes; others were in a doubtful, intermediate position. Unquestionably forces were in operation which looked toward that complete disintegration of the non-noble, free class which was taking place upon the continent. But the important point to note here is that the process had not been completed in England and that the Norman Conquest was reached with a considerable body of non-noble freemen, a true middle class, still existent. The immediate effect of Norman clear thinking and vigorous action upon the broad Anglo-Saxon class which lay between the manifestly servile and the noble was to push many individuals farther down than they had been before, and, on the other hand, to render the free status of the remainder more distinct. Surviving the Conquest, and, in a manner, created by it, was a well-defined class of non-noble freemen.[1]

A second source of the later middle class lay in the lower orders of the nobility. These consisted of the numerous small tenants-in-chief, the so-called minor barons, and the small sub-tenants of the king's greater vassals, or, where the feudal hierarchy extended so far, the tenants of sub-tenants. Any of these might hold only a single knight's fee, or perhaps not even the land requisite to a knight and be reckoned as esquires. As the twelfth century progressed, a split appeared in the

[1] The free classes outside the boroughs are particularly in mind here, for it was in that part of the population that the principles of representation and election, which gave rise to the House of Commons, had their origin. But it should be remembered that the burgesses were largely of free origin, and that burgage tenure was a variety of free socage, the characteristic tenure of the non-noble free classes. For an account of class conditions in the twelfth century, see above, pp. 80–85.

nobility; the interests of these smaller holders were becoming differentiated from those of the greater barons. The strong Norman and Angevin kings, who made wars to cease and kept order in the country, were cutting the lesser nobles off from their feudal activities. Fighting with their neighbours was the normal occupation of small feudatories; if they could not do this, there was nothing left but to stay at home and attend to their estates. The possibility of increased revenue from their estates began to suggest itself to them; the financial side of their position absorbed more of their attention; they were soon on the way to pure land-lordism. This change brought them into closer contact with the class next below them, and their interests became more identified with their localities. There thus began, as early as the twelfth century, the process by which the lower orders of the nobility in England voluntarily dissociated themselves from the higher nobility and approached the non-noble freemen.

Besides these results of their stern rule, there must be noted also the effect upon the whole nobility of what may possibly be termed a policy of the post-Conquest kings. They were able to keep any class of the nobles from attaining such immunities or privileges as to differentiate it in the eyes of the law from the other freemen.

Our law hardly knows anything of a noble or of a gentle class; all free men are in the main equal before the law. For a moment this may seem strange. A conquered country is hardly the place in which we should look for an equality, which, having regard to other lands, we must call exceptional. Yet in truth it is the result of the Conquest, though a result that was slowly evolved.

With the strange complex of classes left from Anglo-Saxon times, a strong king could do what he pleased:

. . . he can make his favour the measure of nobility; they are noble whom he treats as such. And he does not choose that there shall be much nobility. Gradually a small noble class is formed, an estate of temporal lords, of earls and barons. The principles which hold it together are far rather land tenure and the king's will than the transmission of noble blood. Its members have political privileges which are the counterpart of political duties; the king consults them, and is in some sort bound to consult them, and they are bound to attend his summons and give him counsel. They have hardly any other privileges. During the baron's life his children have no privileges; on his death only the new baron becomes noble.[1]

But this is using the word noble in a narrow and very English sense. The formation of this new and limited nobility will be readily recognised as the evolution of the House of Lords. It was a nobility that did not tend to increase, for the title went only with the tenure and the tenure was becoming strictly primogenitary.

The early prevalence of the primogenitary principle was also a result of the Norman Conquest. Primogeniture originated in feudalism. The overlord wanted a certain and undivided source to which he might look for the service owed by the fief; the vassal would naturally divide his holding equally among his sons. Owing to this clash of interests, the growth of primogeniture was slow and was not completely established in Normandy at the time of the Conquest. The Norman kings of England had far more vassals than any

[1] P. and M. i., 408, 409.

other English overlord and were therefore more interested in the enforcement of the principle. They were strong enough to enforce it, and were strong enough not to be afraid to enforce it, that is, they had no vassals so powerful that they were tempted to favour some principle of partition in order to weaken them. Thus England got in advance of the other countries of western Europe in the adoption of primogeniture as the rule of succession in the land law; and the younger sons of barons lacked both the baronial tenure and the baronial title. They went to swell the class of lower nobility, which in England is properly termed *gentry*, a word which indicates nobility. For the gentry were of noble blood and performed only honourable services for their lords. In any country but England, they would have been reckoned every whit as noble as the greatest barons. But the strong kings in England had formed at the top of the general body of nobles a select number, who, being the only ones in possession of political and legal privileges, came finally to be reckoned the only nobles. Thus the gentry were distinguished from the non-noble freemen only by their noble blood, which carried with it the social privilege of wearing coat-armour, a practice which arose in the twelfth century.[1]

The characteristic member of the class of gentry was the knight. But the younger sons of a knight might never attain to knighthood either in tenure or title.

[1] It must not be supposed, of course, that the kings contributed to this change with the conscious intent of fashioning a unique nobility in England; they acted merely as it suited their immediate purposes to deal from time to time with this important part of their population. The thing was done before it was clearly understood what was done.

Title is mentioned, for there were knights—often those knighted on the field of battle—who were not holders of the knight's fee; on the other hand, there were those who possessed knight's fees who had never been dubbed knights. The divorce between tenure and status [1] showed itself everywhere, and intermarriage might easily occur between gentle and simple; notwithstanding the use of coat-armour the line between the gentry and the non-noble freemen was often blurred, and there was a much sharper line of demarcation between the greater and lesser nobles. Upon the continent, there was an impassable gulf between the pettiest noble and the class below; in England, there was a much slighter chasm at this point with many means of crossing.

The sources of a substantial middle class in England (without taking into account the borough population) may now be summarised: a non-noble, free class survived the Anglo-Saxon period; the Conquest resulted in making the status of a portion of that class more distinctly free; there were many small nobles after the Conquest; the masterful post-Conquest sovereigns deprived these nobles of their important feudal characteristics, made them landlords in close touch with their localities and the class below them; royalty also allowed no legal advantages to the nobles as a whole, but made a small class of hereditary counsellors a nobility in a special sense, and finally the only nobility; the gentry, thus lacking the name and distinguishing marks of a nobility, more readily approached local interests and the class of freeholders, and the movement was further aided by the characteristic English divorce

[1] See above, p. 84.

between tenure and status and the early triumph of primogeniture.

In the second half of the twelfth century, the local activity of knights and freeholders in judicial and revenue matters strikingly illustrates the common interests of the two classes and probably itself contributed to their approach. In it lay the origin of the machinery which eventually suggested the calling of local representatives to the centre. With its consideration, we take up the second part of our general theme; having noted the conditions which brought forth a true middle class, we next consider the line of development which led to its representation in a central assembly. When Henry II. incorporated the sworn inquest in the procedure of the royal courts and outlined the work of a presenting jury, he furnished an appropriate sphere of activity for a middle class, a class acquainted with, and interested in, the affairs of the locality.[1] The sources leave one in no doubt as to the classes employed upon these early juries; they nearly always specify knights or free and lawful men. Towards the end of the century, the language often indicates that knights were preferred. These men were regarded as representing the knowledge and opinion of their neighbourhood; indeed, their representative character when they acted in these capacities was always marked.

But the sworn inquest in its original, non-judicial character also continued, and, though no longer called *inquisitio*, was receiving a great extension about the end of the twelfth century. In the Assize of Arms, 1181, a jury of "lawful knights or other free and lawful

[1] See above, pp. 144, 145.

men" were to assess their neighbours' wealth with a view to determining their proper military equipment.[1] This was in principle the same thing as to assess them for taxation. By the Ordinance of the Saladin Tithe,[2] 1188, the same method of assessment was to be used when a man was suspected of having paid less than he ought. In this instance, the machinery was used in connection with a true tax; and from this time, assessing juries were increasingly employed for the new personal property taxes. The itinerant justices' commission of 1194[3] shows the great variety of the information elicited from the knights and lawful men of the hundreds, much of it of a non-judicial character. In this same document, is the first distinct mention of coroners, who had probably been in existence since some time in the reign of Henry II. The coroner was then in the first stage of his development, a minor local justice who disposed of many small criminal cases and held preliminary hearings on more important ones preparatory to the visitation of the justices.[4] The coroners were regularly drawn from the class of knights. Thus there is much evidence that, if the knights had withdrawn from the camp and the court, they were finding plenty to do at home, and that the king regarded them and the class next below them as most useful in developing his court system, his revenue, and the general efficiency of his local control.

In these dealings with the great middle class, the kings were developing little by little a representative machinery and were certainly becoming conscious of it as such. But all this activity was at the king's

---

[1] A. and S., p. 24.
[2] Ibid., p. 28.
[3] Ibid., document 21.
[4] See above, pp. 188, 189.

initiative, and though the country was much benefited by the increasing governmental work and efficiency, there was no immediate prospect of an independent representative body. For these early local representatives were always appointed by a power above them. This might not detract from their purely representative character, but no system of representation can be sure of remaining such unless the appointing power lies with the people represented. Another development must take place before popular representation in a modern sense was even remotely possible.

The first approaches to an election by the people are to be found in the very late twelfth century. The juries of the Assizes of Clarendon and Northampton were probably selected by the sheriffs; but in the commission given the itinerant justices in 1194, great care was taken to specify how the jury should be chosen: "In the first place, four knights are to be chosen" (probably still by the sheriff) "from out of the whole county, who, upon their oaths, are to chose two lawful knights of every hundred and wapentake, and those two are to chose upon their oath ten knights of every hundred or wapentake, or, if there shall not be knights sufficient, free and lawful men, in order that these twelve may together make inquisition on each of the following heads in every hundred or wapentake."[1] This method appears to have been a transition from the entire control of the sheriff to true popular election. The reference to the coroners in this same document is in these words: "Also in every county there are to be three knights chosen, and one clerk, who are to be keepers of the pleas of the crown." In all

[1] A. and S., p. 29.

the later known history of the coroner, the office was elective, and it is probable that at this time the coroners were chosen in the county courts.[1]   This seems to have been the earliest connection between the local use of representative knights for governmental purposes and popular election.   By the time of Magna Carta, nearly twenty years after, the transition had been completed, and undoubted instances are found of the popular election of knights for various local purposes.   In article 18 of the Charter, there is mention of "four knights of each county, elected by the county,"[2] who were to act with the itinerant justices in holding the possessory assizes.   The last word in the quotation might well be translated "county-court," as the Latin *comitatus* means that also, and the county court was the only assembly through which the county could act. In article 48 of the same document, in providing for an inquisition into the bad forest customs, it says that these "shall be enquired into immediately in each county by twelve sworn knights of the same county, who shall be elected by the honest men of the same county."   This language admits of no doubt that there was popular election in the county courts.   As a final example, and one of much significance because it relates to the use of knights in assessing and collecting a tax, the language of a writ of 1220 for collecting a carucage

[1] "The machinery for the election of coroners seems to have been the mould which shaped the representation of the shires in parliament; the coroners were prototypes of the parliamentary knights of the shire.   Elected knights of the shire were also employed for other local purposes, but in a more casual or transitory way than in the case of the coroner.   This latter office was a permanent institution, which must have helped to habituate the nation to the idea of county representation."—Gross, *Select Coroners' Rolls*, p. xxxv.

[2] A. and S., p. 45.

may be cited.   It is addressed to the sheriff of each
county.

. . . two shillings are to be collected by your own
hand and the hands of two of the more lawful knights of
your county, who shall be chosen to do this by the will and
counsel of all of the county in full county court.   And
therefore we bid you and firmly and strictly enjoin you
that, after the convocation of the full court of your county,
by the will and consent of those of the county, you cause
to be chosen two of the more lawful knights of the whole
county who shall best know how, wish, and be able to
attend to this business to our advantage, and when these
have been associated with you, you shall immediately cause
this gift to be assessed throughout your whole bailiwick
and collected from each carrucate.   .   .   .[1]

This identical method of assessing and collecting a tax
was far from permanent, but the use of local knights
for these purposes was permanent and was big with
possibilities.

Why had the king changed the method of selecting
the knights who were attending to his various local
concerns?   Probably because of his inveterate distrust
of the sheriff.   The Norman kings had never been
wholly satisfied with the sheriff.   They had kept this
part of the Anglo-Saxon system as something which
promised to be useful in conducting and safeguarding
the king's interests; but the sheriff was resident in his
shire, and was usually a great noble with landed and
other interests there; he was consequently subject to
the influences, always potent in the middle ages, which
tended to destroy the really public character of the
resident official.   Henry I. and Roger of Salisbury had

[1] A. and S., document 30.

invented the itinerant justice to oversee the sheriff and take part of his work from him. The shortcomings of the sheriffs in Henry II.'s time and what the king thought of them is well shown in the famous "Inquest of the Sheriffs"[1]; and although fewer great nobles were appointed to the office afterwards, the possibility that public interests would be neglected for private interests still existed. The knights or other freemen, when chosen for the purposes just discussed, were doing king's business; they might be called upon to tell the truth about the doings of the sheriff himself. Doubtless the king came to feel that some form of popular choice was a safer way of obtaining these representative men and of being certain of an unbiassed statement from them. A machinery was in existence, independent of the sheriff, for learning the truth about local affairs, getting at the locality's needs, and hearing its complaints.

3. **Origin of County Representation in a Central Assembly.**—Having seen the many local uses to which the king, by means of the jury device, was putting the knights and other freemen, the next development to be examined is the gathering together of local juries at some central point and the earliest connections of such concentrated juries with the Curia Regis. A chronicler's account of something that was done in August, 1213, has usually been interpreted as indicating the first instance of a concentration of juries. The writ of summons itself is not extant, and either the text of the chronicle is corrupt or the writer gave a confused account of what took place.[2] That the king used

---

[1] A. and S., document 15.
[2] For the text, see Stubbs, *Select Charters*, p. 276.

juries on this occasion to assess the damage which he had done the bishops' property is certain, but whether or not it was his intention that these juries should come together at St. Albans and state the facts there it seems impossible to determine.[1]   There is no evidence that they actually came together, while there is much to the contrary.   But it is of almost equal importance to know whether the idea of concentration had suggested itself to the king.   Whether or not it had done so in August, there is good evidence that it had three months afterwards.   In November this writ was issued:

The king to the sheriff of Oxfordshire, greeting.   We direct you to cause all the knights of your bailiwick, who have been summoned to appear before me at Oxford on All Saints' Day, to come in fifteen days with their arms; but all the barons to come in like manner unarmed: and that you cause four discreet men of your county to meet us there at the same time to consult with us about the affairs of our realm.

Witness myself at Witney, the seventh day of November.

Similar writs were directed to all the sheriffs.[2]

The unarmed barons referred to evidently constituted the larger Curia Regis.   There is no evidence that this proposed assembly met; if it had, it would have been of more significance than that of August, for here was county representation, the business seems to have been

---

[1] H. W. C. Davis, *English Historical Review* xx., pp. 289, 290, thinks that the juries were consulted as usual in their localities and that the sheriffs brought the verdicts to the St. Albans meeting; G. J. Turner, *ibid.* xxi., 297–299, believes that it was the intention to bring together at St. Albans juries drawn from the bishops' estates, not from the royal domain, as has been the usual reading.

[2] A. and S., document 27.

of a general character, and some connection between
county representatives and Curia Regis was apparently
contemplated. But at any rate, a concentration of
juries had actually been thought of.

So long an interval intervened before the next instance of concentration that the case or cases of 1213
surely could not have served as precedents.[1] But the
practices and ideas which had made them possible
still continued, indeed grew more vigorous, and were
certain, sooner or later, to produce like results. County
representation in a central assembly had its historical
origin in 1254; by this is meant that from that time
there was a sufficiently continuous use of the practice
to indicate that there was no later invention of it.[2]
Henry III. was in Gascony; an aid was to be levied
and the money sent to him. While the writs were in
the king's name, the assembly was summoned on the
authority of the queen and the Earl of Cornwall, "in
the belief," says Stubbs, "that, as the bishops had
refused to grant money without consulting the bene-
ficed clergy, the surest way to obtain it from the laity
was to call an assembly on which the promise of a
renewal of the charters would be likely to produce the
effect desired." The language of the summons should

[1] It may be argued from this that they are of little consequence:
the continuous use of the device does not date from them; they do
not represent its historical discovery. But they indicate the degree
of development and familiarity reached by the practices and ideas
out of which the new institution grew, and it is no small thing in
understanding the origin of an institution to know the point at
which it was potentially present.

[2] That the smallness of the assessing juries suggested the feasi-
bility of concentration is altogether probable. They ordinarily
consisted of two individuals, while the judicial juries were, of
course, much larger.

be noticed.   The following clauses are taken from the writ sent to the sheriff of the counties of Bedford and Buckingham:

. . . we straitly command you, that besides all those aforesaid, you cause to come before our council at Westminster on the fifteenth day after Easter next, four lawful and discreet knights from the said counties whom the said counties shall have chosen for this purpose, in place of all and singular of the said counties, that is, two from one county, and two from the other, who, together with the knights from the other counties whom we have summoned for the same day, shall arrange what aid they are willing to pay us in our need. [1]

Here were two knights from each county, whose representative and elective character is made particularly clear, formally summoned in the king's name to come before his council and negotiate the levying of an aid. The council before which they were summoned was evidently the smaller Curia Regis.[2]   Though the specific date, 1254, may be used to mark the technical beginning of county representation by elected knights, the foregoing discussions have been wasted if they have not shown how that event was gradually led up to by the growth of ideas and institutions throughout the preceding century, and that what was actually new in the event of 1254, though very important, was very small.

By a peculiar coincidence, the word *parliamentum*

---

[1] A. and S., document 33.

[2] See the first part of the writ for the location and occupation of the general body of tenants-in-chief at the time.   Moreover, the fuller meeting would not have been referred to in the words *consilio nostro.*

had come into use in connection with the work of the Curia Regis only a few years before this. But it is very essential to have in mind the long evolution which lay before the word before it had acquired the meaning with which one is familiar to-day. *Parliamentum* was a quite common medieval Latin word, derived from the ancient popular Latin, and meant a talking or colloquy, especially one of a formal sort and concerning a matter of importance. Speaking of its use as late as the end of Edward I.'s reign, Maitland says:

A parliament is rather an act than a body of persons. One cannot present a petition to a colloquy, to a debate. It is only slowly that this word is appropriated to colloquies of a particular kind, namely, those which the king has with the estates of his realm, and still more slowly that it is transferred from the colloquy to the body of men whom the king has summoned. As yet any meeting of the king's council that has been solemnly summoned for general business seems to be a parliament. . . . The personification of "parliament," which enables us to say that laws are made by, and not merely in, parliament, is a slow and subtle process.[1]

There is no single word or phrase which can adequately describe the confused parliamentary foreshadowings of the thirteenth century; this would seem to make it logically imperative, at every mention of them, to enter into long and repetitious explanations. On practical grounds, it will be expedient to occasionally use the word Parliament in a kind of anticipatory sense, its substance yet being imperfect.

The precedent of 1254 was not lost. In 1261, during

[1] Introduction to *Memoranda de Parliamento*, p. lxvii. and note 1.

the civil war, Simon de Montfort summoned three knights from each county to consult upon matters of common interest, and the king issued writs with the intention of drawing these same knights to a colloquy (*colloquium*) on the royal side. In June, 1264, de Montfort again summoned knights, this time four from each county, "chosen to represent the whole county with the assent of the county . . . to deal with us concerning the business mentioned." In December of the same year, de Montfort's famous Parliament was summoned—famous because, in addition to two knights from each county, the sheriffs were ordered to return two citizens from each city and two burgesses from each borough. Here was something new; the other representative element, which, together with the representative knights of the shire, was eventually to constitute the House of Commons, made its first appearance. It is necessary to examine in the next place the conditions and circumstances which lay behind borough representation.

4. **Condition of the Boroughs in the Thirteenth Century, and the Origin of their Representation in a Central Assembly..**—We have seen the boroughs of the twelfth century striving for various liberties and immunities, their general object apparently an institutional isolation such as was attained in some places by the continental cities.[1] By the middle of the thirteenth century, there were borough governments of the most diverse types, with perhaps a general oligarchic tendency. The corporate character of the older and larger boroughs was more pronounced, and their government was in the hands of a limited circle of burgesses or magistrates; in many of the newer and smaller towns,

[1] See above, Part II., § II., 3.

the government was still very popular, and in some it ever remained so.[1]

But more closely related to the present subject is the question of how far the boroughs had succeeded in cutting themselves off from outside control, from the general government of the country. Here also were various conditions, which grew out of the struggles and negotiations between the boroughs and their overlords; for the dispositions and abilities of the overlords to retain control over the borough governments were extremely diverse. "Some were almost independent republics, some were mere country townships that had reached the stage at which they compounded severally for their ferm, but were in all other respects under the influence of the sheriff and the county court."[2] But the important fact is that the boroughs, as a class, had not by this time progressed so far upon

[1] "Any complete generalisation upon the constitutional history of the towns is impossible for this reason, that this history does not start from one point or proceed by the same stages. At the time at which they began to take a share in the national counsels through their representatives, the class of towns contained communities in every stage of development, and in each stage of development constituted on different principles. Hence, by the way, arose the anomalies and obscurities as to the nature of the constituencies, which furnished matter of deliberation to the House of Commons for many centuries, and only ended with the Reform Act of 1832. The varieties of later usage were based on the condition in which the borough found itself when it began to be represented." The matter "is noticed here in order to show that the obscurity of the subject is not a mere result of our ignorance or of the deficiency of record, but of a confusion of usages which was felt at the time to be capable of no general treatment; a confusion which . . . prevailed from the very first, and occasioned actual disputes ages before it began to puzzle the constitutional lawyers." Stubbs, *Constitutional History of England*, § 211.

[2] *Ibid.*, § 213.

the road to independence as to make the obtaining of
their representation impossible, or to give that representation, if obtained, such exclusiveness and *esprit de
corps* that it could not co-operate with the representatives of any other part of the population. The king
still demanded the boroughs' representation by twelve
burgesses in those full meetings of the county courts
convened by the sheriffs for the itinerant justices, thus
to some extent holding them under the royal jurisdiction. The sheriffs enforced the Assize of Arms within
them, and led their military levies as part of the national militia. And there existed among the boroughs
no leagues or combinations by which they could secure
a common understanding or action.

Juries had been used for obtaining information, and
specifically for assessment purposes,[1] inside the boroughs as well as out; and the regular representation of
boroughs in the great eyre courts, where such varieties
of business were transacted, may well have suggested
to Simon de Montfort the possibility of their representation in a central assembly.[2] The real moving cause
which led him to cast about for such an expedient was
undoubtedly the weakness of his hold upon the upper

[1] See Assize of Arms, art. 9, A. and S., p. 24.

[2] It is interesting to note that these local courts contained all the
elements which constituted the later Parliament. But Parliament
was not being modelled after them for the simple reason that no one
was consciously creating Parliament. A part of the first clause of
a writ to assemble such a court in 1231 reads: "The king to the
sheriff of Yorkshire, Greeting. Summon by good summoners all
archbishops, bishops, abbots, priors, earls, barons, knights, and
all freeholders from your bailiwick, from each vill four lawful men
and the reeve, and from each borough twelve lawful burgesses,
throughout your whole bailiwick, and all others who are accustomed
and ought to appear before the justices itinerant. . . ,"—*Ibid.*,
document 31.

classes. He sought to counterbalance this by getting
the support of the middle and lower classes, and especially this burgher class which might prove very
useful financially. It is hardly necessary to state that
de Montfort's "parliaments" were not national assemblies, but meetings of the adherents and representatives of a party at a time when the country was divided
in civil strife. But the machinery of borough representation in a central assembly was not lost, and credit
for the idea must always be given to Simon de Montfort.[1] Of its future use in true Parliaments or of the
nature and importance of this new institution, Parliament itself, he had, of course, no more conception
than any of his contemporaries.

Having up to this point dealt entirely with antecedent conditions and causes and the bare beginnings
of what may be termed an embryonic Parliament, the
subject now broadens and three rather general divisions
naturally suggest themselves: first, the external history
of the institution, the history of its form and composition through the critical changes of its early years
until it attained some stability in these respects
and had developed the characteristic features which
were the foundation of its success; secondly, the
electorate through the first century and a half of
Parliament's life; thirdly, how Parliament became
conscious of itself, developed its great powers, and

[1] Professor Adams believes that "borough representatives would
have been summoned to the great council by the close of the century
if Simon's writs had never been issued and for reasons very different
from those which influenced his action." His grounds for this
opinion are the rapidly growing importance of the boroughs in the
thirteenth century and the fact that the "stricter feudal ideas" were
passing away.

started upon its work of creating a government by
the people.

5. **Form and Composition of Parliament from 1265 to
the Middle of the Fourteenth Century.**—The thirty years
from Simon de Montfort's Parliament of 1265 to the
so-called Model Parliament of 1295 was a critical and
experimental period in the life of the young institution.
It might perhaps be more truly said that there was no
new institution until 1295 or thereabouts; there was no
concept of it as such in the minds of the men of that
generation.   They knew only of certain new practices
and devices, the questioning of groups of locally elected
representatives about taxation and other matters in
which the king was interested.

To show how wholly lacking was the idea of a new
assembly of any definite form, it is necessary only to
glance at the practice of the period.   In the assembly
of 1273, were present the three elements necessary to a
Parliament in the later sense: the larger Curia Regis, at
this time verging towards a House of Lords; representatives of the shires; representatives of the cities
and boroughs.   But since the purpose of this assembly
was merely to swear allegiance to the new sovereign,
one especially hesitates to call it a Parliament.   The
sources are not clear upon the make-up of the first assembly of 1275; certainly there was a meeting of the
barons [1] in that year, and the language of some of its
enactments indicates that representative elements were
also present; but such language was often used loosely,

---

[1] The term "barons" is used here and in a number of later instances as a relief from the cumbrous "larger Curia Regis."   It thus
includes those greater tenants-in-chief to whom the king was sending
writs of summons.   The prelates were, of course, barons in the sense
that they held baronies.

and, the summoning writs not being extant, it is impossible to tell just what was meant. At a second meeting of the same year, the representatives of the shires were certainly present, and it is interesting to note that this was the first assembly in Edward I.'s reign to make a money grant. In 1283, there were two very peculiar assemblies. Most of the nobles were with the king on the Welsh campaign; hence the first, which met in January in two divisions, one at York and the other at Northampton, was without the baronage. It consisted of representatives of the shires and boroughs. To these were added representatives of the cathedral clergy. The purpose of this was undoubtedly financial; it was characteristic of Edward I., who aimed at a broad representative basis for his money grants, and was consistent with the whole representative movement of the thirteenth century. These representative clergy were not considered a regular part of a lay assembly in 1283, but such a use of clerical representation was not without precedent, as will be presently seen. The two places of meeting, north and south, seem to have been suggested by the Convocations of Canterbury and York. It is particularly interesting to note that it was regarded as nothing extraordinary for knights and burgesses to meet and transact business in the absence of the nobility. A second assembly of this year met in September, at Shrewsbury on the Welsh border. Thus the nobles, who were still under arms against the Welsh, could be present, and to them were added representatives of the shires and of certain specified boroughs. The main object mentioned in the writs was to judge David of Wales, but it was added that "other matters"

were also to be attended to. The statute De Mercatoribus or Acton Burnell was dated October the
twelfth at Acton Burnell, and was the product of the
deliberations of the burgesses who had withdrawn to
that place from the Shrewsbury assembly. But its
language retained the stereotyped form, "the king by
himself and his council hath ordained," etc.[1] This
second assembly of 1283 is then noteworthy in not containing any clergy—apparently because its business
did not concern them—and in its dividing, the nobles
remaining at Shrewsbury to perform their more proper
function in judging the Prince David while the burgesses
withdrew to another place to deal with a commercial
matter. The king was making use of a machinery for
getting together and consulting various classes of his
population; he used it as time and occasion required;
he was certainly not consciously fashioning a general
assembly; on the contrary, he seems to have usually
adhered to the idea that that which concerned only one
class should be dealt with by that class alone. Early
in 1290, a meeting of the barons acted upon the purely
feudal matter of granting the king an aid incident to
the marriage of his oldest daughter.[2] Later in the
year, this same body made the famous statute of Quia
Emptores, a statute which especially concerned the

[1] A. and S., document 41. In this use of the word council, where
consilium seems really to mean a body of men rather than the counsel
which was given, was undoubtedly indicated the smaller Curia
Regis. This body was then taking on such technical and definable
characteristics that it may soon be considered an independent and
self-conscious assembly. See above, pp.287–290.

[2] Though here were feudal nobles acting on a feudal matter, it
should be remembered that there were very many tenants-in-chief
who might be held for the aid who would not be found in the larger
Curia Regis as it was then constituted.

greater landholders. Late in the year, there were added representatives of the shires, apparently for the sole purpose of negotiating a money grant. In 1294, there was a meeting of the barons and the representatives of the shires. The purpose was largely financial, and a "tenth" was granted. The towns were also tallaged at this time, but they were dealt with separately through commissioners. Late in 1295, after an earlier meeting of the barons, was summoned the great assembly distinguished in later history as the Model Parliament.

It is probable that the use of the term Model Parliament has led to the popular ascription to Edward I. of ideas and purposes quite in advance of any which he ever entertained. It is proper to remember this Parliament and its date as marking an epoch in parliamentary history; but such use is subject to the danger always attendant upon fixing any event as marking an epoch, an exaggeration of its epoch-making character. The impelling motive which led Edward I. to summon such an inclusive and, from a later point of view, model assembly was the financial pressure of the unprecedented combination of wars which he had on hand. He needed money as never before, and he used the means to obtain it which the experience of the past thirty years and his instincts as a practical statesman suggested. He needed the help of all classes and, as far as conditions allowed, he took them all into his confidence. It can hardly be thought that the representative elements were really asked to give their consent to taxation, but their good will could be gained and consultation with them certainly facilitated assessment and collection. There was no grand theorizing,

and the high-sounding adaptation from the Theodosian
Code to be found in the summons to the clergy was
probably the insertion of a clerical official in the Chancery.[1]   To suppose it a great principle, weighed and
enunciated by Edward I., would be at variance with
the actual happenings and with the spirit of preceding
and succeeding history. The Parliament of 1295 was
simply a great fact, great in itself, and made particularly prominent by the national crisis which occasioned
it; it worked by its own weight, and, fitting in aptly
with the contemporary trend of events, it was not forgotten and became one of the greatest precedents in
English constitutional history.   The king had been unconsciously working towards the use of the representative principle in national affairs during the past thirty
years and more.   Now events seemed to demand a completer application of that principle than before, and the
great emphasis thus placed upon it permanently affected
both king and people.   With practically no uniformity in
the application of this principle to national assemblies
before 1295, it must not be understood that there was a
close approach to uniformity afterwards, but merely
that a long step had been taken in that direction.[2]

[1] "As a most just law, established by the careful providence of
sacred princes, exhorts and decrees that what affects all, by all
should be approved, so also, very evidently should common danger
be met by means provided in common."—A. and S., p. 82.   See
Riess, *Geschichte des Wahlrechts zum englischen Parlament im Mittelalter*, pp. 1–14, for a discussion of this clause and the author's
conception of the true object of early representation in Parliament.
For the writs of summons to the Model Parliament, see A. and S.,
document 46.   Particular attention should be paid to the last
paragraph of the summons of county and borough representatives,
where the purpose and spirit with which they were summoned is
clearly shown.

[2] The king dealt with individual elements occasionally after

The Model Parliament contained the body of prelates and greater barons which was becoming the House of Lords. The lay members of this body numbered forty-eight in this meeting, seven earls and forty-one barons below the rank of earl. The prelates, summoned by virtue of their baronial tenure, comprised the two archbishops, eighteen bishops, sixty-seven abbots, and the heads of three religious orders, the Hospitallers, Templars, and the Order of Sempringham. The bishops were ordered to cite beforehand (*præmunientes*)[1] the deans or priors of their cathedral chapters, the archdeacons of their dioceses, one representative proctor from each chapter, and two representative proctors from the parish clergy of each diocese. Besides the clergy and the nobility, this Parliament contained a representation of the thirty-seven shires then in existence by two knights each and of one hundred and ten cities and boroughs by two citizens or burgesses each.

A pause must be made here for some explanation of the comparatively new element appearing in the Model Parliament, the representative clergy. While, during the thirteenth century, the representative principle was being applied to lay assemblies, the clergy had been perfecting a system by which the Convocations of their two great archiepiscopal provinces, Canterbury and York, were becoming bodies quite perfectly representing all classes of their order. In taxing the clergy,

---

1295. Note the instance in 1372 when the citizens and burgesses "were commanded to tarry" after the dismissal of the knights.—A. and S., document 81. The last instance in which the Lords met alone was in the seventeenth century.

[1] The clause introduced by this word, which has always been retained in the writ summoning the bishops, is often spoken of as the *præmunientes* clause. See A. and S., p. 83.

the king occasionally made use of this machinery,
which he found ready to his hand, just as he used an
analogous machinery in taxing the laity. It is not
the place here to study in detail the origin and growth
of Convocation, but certain of its features must be
noticed in order to understand the early history of
Parliament.

Before the thirteenth century, there were two principal ecclesiastical assemblies: diocesan synods, which
were quite exhaustive meetings of all the clergy of
the diocese; and provincial synods attended, in each
of the archiepiscopal provinces, by the bishops, some of
the abbots, and later the archdeacons.   Until the thirteenth century, as far as the clergy had been consulted
at all concerning money grants, there had been negotia-
tion by the royal officials with the individual dioceses,
sometimes undoubtedly through the diocesan synods.
But this had been much more a matter of demanding
and collecting than of consulting or asking consent.
If there were to be a real consultation of the clergy,
it must be in a body where concerted and effective
action of the higher clergy would be possible, namely,
in the provincial synod. The intense opposition to
John's misrule and exactions made it necessary for
him to treat the clergy with more consideration, and
he was the first king to make any approach toward a
consultation of the provincial synods on money grants.
The stand taken by certain bishops against the unusual
aid proposed in the last year of his brother's reign
shows that the time was ripe for such a development.
It was the new importance attaching to the provincial
synods, as bodies consulted in matters of taxation, that
led to their development into representative Convoca-

tions in the course of the century. In 1225, proctors representing the cathedral chapters and the monasteries were added to the old elements. But the parochial clergy were not represented till 1283, although more than once before this such representation had been virtually demanded by the refusal of the represented elements to bind the unrepresented in the matter of a money grant. In 1283, the organisation was completed; all elements of the clergy were either present in person or by representatives, and the two old provincial synods had become two representative Convocations. These usually met at the same time and were often thought of and spoken of as the Convocation of the whole church.

These Convocations consisted of the following, who attended in person: bishops, abbots, priors, the deans of cathedral and collegiate churches, archdeacons, and the heads of certain religious orders. The representative elements were the two proctors from each diocese, representing the parish clergy, and one proctor for each cathedral and collegiate chapter. Of course Convocation was a purely ecclesiastical body in purpose and make-up, although the king might consult it on civil matters, especially taxation. But during the same century that this body was coming into existence, a parallel and related development was in progress which culminated in the complete ecclesiastical representation in the Parliament of 1295. The king was showing a greater and greater inclination to summon clergy to lay assemblies, but the manner of summons and the elements summoned were largely determined by the contemporary development of the Convocations. Twice in the reign of John were representative clergy summoned to his councils: the first time, abbots for the monastic clergy; the second time, the deans for the cathedral chapters. It is not to be supposed that John intended to make them a regular part of his council, any more than in 1254 did Eleanor and the Earl of Cornwall intend to make the knights; but if the thing were done enough times and proved a sufficiently helpful expedient, it might result in that in the one case as well as in the other. Simon de Montfort summoned the cathedral deans to his Parliament of 1265, and there were a few other cases, which it is not necessary to notice individually, before the very important one of 1283. It can be understood now that the importance of that case lay largely in the fact that the king used this system of clerical representation in a lay assembly in the very year that it was perfected in the ecclesiastical assemblies. It might fairly be expected that if the king were to continue the lay use of the system, it would be in the completed form which it had just attained. In 1294, Edward summoned a practically complete assembly of the clergy, with all the representative elements then used in Convocation, but it seems to have met at a different time from the lay portion of his Parliament, although summoned for substantially the same purpose, namely, revenue. The next year in the Model Parliament, the full clerical representation was summoned at the same time as the other elements, and perhaps with the dawning conception that all these elements constituted, for the time being at least, a single body. Thus the clergy became a distinct estate in the embryonic Parliament; part of them were present as a new element, purely as clergy, while the prelates were there upon the old ground of their baronial tenure.

In studying the origin of the English Parliament, one is too likely to pause for congratulation at the date 1295, as if the great institution were then already completed or nearly so. It should not be forgotten that had Parliament remained what it was in that year there would have been little cause for congratulation. Certain very fundamental changes in its make-up and internal arrangement must take place, some of which appear entirely accidental, before it could become effective in winning power and liberty for the people. In language appropriate to the ideas of the time, the Parliament of 1295 met as three estates: the first estate, clergy; the second estate, lay nobility; the third estate, burgesses. The first estate would, of course, include the prelates, who were there also as barons, as well as the representative clergy. If the second estate comprised all lay nobles, it must include not only the barons but the representative knights of the shire as well. For the knights were technically nobles, and, though they came distinctly and consciously representing the counties that chose them, their formal and historical position seems at first to have drawn them to the barons and away from their more natural associates, the burgesses. Just how this distinction of estates manifested itself in the Parliament of 1295 and those following it is impossible to say.[1] Probably

[1] The use of the term "parliament" at the beginning of the fourteenth century is admirably illustrated by the meeting of 1305. Maitland says of it: "It was a full parliament in our sense of that term. The three estates of the realm met the king and his council. The great precedent of 1295 had been followed and, if the writs of summons were punctually obeyed, the assembly was a large one."

the different elements sat in different parts of Westminster Hall; at any rate they deliberated and acted
separately. If the mobile material of 1295 had hardened into a three-house assembly with the distribution
of elements just noted, one might expect its failure on
at least two grounds: in the first place, three-house assemblies have generally proved inefficient, as such—two
of the houses are likely to intrigue against or outweigh
the third, and an assembly ill-balanced and divided
against itself results; in the second place, if the knights
were to continue to sit with the barons, it left the
burgesses the only true representatives of the non-noble
class, the only element in the assembly that could be
termed *commons;* and in the middle ages, the urban
population was not of sufficient consideration or
strength to make by itself a struggle for constitutional
liberty. The knights would have been left in an unnatural and ineffective position; and these representative knights, as has been shown, were the most valuable
and *English* of all the elements in Parliament; they
stood for what was then to be found in no other country,
a substantial middle class outside the city walls, and

It was opened at Westminster on the 28th of February. "This
assembly was kept together for just three weeks. On the 21st of
March a proclamation was made telling the archbishops, bishops
and other prelates, earls, barons, knights, citizens, and burgesses in
general that they might go home, but must be ready to appear again
if the king summoned them. Those bishops, earls, barons, justices,
and others who were members of the council were to remain behind
and so were all those who had still any business to transact. But
the 'parliament' was not at an end. Many of its doings that are
recorded on our roll were done after the estates had been sent home.
The king remained at Westminster, surrounded by his councillors
and his parliament was still in session as a 'full' and 'general' parliament as late as the 5th and 6th of April."—Introduction to
Memoranda de Parliamento, pp. xxxv., xxxvi.

without that, whatever governmental machinery might
be in process of formation, no constitutional government could have been evolved and maintained. And
unless the middle class outside the city walls could,
through its representatives in Parliament, unite with
the middle class inside the city walls through its representatives, thus forming one great middle class with
an effective representative machinery, there could be
little to guarantee the rights and liberties of the English
commons against the encroachments of nobility and
crown. The great historic English Parliament was no
foregone conclusion in 1295, and the half-century following that date was as critical as the half-century
preceding.[1]

The first great change after 1295 was the withdrawal
from Parliament of the clergy as an estate. It happened to be a time when the clergy were very sensitive
on the subject of taxation by the state. Boniface VIII.
was pope, whose momentous conflict with Philip IV.
of France was opened upon this very issue. The clergy
knew that the king summoned them to a lay assembly
that he might the more readily tax them. The idea
that any honour attached to representative membership in such an assembly was foreign to the time; there
could be no glory attached to a thing which did not

[1] It should not be supposed that the separation of the lesser from
the higher nobility was complete in 1295: if it had been, it would be
difficult to account for the position taken by the knights when summoned to Parliament. In fact it was just at this time, aided by the
Statute of Quia Emptores, that the process was going on most
rapidly. Let it not be forgotten, however, that it was not in anything belonging to this immediate period that this most fateful
movement had its source, but, as has been shown above (pp. 307–
311), in time long anterior and in events and conditions lying at the
basis of English history.

22

exist, and Parliament was a potentiality rather than an actuality; to representative clergy or laymen or their constituents the royal summons imposed a burden which was assumed with reluctance. All the prejudices of the clergy drew them away from this kind of association with laymen; the whole trend of events since the Norman Conquest had been towards separation between clerical and lay institutions under the impulse of the "reform" movements on the continent. The clergy were becoming conscious of themselves as a distinct and superior estate; they looked down upon secular legislation and the common law. Moreover they had just perfected their own Convocation, where they could negotiate taxes equally well and without compromising their dignity by becoming members of a secular assembly. Their reluctance to attend Parliament was probably at first regarded by the king as a kind of insubordination; but money was what he wanted and, if he could gain that as well from Convocation, he was hardly in a position to fight out a purely theoretical issue with them. The representative clergy began to show their disinclination to come to Parliament soon after 1295, and for about forty years the king made some attempt to secure their presence; then, although the *præmunientes* clause was retained in the writs to the bishops and there was an occasional attendance of a few, the matter ceased to be an object with the king, and the clergy in their Convocation granted subsidy for subsidy as granted by Lords and Commons in Parliament.[1]

The withdrawal of the clergy as an estate left Parliament a two-house body. The clergy who remained,

---

[1] For an illustration, see A. and S., documents 66 and 67.

the bishops and part of the abbots, had always been members of the larger Curia Regis; they remained as barons, not as clergy. There were left then the second estate and the third estate, the nobles and the burgesses. Though a two-house assembly may be superior, as such, to a three-house assembly, yet it cannot be effective unless there is some degree of equality between the houses. If the knights continued to rank themselves with the nobility, the houses of this English assembly would be too unevenly matched to work well together, and the question whether the knights of the shire would permanently cast in their lot with the lords or with the burgesses was perhaps the most critical in the whole history of Parliament. There is evidence of uncertainty upon their part from the beginning and, although there are several specific instances in which it is known that they sat and voted subsidies with the barons, and this may be fairly considered their normal action in the early years, they sometimes seem to have regarded themselves almost as a separate estate and to have sat and voted alone. Their first distinct approach to the burgesses was to join them in petition while still voting with the barons. This well illustrates their situation: they were naturally with the burgesses, for they found themselves wanting to ask for the same things, while formally they were nobles and in formal action still took their position as such. But the transition once started did not require long for completion, and before the middle of the fourteenth century the representative knights of the shire were sitting and voting with the representative citizens and burgesses.[1] A House of Commons had been created.

[1] "In 1341 the 'grantz' and the commons seem to have definitely

There was nothing striking or spectacular connected
with the accomplishment of this change, one of the
greatest single events in the history of the English
government; it was the inevitable working out of forces
and conditions, some of them centuries old, some of
them recent, but very numerous and working silently
and irresistibly. No one was conscious that anything
remarkable was taking place. We pause to emphasise
it because we know the infinite possibilities for good,
not only to the English people, but to the world that
lay in that small change.

A money consideration was the chief immediate
cause of this transfer of the knights. They felt that,
like the burgesses, they stood for the poorer parts of
the community; united action would be a great advantage in the attempt to control taxation, and this
united action seemed possible and not entirely unnatural as the result of all previous English history.
It must be remembered that these representatives
were not legislators or counsellors as yet; they were a
concentration of juries as they had been fifty or seventy-
five years before. And what were the uses of the
primitive jury? Mainly to give the king local information bearing on his revenue, and then later to
help and advise in its assessment and collection. To
be sure the representatives in Parliament in the early
fourteenth century did a little more than this; they did,
in some sort, consent to taxation, although this function could be easily overstated; and they certainly
furnished the king, through petition and otherwise,

---

assorted themselves in two chambers; and in 1352 the chapterhouse
is regarded as the chamber of the commons."—Stubbs, *Constitutional
History of England*, § 426.

with local information which proved a valuable check
upon the work of his officials, especially the sheriffs.
These he still distrusted and their arrogant and oppressive behaviour often bore heavily upon the people.
This last-mentioned use of representatives was rapidly
increasing in importance.[1]

6. **The Electors, the Elected, and the Election in
County and Borough during the First Two Centuries of
Parliament.**—Having watched the form and make-up
of Parliament through the tentative and changeable
period and seen the beginnings of the House of Lords
and the House of Commons, the next enquiry is naturally about the election of the elements which have come
to form the constitutionally significant part of Parliament, the lower house. The ideas of representation

[1] Riess, in his *Geschichte des Wahlrechts zum englischen Parlament*, ch. i., regards the checking and controlling of the royal officials
in their local administration as the first object with Edward I. in
summoning local representatives to Parliament; he believes that in
Confirmatio consent to taxation was not extended, except in a purely
formal and empty manner, beyond tenants-in-chief, but that this
formal consent came gradually by force of custom and favouring
circumstances to have a real significance. See also Riess, *Der
Ursprung des englischen Unterhauses* in Historische Zeitschrift, lx.,
1–33. On p. 3, he says: "To attain a genuine and regular control
of the local administration and to carry out especially the assessment and collection of taxes with the least possible friction were the
most substantial reasons for which Edward I. added to the English
constitution as a perfected and enduring institution the system of
representation that had earlier been only sporadically connected
with it." In speaking of what the Commons did in the Parliament
of 1305, Maitland says: "The king, so far as we know, did not ask
them for money, nor did he desire their consent to any new law.
The doctrine that in these days the representatives of the shires and
towns were called to parliament not in order that they might act in
concert on behalf of the commons of England, but in order that each
might represent before the king in council the grievances and the
interests of the particular community, county or borough, that sent

and election have such a definite content in modern
times that there are few matters in connection with
which there should be greater care in clearing the mind
of preconceptions than in dealing with the early phases
of these practices.   We have noted the representative
idea in connection with the primitive use of juries,
have seen the practice of electing certain kinds of
juries in the county courts take the place of appointment by the sheriff or other royal officer; have also
seen knights elected for other local purposes, and how
these usages finally suggested a concentration of juries
at some central and convenient point.[1]   As to borough
representation, at least a hint of its origin has been
seen in the burgesses sent to the full meeting of the
county court assembled for the itinerant justices.[2]

---

him thither, may easily be pressed too far, but we shall probably
think that there is no little truth in it, if we ask what the knights
and burgesses were doing, while the king and his councillors were
slowly disposing of the great mass of petitions, many of which were
presented by shires and boroughs.   Official testimony the council
can easily obtain; but it wants unofficial testimony also; it desires
to know what men are saying in remote parts of England about the
doings of sheriffs, escheators, and their like, and the possibilities of
future taxation have to be considered.   Then again there are many
appointments to be made; for example, it is the fashion at this time
to entrust a share of the work of delivering the county gaol to some
knight of the county, very often one of the knights who is representing or has represented that county, at a parliament.   Without
denying that the germ of a 'house' of commons already exists,
without denying that its members hold meetings, discuss their
common affairs and common grievances,   .   .   .   we may still
believe that the council often gives audience, advice, instructions
to particular knights and burgesses.   After all we shall have to fall
back upon the words of the writ of summons:—the commoners have
been told to come in order that they may do what shall be ordained."
—Introduction to *Memoranda de Parliamento*, pp. lxxv., lxxvi.

[1] See above, pp. 312–320.   [2] *Ibid*, p. 324.

But in all this, nothing has been said of the manner of election or the way in which it was regarded, and very little of the personnel of the elected. [1] The representatives of the shires were probably always knights in the very early Parliaments; but the burdens of representation so far outweighed any advantages that seemed possible that those whose property made them eligible to knighthood, through the provisions of the Distraint of Knighthood, often paid the fine required by that act rather than assume the local duties which knighthood entailed or risk an election to Parliament. The result was that, throughout the fourteenth century, many below knightly rank were returned from the counties. No positive law upon the subject was enacted, but the kings made various ineffectual efforts to have knights returned, the writs of summons usually demanding that "belted" knights be chosen. Beyond this, the positive requirements and disabilities seem to have been these: the county representatives must be inhabitants of the county electing them and must be men of ability, consideration, and substantial property; and in the fourteenth century statutes were passed excluding sheriffs and lawyers from Parliament on the ground that with them more particular interests than those of the community in general were uppermost. [2] A statute of 1445 summed up most of the ideas of previous times, but shows that the king had had to con-

---

[1] Probably not much detailed information upon these subjects will ever be obtained. For the fact, already often emphasised, that Parliament had an obscure and unappreciated beginning goes far to account for the lack of records of its elections. However, enough has been ascertained to establish with some certainty the leading features of the elective process.

[2] A. and S., document 80.

cede the point respecting belted knights. It states that "the knights of the shire for the parliament . . . shall be notable knights of the same counties for the which they shall be so chosen, or otherwise such notable esquires, gentlemen of birth of the same counties, as shall be able to be knights."[1]

The knights of the shire (the elected representatives of the counties had come to be called such whether they were actually knights or not) were elected in the county courts. There has been considerable discussion as to whether or not these minor tenants-in-chief, as it may be supposed most of the county representatives normally were at the beginning, were originally elected solely by their own class and went to Parliament as representatives of that class. There has seemed to be an *a priori* logic in supposing, when the minor tenants-in-chief ceased as a class to receive the special writs of summons and elected members of the class went up from the counties, that their class only was concerned in the transaction. The theory falls to the ground however when tested by the evidence of the sources. In all the local activities of elected knights, activities which suggested and led to representation in a central assembly, the knights were certainly regarded as standing for the best knowledge and judgment of the whole community; and knights were very often associated in this work with the non-noble freemen below them, the provision appearing repeatedly that when there were not knights sufficient the number was to be filled out with free and lawful men.[2] Moreover, the business

---

[1] A. and S., document 125.

[2] For examples, see art. 1, Assize of Northampton, A. and S., p. 20; art. 9, Assize of Arms, *ibid.*, p. 24; the commission of 1194, *ibid.*, p. 29.

upon which they were employed had no limitation to a single class. And in coming to the later representative activities of the knights in Parliament, the language is exceedingly explicit to the effect that they were to be elected in *full* county court. This idea is expressed so many times and in such a variety of ways as to leave no doubt that the whole court was supposed to be concerned in the electing.[1] There is no doubt then that the knights went up to Parliament representing all the elements of the county as found in the county courts.

What were the elements in the county court? It is impossible to answer by a definite enumeration; for long before this, suit of court had become attached to certain holdings of land, and the tenants of these were bound to this duty by the terms of their tenure. It would not often be the large meetings of the county courts, summoned to meet the justices, that elected the knights; only forty days intervened between the issue of the summoning writs and the meeting of Parliament; so it was usually the ordinary monthly meeting of the court, at which there was likely to be but a small attendance beyond those concerned in the cases to be tried and those who served on the juries. There would be no flocking to an election in which, in the nature of things, there could be no interest.

As to the electoral process, one's mind is so prepossessed by the whole modern paraphernalia of ballot-boxes or voting machines, election judges, accurate counts, majorities, and pluralities, that he is likely to forget that such things are the product of a very long

---

[1] See the first summons of knights to a central assembly, A. and S., document 33; and the anticipations of this action in the use of knights illustrated by document 30.

evolution. These thirteenth and fourteenth century elections, which antedate party and interest and all consciousness of the value of the franchise, may seem unworthy to be reckoned popular elections at all. Yet modern popular elections are their lineal descendants. Names were probably proposed to the assembled court by the sheriff or other influential man of the county. If they met with approval, there was a general acclamation and the election was complete. But some one might be bold enough to object; if his objections seemed valid and he was influential enough to gain a considerable backing, his point was made good and other names were proposed. It was thus only in the acclamation and in the right to dissent that the popular element consisted. And yet in theory—and this is very important—these elections were purely popular; any member might propose names and any might dissent.

No one cared to take part in these elections, not only because there was little inspiration in electing people to places they did not want, but because wages had to be paid them. These became fixed under Edward II. at four shillings a day for the knights of the shire and two shillings for the burgesses. Abstention from the election might be urged as an excuse for not sharing in the payment of the wages. Few were able to make good such a claim, but the possibility worked with other forces to so belittle the election that the sheriff often practically named the knights who were to be returned, and, when he had an object for doing so, he could usually manipulate the elections to suit himself.[1]

[1] In 1376 a petition was sent to the king by the House of Com-

In this condition the shire elections remained until
the one thing which could cause development occurred.
At the end of the fourteenth century, places in the
House of Commons were no longer matters of indifference; hence an increased interest in electing men to
those places and developments in the electoral process.
There were two things in the reign of Richard II. that
begin to threaten the influence, both general and local,
of the class of knights and esquires, the country gentlemen, the smaller landlords. The great peasant agita-
tions then culminating showed that there was a class
below whose rights and power must be reckoned with,
and the long war with France had resulted in an increased power and arrogance of the great nobles.
Livery and maintenance were beginning; the nobles
returned from the continent with large bands of followers whom they were loath to dismiss; they often
brought greatly increased wealth, and always high-
flown ideas of their importance and their superiority
to the classes below them. They were the essence of
the tawdry and decadent feudalism of the English and
French courts of that period. The knights felt themselves in danger of being crushed between the upper
and nether millstones; the House of Commons was
the only place where they could make themselves felt,
where they could enact "statutes of labourers" on the
one hand or join the king in his attempts to curb a

---

mons asking that the knights be chosen by the better folk of the
shires and not by the sheriffs alone. The king replied that they
were to be chosen by the whole county. This shows the continuance
of the sheriffs' undue influence, but undoubtedly also indicates an
increasing interest on the part of the people. As late as 1410, an
act was passed restraining abuses by the sheriffs in the election
returns. See A. and S., document 113.

grasping aristocracy on the other.[1]   This approach of king and Commons was one of the most striking and novel features in the politics of this reign.   In fact, the Commons began to assume the consciously independent position between Lords and king which became characteristic in the fifteenth century.   An entirely new significance began to attach to their election to Parliament.   Should the rising peasant class, whose interests they thought so contrary to theirs, or the insolent followers of the great nobles share in the county elections?   From the end of Edward III.'s reign, there is evidence that numbers of people attended the elections who were not properly suitors to the county court.   An act of 1406,[2] decreeing that knights be elected not only by suitors duly summoned to the court for the purpose of election but by all who might be present, appears so out of harmony with the more definitive legislation soon to follow and with what one would naturally expect from the Commons as to suggest an exceptional situation just at that time. The Commons had been bringing forward an unusual number of petitions looking towards an interference in the government and a limitation of the royal power. It has been suggested that a temporary estrangement, arising between king and Commons because of this, was made use of by the Lords to carry through an act by which they hoped in the end to gain virtual control of the lower house.   If no restrictions were placed upon the county electorate, they might expect, by means of the votes of their retainers, not only to prevent the

[1] See the Statute of Maintenance and Liveries, 1390, A. and S., document 96.

[2] A. and S., document 111.

return of specially obnoxious knights, but possibly to
compass the election of some of these retainers themselves.[1]   But by 1413, the situation had changed:
Henry IV. was dead and the new king and Commons
were in harmony.   A statute of that year decreed that
knights elected to Parliament be resident at the time
of election in the counties which chose them and that
the electors be of the same county in which they voted.[2]
This removed much that was dangerous in previous
practice and which was sanctioned by the act of 1406,
but not all.

In 1429, was passed the famous disfranchising
statute.[3]   It leaves no doubt of the interest now taken
in the county elections.   The statute mentions great
troops of people, residents of the county, who come to
elections, and, by their presence, cause danger of
"manslaughter, riots, batteries, and divisions"; and
there is this significant clause: whereas the elections of
knights "have now of late been made by very great
and excessive number of people . . . of the which
most part was by people of small substance, or of no
value, whereof every of them pretended a voice equivalent, as to such elections to be made, with the most
worthy knights and esquires."   In these words, confirmed by the disfranchising provision which follows,
one comes upon the first recognition in English history
of election as a political right.[4]   After there had been
a representative Parliament for nearly one hundred
and fifty years, is first found this idea which, at first
thought, would seem its inevitable accompaniment
from the beginning.   The disfranchising clause limited

---

[1] Riess, *Wahlrecht*, pp. 87, 88.   [2] A. and S., document 115.
[3] *Ibid.*, document 121.   [4] Riess, *Wahlrecht*, p. 91.

the electorate to residents of the county, "whereof
every one of them shall have free tenement to the value
of forty shillings by the year at the least above all
charges." Then follows another statement of great
significance: "and such as have the greatest number of
them that may expend forty shillings by the year and
above, as afore is said, shall be returned by the sheriffs
of every county, knights for the parliament." This
has been regarded as the first legal expression of the
majority principle to be found in the middle ages.[1]
All the election writs in the remainder of Henry VI.'s
reign repeated the provision. The statute of 1445,
requiring county representatives to be of gentle birth,
completed this important line of legislation. That
the disfranchising statute was a thoroughgoing measure
is shown by the reflection that forty shillings of that
time had the purchasing power of over £30 to-day.
A large and worthy class of people was kept from political rights for four hundred years; but the Commons
were dealing with very real dangers in the fifteenth
century; they were fighting for political existence. It
must be acknowledged that in the centuries following
the forty-shilling freeholders exercised well the great
power vested in them.

The subject of the electorate in the boroughs presents
a serious problem at the outset. The normal writs of
early times simply ordered the sheriffs to return so
many citizens and burgesses from such cities and
boroughs as lay in their respective counties.[2] It was

[1] Riess, *Wahlrecht*, pp. 91, 92.

[2] Simon de Montfort dealt with the boroughs directly, and
the same thing was done in one or two instances in the reign of
Edward I. but it soon became the unbroken rule to deal with them
through the sheriffs.

not long, however, before certain cities and boroughs are found always represented in Parliament, whereas in the case of certain others the right or rather the burden of representation has disappeared. So anomalous and haphazard has the line of demarcation between these two classes appeared that many investigators have been at a loss to account for the distinction. Probably an important source of error in dealing with the subject has been the attributing of more value to borough representation than it had at the time either in the thought of the king or of the boroughs themselves. It has been thought that if in so weighty a matter as representation in Parliament some boroughs were almost always represented while some were not, the central government must have had a weighty reason for making the distinction. But it was not a weighty matter; the king levied taxes upon the boroughs whether they were represented or not [1]; and, if he found representatives of a respectable number of them present, enough to give necessary information and confer with him concerning his proposed exactions, the fact that the others had failed to return members was a matter of indifference. It is a significant fact that the responsibility of dealing with the individual boroughs was left to the sheriffs, and there is but slight indication that penalties were ever imposed by the king upon the boroughs that failed to respond. The boroughs certainly regarded representation as a burden, and there are several instances in which the king formally granted relief from it for specified reasons.

The growth of a definite and somewhat limited class

[1] But of course the boroughs which escaped representation escaped the payment of wages to representatives.

of represented boroughs is therefore to be explained
through the relations between the sheriffs and the
boroughs in their respective counties. Some boroughs
had become entirely independent of the hundreds in
which they lay, not only in internal administration,
which was true of all, but in external relations. In the
matter of the summons to Parliament, the sheriff dealt
with such boroughs directly and not through the hundred's officers. Dealing directly with so powerful a
king's officer as the sheriff, these boroughs were the
ones most regularly represented. In some of the distant counties, as Somerset, Devon, and Cornwall, the
sheriffs adopted the same direct summons in the case
of boroughs not independent of their hundreds and
these were thus brought into the class of regularly
represented places. When the sheriffs communicated
with boroughs through the hundred's bailiffs, there
was a tedious procedure, subject to many chances and
interruptions, before the names of the chosen representatives, in case any were chosen, were ready to be sent
to the Chancery. Apparently in these distant counties,
the addition of the long and slow journey from and to
London made it impossible to get the returns in before the meeting of the Parliament concerned. Hence
here the sheriffs came to deal over the heads of the hundred's bailiffs. A third class of boroughs lay in the
great "liberties" (usually much larger than hundreds):
these must be dealt with through the bailiffs of the
"liberty." In this case, not even in the distant counties did the sheriff venture to disregard the medium-
ship of the bailiffs, and these boroughs, almost without
exception, early ceased to be represented in Parliament. Thus the boroughs dealt with through the

minor officials found it easier to dodge the disagreeable
duty. It may seem a trifling matter to have produced
so marked a distinction among the boroughs of England, in the course of time the source of marked political
results; but in the early years of an institution, when
everything is in flux and small importance is attached
to the beginnings of things really great, petty and obscure influences may play a great rôle.[1]

The sheriff had about as much opportunity to manipulate borough as county representation. The writ
ordering the election passed through his hands and he
might be induced not to send it. Such suppression of
writs seems to have occurred occasionally in the last
half of the fourteenth century and later, when the list
of boroughs that commonly sent representatives had
become quite fixed. Moreover, it was possible for
the sheriff, since the names of the borough members
had to be returned through him together with the results of the shire elections, to change the names. This
left the boroughs quite powerless since the Chancery
did not ordinarily go back of the sheriff's returns.
There was no temptation to such abuse until seats in
Parliament were regarded as worth something. The
abuse was in part mitigated through the petitions of
individual boroughs or actions originating in the House
of Commons, and these means were supplemented by
the effect of the new charters of incorporation granted
to some boroughs; these virtually placed the electorate
in oligarchies which carefully guarded their rights and
created a greater *esprit de corps*. By the end of the
fifteenth century, about eighteen important boroughs

[1] For a full discussion of this subject, see Riess, *Wahlrecht*,
ch. ii.

had been granted the organisation of shires with sheriffs of their own.

The variety in borough governments, the slight intercommunication, and the small value set upon representation in Parliament resulted in lack of uniformity in the manner of election. The sheriff sent to the borough's bailiffs a copy of the writ received from the king requiring that borough to send two representatives to the ensuing Parliament. Ordinarily the choice was then made in one of three ways: the bailiffs themselves made the choice; they called a meeting of the most important burgesses and consulted them in the matter; they called a general meeting of the burgesses, in which case the election was conducted much as it was in the county courts, with a real, if slight, popular element in it. The bailiffs sent the result to the sheriff, who included it in his statement of the county election which was sent to the Chancery.[1]

7. **Origin of the chief Powers of Parliament: Control over Taxation; Legislation; a Share in Administration.—** What has already been said incidentally of the functions of the representative elements in the early Parliament has represented them as narrow and somewhat undignified and subordinate. The Commons were present to vote taxes—which, paradoxical as it may seem, scarcely implied an ability to refuse them; to humbly petition; to answer questions. The almost servile part played by the third estate in the French Estates General of the same period was not very different from that of the corresponding element in the English assembly. To be sure, the knights of the shire, from their antecedents and local influence, were always accorded more

[1] Riess, *Wahlrecht*, pp. 59–62.

consideration than the burgesses, and in the union of these elements lay infinite possibilities. But it was all possibility at the beginning of the fourteenth century and it is now to be noted how, from so humble a beginning, Parliament developed the great attributes of power which one now associates with the name, how through Parliament the English people preserved, and in part gained, a constitutional monarchy. Only the beginning of the development is dealt with here, substantially that which was included in the fourteenth century; but in that period nearly all the activities of Parliament were outlined.

A preliminary consideration claims attention at the outset. How can the early remarkable vitality of Parliament be accounted for? In order that Parliament should gain power of any sort, there must be reasonably frequent meetings; the more frequent they were in the early days, the more rapidly would grow the general esteem in which the institution was held, the more necessary and regular a part of the government would it seem. A new and unrecognised institution is so easily killed by adverse circumstances or long interruptions, that it was of prime importance that during the first century of Parliament's history political conditions demanded almost yearly sessions. The battle of an institution is half won when it has become to the popular mind something regular and necessary.

The misrule and inefficiency of Edward II. caused local oppressions and a corresponding demand for frequent meetings of the body in which complaints might be made and remedies sought. An article in the New Ordinances of 1311 says: "Inasmuch as many people are oppressed by the king's ministers, . . . and for such oppressions can find no remedy, save through the common parliament: we do ordain, that the king shall hold a parliament once in the year, or twice, if need be, and that in a convenient place." In 1322, when the Ordinances were revoked under the leadership of the Despensers, these royal favourites found it convenient, on purely selfish grounds, in taking their stand against the barons, to uphold the parliamentary tradition. In the act of revocation is found this great principle, which surely did not represent the practice or even the general theory of the time, but the statement of which must have had its importance: "but the matters which are to be established for the estate of our lord the king and of his heirs, and for the estate of the realm and of the people, shall be treated, accorded, and established in parliaments, by our lord the king, and by the assent of the prelates, earls, and barons, and the commonalty of the realm; according as it hath been heretofore accustomed."[1] Early in the next reign, 1330, while local abuses were still grievous, and from the context of the clause undoubtedly because of them, again is found the enactment "that a parliament shall be holden every year once, or more often if need be."[2] Then began the great drama of Edward III.'s reign, a war drama from beginning to end, a reign of fifty years, during which there was constant and unusual need of money. Taxes must be negotiated through Parliament, and the letter of the statutory requirement

[1] A. and S., p. 97.

[2] *Ibid.*, p. 101. This was confirmed in 1362: "For redress of divers mischiefs and grievances which daily happen a Parliament shall be holden every year, as another time was ordained by statute." Cited in Taswell-Langmead, *English Constitutional History*, p. 217.

of 1330 was almost kept, for there was the remarkable
record of forty-eight Parliaments in fifty years. The
late years of this reign and the whole of the following
reign were another period of factional strife, and in
another connection has already been noted the importance in the history of the House of Commons of
Richard II.'s intrigues with it against the Lords.[1]
Thus for a full century after 1295 one cause or another
was keeping Parliament alive and active.

The knights of the shire and the burgesses were from
the beginning conscious of the financial purpose which
drew them to Parliament.   Especially was this purpose
emphasised by the circumstances which attended the
summons of the Model Parliament and the events of
the two succeeding years. Parliament was distinctly
a taxing body from the first; it was more this than anything else.   It was natural then that Parliament's first
great contest with the king should have been financial
and that its first great power to be developed should
have been control over taxation.   Legislation, in point
of time its second line of development and which became its characteristic function, began very gradually,
was really exercised by Parliament before that body
was fully conscious of its character and import, but
became a great and recognised attribute in the course
of the fourteenth century.   A third activity beginning
in the same period, the interfering in and seeking to
control certain lines of public business, Parliament was
drawn into through its attempts to gain a mastery in
the other two departments, especially the first.   The
origin and early growth of these three fundamental
powers will now be considered in the order named,

[1] See above, pp. 347, 348.

though their interrelations will render entire separateness of treatment impossible.

A.—The king got together the different estates in Parliament, not so much to consent to taxation, though they may have formally done that, as to provide ways and means for its assessment and collection; he consulted them on the form the proposed levy should take and how it should be apportioned among the elements represented. But this implies a conception of taxation as a thing in which all classes were concerned, a national taxation. It has been shown that for a considerable period after the Norman Conquest there was no understanding of taxation in the modern sense.[1] The king had various sources of revenue and means of supplying the needs of government, but his attention was always fixed upon classes of men. Each class had a specialty, in some cases based upon private contract or proprietary relations, for supplying the royal needs. The king made his demands upon this, that, and the other class of the population as opportunity dictated and upon this, that, and the other different ground. This system gradually passed into disuse as feudal ideas waned, and out of it national taxation did not grow. National taxation is characterised by fixing the attention upon kinds of property rather than upon classes of men, by taxing at one time all of a certain kind of property irrespective of who holds it. Its scope is the nation, not the class. It is necessary at this point to say a word upon its origin.

Of the two well-known varieties of tax, direct and indirect, the former made its appearance first and carries us back to the reign of Henry II. and the eve

[1] See above, pp. 105–109.

of the third Crusade.　How large a part in the origin
of taxation was played by the Crusades and the popes
as their managers is coming to be well understood.　The
situation in the East constituted a need international
and pressing, in meeting which the state was ready to
co-operate with the church; and feudalism, efficient
only in local undertakings, was found wanting.　The
management of the third Crusade was openly and
effectively undertaken by the church, and money was
to be raised by a tax on revenue and movables.　This
was the famous Saladin Tithe.[1]　An ordinance of 1188
imposed it upon England; the first clause reads, "This
year each one shall give in alms a tenth of his revenues
and movables."　This new scheme for raising money
was not likely to be lost sight of in such a reign as
Richard I.'s; and when his great ransom was raised it
was used for the first time in a domestic concern, and at
a higher rate.　From this time, the tax was levied with
more or less frequency and at greatly varying rates;
and the difficulty in assessing personal property gave
rise to the use of juries of neighbours that has been
noted as so important in leading to the origin of
representation in Parliament.[2]　At first some account
was taken of the different classes of people, as
clergy, barons, knights of the shire, burgesses; but
partly owing to the union of the last two elements in
Parliament and partly as a result of the inherent neces-
sities of such a tax, "the old distinction between Estates
gave way to a new distinction based on the difference
between town and country, or, roughly, between real
and personal property; and while the ordinary propor-
tion granted for dwellers outside a chartered town

[1] A. and S., document 19.　　[2] See above, pp. 313, 315, 316.

was one-fifteenth, one-tenth was the settled share of inhabitants of a parliamentary borough."[1] After 1332, because it was felt that this tax was being excessively levied, it was really decreased by allowing no new assessment. So the actual sum levied on the basis of the assessment for that year, £39,000, became a fixed charge properly proportioned between town and country, and was always known as the *tenth and fifteenth.*

Of the indirect taxes, import duties originated in the immemorial right of the king to regulate trade with foreign countries; he received some portion of the imported goods in return for his countenancing and protecting the traders, whether native or foreign. The seizures made under this right were very arbitrary in the early days, but in the reign of Edward I. there was some attempt at regularity by levying 2s on every tun of imported wine and 4s on every pound's worth of other imports. This was the origin of *tunnage and poundage.*[2] The duty on exports arose from the right to tax movables. Their passing out of the country afforded a specially easy and effective means of assessing certain kinds of movables. The great exports of England were wool and leather. By the early thirteenth century, it was customary for the king to receive 6s 8d (half a mark) on each sack of wool and a mark on each last of leather. He took more than this when he could, but the higher levy was known as an evil toll (*maltote*). Of course this taxing of exports was only possible because there was at that time no country able to compete

---

[1] Medley, *English Constitutional History*, p. 511

[2] This was the New Custom of 1303, when the foreign merchants consented to pay an import duty in exchange for certain trading privileges. It was not called *tunnage and poundage* until 1373.

with England in the production of these particular commodities.

In general, war has been the necessity that fathered taxation. With the exception of the resistance to the Danish invasions, the wars of the Anglo-Saxon period were petty. Those invasions resulted first in a wider and more regular enforcement of the *trinoda necessitas*, and finally brought forth the Danegeld. The Norman dukes had fought at no great distances, and feudalism served the military requirements of the duchy fairly well. After the Conquest, one of the most important roots of taxation and of resistance to taxation in England was the attempt to make feudal service extend across the Channel. Hence in the early resistances the nobility naturally took the lead.[1] But the income and personal property taxes, also the offspring of war, were being more and more used. All classes were concerned in these; and as the indirect taxes were developed during the thirteenth century, and gained recognition in the reign of Edward I., powerful special interests became involved in the problem of taxation. In the struggle of 1297, the great nobles still led, but all classes were more consciously concerned than in any preceding conflict and were learning the lesson of resistence to taxation as they could not have done in 1215. Thus, just as Parliament was coming into existance, the people of England were gaining their first true insight into the possibility and necessity of controlling the king's taxing power.

The vital promise made by the king in Confirmatio Cartarum reads:

[1] For a discussion of the transformation of feudal service into taxation and the resistance to the process, see above, pp. 107-109; 258-260.

Moreover we have granted for us and our heirs as well to archbishops, bishops, abbots, priors, and other folk of holy Church, as also to earls, barons, and to all the commonalty of the land, that for no business from henceforth we shall take of our realm such manner of aids, tasks, nor prizes, but by the common assent of all the realm, and for the common profit thereof, saving the ancient aids and prizes due and accustomed.[1]

It is interesting to note the somewhat grudging and slight mention of the Commons' right to consent to taxation, and that in the excepted "ancient aids" they had never had any share, and hence, as far as this law was concerned, would not in the future.   One is reminded that, despite the great changes of the thirteenth century, the revolt of 1297 was much a barons' affair, and that the difference in spirit between this provision and the long-omitted article twelve of Magna Carta, which it really replaced, was not as great as has often been represented. The Commons were upon the brink of obtaining a great right in 1297 rather than in possession of it.

[1] A. and S., document 48. It is interesting in estimating the value and inclusiveness of this famous promise to compare its language with that of the document known as De Tallagio non Concedendo.   This was an unofficial statement of the demands of the discontented elements and is found in the chronicle of Walter of Hemingburgh; it was mistaken for a statute in later centuries and was cited as such in the Petition of Right (A. and S., document 189). Its first article reads: "No tallage or aid shall be laid or levied by us or our heirs in our realm, without the good will and assent of the archbishops, bishops, earls, barons, knights, burgesses, and other freemen of our realm."   Here was a statement without qualifying words and which expressly mentioned the individual elements of the commonalty as well as of the nobility.   It would be useful to know the exact source of these words, who it was that in 1297 stated the great principle so perfectly.

The language of Confirmatio was loose, and the kings, even Edward I., were quick to see and use the loopholes which it afforded them. It was without doubt the intention, under the words *aids*, *tasks*, and *prizes*, together with the succeeding article dealing with the customs duties, to include both direct and indirect taxation. But the kings presumed themselves permitted, without consulting anyone, to levy the regular feudal aids and scutage, to tallage their domain towns, and to dodge the customs article by entering into private negotiations with merchants, especially foreign merchants who would be in no wise covered by Confirmatio. These merchants were granted valuable privileges in return for the increased duties which they agreed to pay.[1] This veiling of a real tax under the form of a private bargain, in which, however, one of the parties had small chance of dealing on an equality, was the most important of these subterfuges; for the export of wool, comparatively small before this, was growing with great rapidity. Feudal aids, scutage, and tallage of the royal domain were already antiquated, played little part in the coming conflict, and were of no consequence after the three Edwards.

The first real issue was upon indirect taxation. The Commons, conscious that they were not strong enough to absolutely prohibit the king's breaking the letter or the spirit of the customs article, adopted the shrewd device of formally voting the money that he had arranged for and would obtain anyway. They thus

[1] Purveyance, Commissions of Array, and Distraint of Knighthood were minor forms of indirect taxation retained by the king for a considerable time. See Medley, *English Constitutional History*, pp. 238, 239.

tacitly asserted the principle that no money grants could be made without their consent. The king made no objection to this assumption of authority, provided he obtained what he wanted; but Parliament must have had a dawning perception that such repeated assertion of principle was bound sooner or later to bear fruit. Edward III., under the pressure of the new war with France, manifested, in 1340, his intention to levy a generally increased custom on wool and leather, similar to the *maltote* of his grandfather. Parliament, to prevent the arbitrary action, made a regular grant of the custom to be in force for a specified time, and containing a provision that after the expiration of that time no custom, beyond the ancient custom, that is, the one established early in Edward I.'s reign, should again be levied. This was almost immediately followed by a statute which contained a broader prohibitive provision. Referring especially to a large subsidy granted at the same time that the increased tariff had been arranged, it stated that the people should not "be from henceforth charged nor grieved to make common aid or to sustain charge, if it be not by the common assent of the prelates, earls, barons, and other great men, and commons of our said realm of England, and that in the parliament."[1] This was a reassertion, after nearly half a century of intermittent conflict, of the principle of 1297, and the added clause respecting Parliament is very significant. That Parliament was strong enough to gain this acknowledgment from Edward III. indicates that the victory was practically won, the great principle of parliamentary control of taxation established. Scarcely ever after was

[1] A. and S., document 59.

it called in question; the energy and ingenuity of kings was expended rather in dodging it. The date 1340 is, therefore, a most important one in the growth of parliamentary power. An act of 1362, confirmed in 1371, to the effect that no one, without the consent of Parliament, could negotiate any charge upon wool, seems to have brought to an end the private dealings with merchants.[1] However, the results of those dealings, having passed into custom, continued to advantage the king, and the *maltote*, so resisted in 1340, became a regular charge upon wool through parliamentary action before the end of the reign.[2]

B. Before there was a Parliament, laws had been made by the king acting through his court, Curia Regis; he made *ordinances* with the advice and consent of his counsellors. But the Curia Regis was no national assembly standing over against the king and representing another interest in such action. When the barons resisted the king's power, they did it individually or in groups with force of arms, they did it as a feudal nobility; they did not fight out the issues in parliamentary manner in an assembly. And up to the late twelfth century, at least, such resistance was rather against the power of the king in general than a calling in question of specific manifestations of his power.[3] In the legislative act, king and Curia were one; when he acted formally, the king always acted through his

---

[1] For a specific instance of resistance to such dealings, 1343, see A. and S., document 65. The Ordinance of the Staples, 1353, shows something of the "merchants strangers" and of the rate of the customs duties in that year; *ibid.*, document 74.

[2] Parliament was bound in time to recognise that the so-called *maltote* was not an exorbitant charge.

[3] See above, pp. 253-259.

Curia; it was the king in action. The king was the source of legislative authority—a Roman idea, vaguely present in England from very early times, but reinforced from the continent at the Conquest.

During the thirteenth century, the oneness of king and Curia in legislation was less marked than formerly. A distinction was being drawn between modifying or applying old law and making absolutely new law. While the king could do the former upon his sole authority, it was felt that there was an impropriety in his doing the latter without the consent of the barons; and in this consent, there was a consciousness of voluntary collaboration which anticipated a new theory of lawmaking. But when representatives of the counties and boroughs came to be added to the changing Curia, there was introduced an element of confusion so great as for a time to do violence to any theory whatever. The king might gain, or rather demand, the consent of any element of his people thus brought to the centre, and the ordinance, or whatever one may choose to call it, based upon this action, was law. But this constituted no recognition of a right on the part of these elements to a share in legislation. The idea of legislation as a right to be sought or shared was not in existence. Moreover the matters with respect to which the king asked information or confirmation were not of a varied character; they usually were related in some way to the royal revenue. So the old form of ordinance by king and Curia continued, with perhaps something of a narrowing of scope to the things of special interest to the barons, and supplemented by these occasional and anomalous actions in connection with knights of the shire or representatives of the boroughs. The Statute of Quia Emptores, 1290, relating to a subject of special interest to the barons, was made by king and Curia alone, while the Statute of Merchants, 1283, though bearing the form and wording of an ordinance, was the product of deliberations with the burgesses alone. At this time, there was no Parliament, merely the ingredients of Parliament, and the idea of a new source of legislation could not exist until the body which was to be that source had taken shape; for, as has been shown, it was not for a legislative purpose that the new body was called into existence.

The first distinct recognition of Parliament as a regular source of legislation is found in the revocation of the New Ordinances, 1322. The important clause already quoted in another connection must be repeated here: "but matters which are to be established for the estate of our lord the king and of his heirs, and for the estate of the realm and of the people, shall be treated, accorded, and established in parliaments, by our lord the king, and by the assent of the prelates, earls, and barons, and the commonalty of the realm; according as it hath been heretofore accustomed." [1] But this was probably a bit of political theorising by the antibaronial party; regular parliamentary legislation can scarcely be said to have begun at that time. But it is significant that such a theory could have been formulated. Supposing, however, this theory to have become realised most perfectly, it could still only have meant that the king had to obtain the consent of Parliament to measures he himself proposed; there was nothing in it to interfere with the monopoly of initiating legislation which he had always possessed. No legislative body

[1] A. and S., p. 97. See above, p. 356.

is worthy the name, nor can it be at all useful in winning for the people political liberty, unless it has the right to introduce measures of its own.

The origin of Parliament's right to initiate legislation was in the right of petition for redress of grievances. The right of every subject to petition the sovereign had always existed. Petitions before the existence of Parliament may be divided roughly into two classes; most petitions came from individuals or very small groups and dealt with individuals' wrongs: but occasionally there had been petitions, or perhaps remonstrances, presented by large bodies of men acting together and dealing with matters of quite general concern. Such had been the barons' articles upon which Magna Carta was based, and the petition of 1258 which resulted in the Provisions of Oxford. After there was a Parliament, these two kinds of petition continued. Of the private petitions, some were now brought to Parliament for consideration before being presented to the king, others went directly to the king or some official near him. An increasing number would naturally be the product of Parliament itself; it was representative and, if in session often enough, was exactly the kind of body needed to express public sentiment; it was an organised and regular body, quite in contrast with the irregular and revolutionary risings which had previously been the only means of voicing general grievances.

But this use of Parliament, like Parliament itself, was a new and untried matter in the early fourteenth century.[1] Parliament could only petition—the word

---

[1] Speaking of this period, Maitland says: "By no sharp line can the petitions of the assembled lords and commoners be marked off

itself is significant—petition a sovereign who, on the precedent of all past history, was perfectly free to reject or ignore. As Parliament gained self-consciousness and recognition from frequency of meeting and financial importance, a contest with the king on the matter of petitions was inevitable. We have now to examine the weapons used by the parties to the conflict, and note how Parliament gradually prevailed and, in the course of the century, became an acknowledged legislative body.

As it became more thoroughly established that the king could not tax without Parliament's consent, that body found itself possessed of a valuable commodity in exchange for which it might expect something of equal value from the king; Parliament had money or the power to grant money and the king had the right to grant petitions. Here were the elements of a bargain of which Parliament became aware early in the fourteenth century, and which have perhaps proved the most potent factor in building up its power. The grant of money was postponed until after redress of grievances. The first clear instance of this device is found in 1309,[1]

---

from the general mass of those petitions which are to be expedited in the parliament by the king and his council. At a somewhat later date the line will be drawn; the petitions of the assembled commons, the petitions of 'the community of the land,' will be enrolled along with the king's answers to them; petitions addressed to either of the two houses will be enrolled, if they have received the assent of both houses and of the king; but the ordinary petitions presented to the king and council by those who have grievances will not be enrolled, though as of old many of them will be answered in parliament by committees of auditors." Introduction to *Memoranda de Parliamento*, pp. lxxiv., lxxv.

[1] Taswell-Langmead, *English Constitutional History*, p. 215 and note 2. The Commons allowed a tax "upon this condition that the king should take advice and grant redress upon certain Articles,

and it soon became customary to postpone money grants until the end of the session.

The king, however, possessed several methods of rendering these granted petitions ineffective, and he used them with great skill and persistence, some of them lasting long after the infant stage in parliamentary legislation. The most important at this time was his use of ordinances. When the king granted a petition, it practically lay with him whether, when it was engrossed as a law, it should take the form of an ordinance or a statute. The use here of the term statute implies that there was a consciousness of a new kind of legislation; just as soon as the idea existed that there could be a specially weighty and permanent kind of law because it had been sanctioned in a specially large or varied body, the statute was in embryo. Several acts in the early time, especially in the reign of Edward I., have been called statutes, which were not consented to by all the elements necessary to a statute on later theory; but the diversity in size and make-up of the assemblies in that reign favoured the growth of the idea of a new source of law.[1] In the course of half a century of frequent Parliaments, it was natural that this

---

in which their grievances were set forth." The list of grievances is an interesting one. In A. and S., document 66, is a grant of *tenths and fifteenths* for a limited time and on conditions, and document 68 is an excellent example of a grant on conditions. A much later instance is found in document 114. See also Gneist, *History of the English Constitution*, p. 367, note. In the reign of Richard II., the postponement of money grants to the end of the session was one of the matters dealt with in the famous replies of his servile judges to the list of questions put to them by the king. The time of his tyranny proved but a temporary setback to the attempts of the Commons in this line.

[1] See above, pp. 235-237.

idea should begin to take definite shape, and it became the accepted theory on the part of the Commons that measures of permanence and importance must have the concurrence of king, Lords, and Commons, and measures so established were called statutes.[1] Such measures might be introduced by the king or originate as petitions in the House of Commons. If the king, then, gave the form of an ordinance to that which had originated in a petition, or indeed to anything which had been confirmed by Parliament as a whole, it was regarded as doing violence to the distinction then taking shape. There are, however, but few instances of such action by the king after the distinction had become generally recognised. But king and Council could still make ordinances, and use was often made of these to limit or injure a statute which the king had not been able directly to prevent.

A further difficulty lay in the king's assumption of the right to annul a statute. This illustrates well the difference between ordinances and statutes and worked powerfully at the time to clarify thought upon the matter. The king had always been able to annul an ordinance because he had created it. He created it because he was the source of law, and he could destroy that which he was alone concerned in creating. Edward III. tried to annul a statute. In 1341, a radical measure was passed, an important provision of which was that ministers and judges be appointed by Parliament; the king, under threat of no subsidy, was forced

---

[1] How clearly this had become recognised is shown by the protests and requests of the years 1353 and 1354. See A. and S., documents 75 and 76.

to assent to it, and it became a statute.[1]   After Parliament was dissolved, the king declared the statute null and sent a notice to that effect to all the sheriffs.[2] That this was regarded as an unwarranted action is shown by the facts that the next Parliament regularly repealed the statute and that this is the only known instance in which the king went to such an extreme. When the king, by countenancing Parliament's repeal, acknowledged that he could not annul a statute, he acknowledged that there was now in England a second source of legislative authority.   It was no longer a matter of a specially solemn kind of ordinance with a large backing, with the king still in theory the one source of law; but a statute, to make which entirely independent elements acted in common, any one of which, king, Lords, or Commons, could, by refusing to co-operate, exercise a veto power.   The old Roman theory had been broken, and the people, through their elected representatives, made written law.   Ordinances decreased in number and importance; always somewhat temporary in character, meeting conditions as they arose but without much reference to the future, they became after this more strictly such.   There has always been a field for them in the intervals between Parliaments or upon occasions when immediate action was necessary.   They are known to-day as Orders-in-Council.   Even in this limited scope, they did not remain a permanent means of infringing upon statutes; for Parliament eventually gained such control over king and Council as to control their legislation.

While the king only once attempted to annul a statute, he had, besides his use of ordinances, other

[1] A. and S., document 62.   [2] *Ibid.*, document 63.

less radical means of attack. An important and long-continued one was his use of the *dispensing* and *suspending* powers. These grew out of the same Roman root as his power to create or annul an ordinance. The maker of law could dispense with its operation in individual cases or suspend it for a time in certain classes of cases. Some exercise of a dispensing power is necessary for any executive; for no body of law, however good, can be enforced with absolute rigidity without working much actual injustice. The right to pardon those convicted of crime is the commonest illustration of such necessary power. But evidence is abundant that the fourteenth-century kings so used the dispensing and suspending powers as to make Parliament feel that its law-making function was being seriously crippled. How consciously they did this to fight Parliament it is hard to tell. The dispensing power, which was then the more common, was, in the eyes of Parliament, as truly an invasion of the legislative domain as the creation of a new writ in Chancery or the extension of the jurisdiction of the Council.[1] It was often used in the reign of Edward III. practically to license crime, pardons being given before the accused were brought to trial; while the frequency of its use and the character of the crimes, of which the king seems often to have known little, discredited it still further. Attempts were made by the Commons in 1328,[2] 1330,[3] 1347, and 1351 to do away with the abuse, but, despite the promises made by the king, it continued. Under Richard II., a statute was passed forbidding the issue of pardons in the case of serious crimes, unless

[1] See above, pp. 208, 214, 215.   [2] A. and S., document 56.
[3] *Ibid.*, document 57.

they specified the nature of the crime and contained the name of the culprit. This principle, although often violated, has remained an element in the law of pardons. At the end of the century, nothing had been done to regulate the dispensing power outside the matter of pardons, and it remained a vague and dangerous factor in the royal prerogative. The suspending power was then seldom used, but in it there lay even greater possibilities of despotic action.

Since all legislation which Parliament initiated in the fourteenth century was introduced in the form of petition, it was necessary in engrossing the granted petition as a law, putting it in statutory form, to make changes in its wording. This work was entrusted, as was natural, to the judges of the common-law courts. In this connection, is one of the earliest illustrations of the subservience of the judiciary to the executive, with a resulting tendency upon the part of the two to unite against the legislature.[1] Advantage was sometimes taken of this necessary change of the petitionary form to alter the meaning of the act or even to make substantial additions or omissions. This was a danger from which Parliament could never feel entirely free; it was inherent in the system of initiating legislation by petition, and not until a new method was substituted in the next century did it cease. As a result of these varied experiences in law-making, Parliament became fully conscious of itself as a legislative body and of a profound distinction between its legislative product and that of king and Council.

[1] The possibility of this combination has been one of the very late serious faults in the English constitution to be removed.

C. In its endeavours to control taxation and legislation, Parliament was drawn into some interference in the executive functions of government. How inevitable this was has already been incidentally shown. It remains now to notice more directly the beginning of a line of development which has, in modern times, resulted in complete harmony between the executive and the legislature, with the latter, representing the people, in substantial control. In using these terms for departments of government, it must be remembered that men in the fourteenth century were only in the vaguest way conscious of such distinctions. One is prone to think that a struggle for liberty on the part of the people began at this time, the people for the first time being able to act in an effective way through a representative Parliament; and in one sense such a struggle did begin. But the participants were not conscious of it as such. The king was not upholding royal prerogative against government by the people; he was simply resisting something which was taking away his power, without seeking to justify or explain his action upon any dogmatic basis. The House of Commons was conscious of administrative abuses; its constituents were actually suffering from them; it sought an extension of power to remedy these abuses, but uninfluenced by a theory of government by the people. And there was no limit to the extension of power it sought; for, being unconscious of any categories of government, it could know of no propriety or expediency in observing limits beyond which the legislature should not extend its activities. So king and Parliament began their long conflict in the naïve, shortsighted, unidealistic fashion in which nearly all

medieval conflicts were fought.   However, the relations
between the two in the fourteenth century were far
from continuously hostile; in many instances, they
worked together for common ends with much good
feeling.

As the first business of Parliament was to grant
money, an early and natural extension of its activity
was towards ensuring honesty and accuracy in its
collection and in showing an interest in its expenditure.[1]
In 1340, parliamentary commissioners were appointed
to audit the accounts of the collectors of recent subsidies[2]; and in 1353 a subsidy was granted with the
stipulation that it was to be used only for the war.
This interest in public business, in the character and
work of public officials, contributed largely to the
radical statute of 1341[3]: the auditing commissions
were renewed, the appointments of important public
officials and judges were to be sanctioned by Parliament, and in that body these men were to swear to the
observance "of the Great Charter, and the Charter of
the Forest, and all other statutes, without breaking any
point."[4]   This act was premature, and in the following
Parliament the king secured its repeal.   When, in
modern times, control of the ministry was finally secured, it was by a different method, but the statute of
1341 is an interesting prophecy of one of Parliament's
most important achievements.

Another product of the same general line of activity
was parliamentary *impeachment*, the first instance of

---

[1] See the closing words of article 1 in the famous statute of 1340,
A. and S., p. 105; also document 61.

[2] *Ibid.*, document 61.   For later examples of parliamentary
supervision of accounts, see *ibid.*, documents 83–86.

[3] See above, pp. 371, 372.   [4] A. and S., p. 108.

which was in 1376.[1] Impeachment was the trial
before the House of Lords of persons, generally officials,
accused by the House of Commons of a public offence;
the House of Lords judged, the House of Commons
prosecuted. This right to bring to trial the king's
most powerful ministers, in a manner calculated to
secure justice as it could not be secured in the royally
dominated or locally intimidated courts, and for
offences which, though serious, might not be technically
admissible there, was one of the most substantial and
beneficent extensions of power made by Parliament in
this or the succeeding century. Parliament found by
experience that the control of the king's ministers was
the best way to control the king.

Two more general and less important ways in which
Parliament touched the administration remain to be
mentioned. Throughout the fourteenth century, the
Commons were very diligent in pointing out administrative abuses, the burden of the complaint being that the
king's judges and other officials, especially the sheriffs,
were not vigorously and impartially administering the
laws.[2] To get such information was one of the original
objects with the king in summoning a representative
assembly, and he made much use of it in early times.
He took the Commons into his confidence and quite
regularly asked their advice upon judicial matters and

[1] A. and S., document 82. See also the interesting impeachment
of Suffolk in 1386. *Ibid.*, document 93. Treason was first defined
by statute in 1352. (A. and S., document 72.) This may have
suggested the propriety of indicting men for treasonable offences in
Parliament. On the origin of impeachment, see Medley, *English
Constitutional History*, pp. 162, 163.

[2] Taswell-Langmead, *English Constitutional History*, p. 215, note
2; A. and S., pp. 94, 95, and documents 56 and 57.

upon the best methods of holding his officials in check. The second matter has to do with Parliament's participation in foreign affairs. In the reign of Edward III., the war with France was the one great subject of popular interest, while the troubles with Scotland were of no small importance. The voting of money to maintain these great undertakings almost necessarily made Parliament a counsellor at the crises, when it came to questions of concluding peace or continuing the strife and concerning the great public expense entailed. Parliament was thus consulted many times and, on several occasions, did not hesitate to express its mind pretty freely; but in the latter part of the reign it showed a disinclination to give positive advice; it shrank from the responsibility and preferred not to be hampered in its financial dealings with the sovereign by too avowed a partnership in his enterprises.[1]

8. **Parliament in the Fifteenth Century. The Lancastrian Constitution.**—The distinctly creative period of English constitutional history ended with the fourteenth century. While by no means denying that things of constitutional importance originated in the fifteenth century, it is nevertheless true that that period, contrasted with the three preceding centuries, was eminently a time of practice and precedent, of adjustments and accommodations and the working out of details. It was a time also of dawning understanding and appreciation of the great things which had been unconsciously wrought, and hence contained a prophecy of the struggle for their preservation. The fifteenth

[1] For Parliament's great efforts and considerable accomplishments in controlling the Council early in Richard II.'s reign, see above, pp. 292–294.

century has already been several times trespassed upon in order to maintain an integral treatment of certain themes, and the purpose here is largely supplementary, to deal with those matters which especially characterise the period and which have found no logical place in the preceding divisions.

Two acts of the fourteenth century have been noted which provided that Parliaments be held annually or more frequently if necessary.[1] The king had been in the habit of assembling his feudal court at least three times a year, and when representatives came to sit with the Curia Regis, it was natural that the time and frequency of meeting should have been influenced by the older practice; moreover there was much for the larger assemblies to do and expedients for economising time and labour had not been devised.[2] The sessions were usually short, for the House of Commons was made up of men who had much business to attend to at home; prolonged absences were serious and harvest time must not be encroached upon. But as election to Parliament became a thing more to be desired, richer men were returned both from county and borough, men who were not so anxious to get home. Also the scheme of voting taxes for more than one year began to be used in the reign of Edward III.; and before the end of the fourteenth century, it was found that a Parliament might on occasion be prorogued instead of dissolved, thus making it unnecessary to have a new election for every new session. For these reasons,

[1] See above, pp. 355, 356.
[2] "In 1328 no less than four assemblies had been called. In 1332 and in 1340 Parliament came together three times within the twelve months, and twice in 1334 and again in 1352."—Medley, *English Constitutional History*, p. 259.

annually elected Parliaments ceased. Sovereigns never seem to have felt obliged to adhere strictly to the statutes requiring them, and in the fifteenth century these fourteenth-century statutes, though still unrepealed, were entirely unheeded. The frequency of new Parliaments and the frequency and length of sessions came to be determined almost wholly by the circumstances and needs of the time. The power of the king to summon, prorogue, or dissolve Parliament at pleasure was unquestioned. Under the Yorkists, there were longer intervals without Parliaments than ever before. It was to be expected of a family with such consciously legitimate claims to the throne, and although the Yorkists were not strong enough seriously to attack the constitution, their policy with respect to Parliament contained a hint of what might take place in the case of some future legitimists.

An important indication of the growing maturity of Parliament was the acquisition of the Speaker by the House of Commons. There is no better evidence of the very gradual and unconscious development of that body than the fact that more than a century passed after the king first summoned representatives to a central assembly before those representatives had a presiding officer. The Speaker originated at the beginning of Richard II.'s reign, but during that reign can hardly be regarded as representing the body over which he presided, being usually controlled by one or other of the masterful factions of the nobility characteristic of that stormy period. Under the Lancastrians, the Speaker really represented the Commons. He was nominated by them, the nomination having to be confirmed by the crown. There was usually little *esprit de corps* among the Commons and so little mutual acquaintance in the case of a newly elected House that a sovereign who so desired could practically name the Speaker. This was regularly the case during most of the Tudor period. The political importance of the Speaker might be very great, for he was the official medium of communication between the Commons and the king; a servile Speaker could render the work of the House abortive in very many ways. The members of the lower House did not enjoy the right of individual access to the sovereign possessed by the Lords, and the Speaker was their mouthpiece, bound to represent truthfully their sentiments. In the fifteenth century, he was almost always a knight of the shire, but with the rise in importance of the borough members at the end of the century this ceased to be the rule.

Fifteenth-century changes in Parliament's exercise of power and in the relations of its Houses are now to be considered. The interruption to the practice of postponing money grants to redress of grievances, occasioned by the absolutist tendencies of Richard II.'s reign, was a matter of concern in the early years of his Lancastrian successor. In 1401, the Commons prayed the king that they might learn his responses to their petitions before any grants were made. Henry refused to accede to this on the partially unhistorical ground that it had not been the practice of his ancestors and predecessors.[1] But the futility of this attitude on the part of the king is shown by a consideration of the essential elements in the transaction: a determined House of Commons could, under all ordinary circum-

[1] A. and S., document 109.

stances, hold out longer without the king's favourable responses than the king could without the money which it alone could give.   There was a quite steady growth in the practice of postponing grants throughout the fifteenth century, and grants with more or less specific conditions attached were the rule.

There arose, however, in 1407 a problem anent the manner of granting supply in which inhered some constitutional questions very briefly and easily disposed of in favour of the Commons, but nevertheless of considerable importance.   The king and Lords had had a conference relative to a grant of money to be made by the Parliament then in session and had concluded upon a *tenth and fifteenth* and a half.   This was evidently regarded as settling the matter, but of course the Commons would have to assent.   Accordingly they were asked to send a deputation to the conference, and the twelve men sent were told what the king and Lords had determined and were then bidden report it to their associates, with the implication that speedy acquiescence was expected.

Which report having been made to the said commons, they were greatly disturbed, saying and affirming that this was in great prejudice and derogation of their liberties; and when our said lord the king heard of this, not wishing that anything should be done at present or in time to come, which could in any way turn against the liberty of the estate, for which they were come to parliament, nor against the liberty of the lords aforesaid, willed and granted and declared, with the advice and assent of the said lords, in the following manner.   That is to say, that it is lawful for the lords to discuss among themselves assembled in this present parliament, and in every other in time to come, in the absence of the king, concerning the estate of the realm and the remedy needful to it. And that in like manner it is lawful for the commons, on their part, to discuss together concerning the state and remedy aforesaid. Provided always that the lords on their part and the commons on theirs, make no report to our said lord the king of any grant granted by the commons, and agreed to by the lords, nor of the negotiations of the said grant, before the said lords and commons shall be of one assent and of one accord in the matter, and then in the manner and form customary, that is to say by the mouth of the speaker of the said commons for the time being, to the end that the said lords and commons should have the agreement of our said lord the king.[1]

The words "granted by the commons and agreed to by the lords" certainly show that it was the intention to have the initiative in money grants lie with the Commons, and it became, in the fifteenth century, a recognised part of the constitution that all money bills must originate in the lower House as standing for the poorer part of the community. This episode of 1407 resulted in the first conscious formulation of the principle. To be sure, the Commons had the right not to concur in a grant originating with the Lords or, as in this case, with the king and Lords, but they recognised the amount of pressure which might be brought to bear in favour of a money bill once formulated and that the right to formulate it was no empty one. Another right brought out with great distinctness was that of each House to carry on its preliminary discussions independently of the other and both independently of the

[1] This is part of the so-called "schedule of indemnity" which the king ordered entered on the roll of Parliament. A. and S., document 112.

king, and that the king was to have no concern in a
bill until the Houses had become a unit.   These principles, at the present day axiomatic in the relations of
any executive and legislature, were then just being
worked out under the favouring Lancastrian conditions.   They were broken many times in the despotic
sixteenth century; but their memory and practice were
at no time entirely absent, and when the final struggle
with the Stuarts came, there was a "medieval, Lancastrian constitution" to look back to for precedent
and inspiration.

In leaving the subject of money bills, it should be
added that, before the end of the middle ages, the king
had invented two famous methods of dodging the principle, established in 1340, that there could be no taxation without the consent of Parliament.   *Forced loans*
originated with Richard II.; they were, as the name
implies, negotiated without the option of the lender,
and their payment was always a precarious matter.
In the reign of Edward IV., the *benevolence* was invented.
This was theoretically a free, but actually a forced,
gift taken by the king from the wealthier people of the
realm.   Benevolences were often winked at by the
Commons, who felt that if the king got his money in
this way he would be less likely to burden the poorer
classes of his people with regular taxation.   "The
difference between a forced loan and a benevolence or
free gift is not easy to grasp; for a loan taken at the
king's pleasure might also be repaid in his own good
time, and with a complaisant Parliament to back him
the distinction entirely disappeared."[1]   These devices
were used to great effect by Tudors and Stuarts and

[1] Medley, *English Constitutional History*, p. 536.

were supplemented by that last and most famous dodge of constitutional taxation, the Stuart "ship-money." They were not used after the Great Rebellion.[1]

It has been seen that a vexatious means of defeating Parliament's legislation was the alteration of the wording of granted petitions by the judges who engrossed them as statutes.[2] At the beginning of the second Lancastrian reign, this was made a matter of formal protest by the Commons. The king replied that nothing should be "enacted contrary to their asking whereby they should be bound without their assent."[3] But despite this promise, there was still danger that the thing might be attempted by a despotically inclined king. The really effective remedy of this evil was hit upon by the Commons in the third Lancastrian reign; it was the simple expedient of doing away with the petitionary language and introducing *bills*, which were, in form and language, completed statutes and became such by the united assent of Commons, Lords, and king. "Later on the House of Lords also began to originate Bills, which were sent thence to the Commons; and it gradually became the established rule of Parliament, that with the exception of Money Bills, which must come from the Commons, and of Bills affecting the Peerage (*e. g.* for the restitution of forfeited honours), which must come from the Lords, all other Bills might be originated in either House."[4]

---

[1] In the reign of Richard III., a statute was passed abolishing benevolences (A. and S., document 133). This was afterwards disregarded on the ground that Richard was a usurper, which made laws passed during his time invalid.

[2] See above, p. 374.

[3] A. and S., document 117.

[4] Taswell-Langmead, *English Constitutional History*, p. 250.

25

The courts attempted during the Lancastrian period to supplement fourteenth-century legislation on the dispensing power, another of the means of defeating Parliament's law-making which survived that century. [1] Very subtle distinctions were drawn between the cases in which the king could and could not exercise the pardoning power. It was found difficult to apply these in the practice of the courts, and perhaps their only important net result was the evolution of the principle that the pardoning power could not be so exercised by the king in behalf of an offender as to deprive a third party of any claim which might have resulted from the offence. As to the suspending power, various attempts were made to limit it, but little progress was made. Both of these powers remained to play a great part in the unconstitutional efforts of later sovereigns, especially the Stuarts. By the Bill of Rights, the suspending power was abolished, while the dispensing power was placed under effective parliamentary control. [2]

The advances which Parliament made in the Lancastrian period in its control over taxation and legislation were small in comparison with the easy and sweeping successes which it seemed to gain over the administration. The hard-fought beginnings in this line which have been noted in the fourteenth century, where masterful kings resisted and, in some lines, Parliament drew back from the assumption of too great responsibility, gave place to such sudden and thoroughgoing control over king and ministry, such

[1] See above, pp. 373, 374.
[2] A. and S., pp. 464, 469. For further information on the dispensing and suspending powers, especially in modern times, see Anson, *Law and Custom of the Constitution* i., 297–305; ii., 228–230.

modern constitutionality, that one begins to question
its genuineness. Henry IV. was of necessity a parliamentary sovereign in a sense in which none of his predecessors had been; to secure his family upon the throne
he felt obliged to be on good terms with the people as
represented in the House of Commons. The first and
most conspicuous attempt of Parliament in the administrative line was to control the appointment of ministers
and hold them strictly responsible for their acts. This
was a resumption of a policy that was very marked
in the early part of Richard II.'s reign.[1]   Formally,
Parliament seldom, if ever, attempted to come quite
so near the actual appointment as had been rashly proposed back in 1341[2]; but during most of the Lancastrian period, the king's appointees were practically
nominated by Parliament.

In 1406, the Commons gained the king's assent to a
lengthy petition of thirty-one articles that, at first
sight, implies as great an achievement in constitutional
government as anything gained in the seventeenth
century. In the first article, the king was required to
"elect and name sixteen counsellors and officers pleasing
to God and agreeable to his people, on whom he could
rely, to advise him and be of his Continual Council until
the next Parliament, and a reasonable number of
whom should be continually about his person." One
cannot read of this limited group of counsellors and
officers, some of them to be specially near the king,
and of the implied dependence upon Parliament without
the thought that here was a suggestion of the Cabinet.
It indicated the direction which governmental development would take when, after long and hard experience,

[1] See above, pp. 292, 293.   [2] *Ibid.*, p. 371.

the people through Parliament came to their final and maturer control of the executive. In the articles following, there was much about the limitations, functions, and responsibility of the members of the Council and the officials, even providing for their being sworn in Parliament to observe the common law and the statutes, and much about economy in the administration and the king's household.[1] "These articles comprise a scheme of reform in government, and enunciate a view of the constitution far more thoroughly matured than could be expected from the events of late years."[2] For a time in the reign of Henry IV., king, Council, and Parliament worked together in an apparent, if somewhat artificial, harmony that anticipated the days of William III.

Notwithstanding this activity in holding the ministry responsible, it so happened that, after the reign of Richard II., Parliament found few important occasions to exercise its power of impeachment until the case of the Duke of Suffolk in 1449. But during the rapidly changing Parliaments in the period of civil war and bitter personal animosities immediately following, the judicial procedure of impeachment was found too slow and cumbersome in dealing with political enemies. *Bills of attainder* came into use, and until 1621 there was not another impeachment. These bills contained the accusation and provided for the punishment of the individuals against whom they were instituted, and were introduced and passed like other bills.[3] Thus

[1] For the provision quoted and a summary of the articles, see Taswell-Langmead, *English Constitutional History*, pp. 252, 253.

[2] Stubbs, *Constitutional History of England*, § 313.

[3] On the origin of Bills of Attainder, see Stubbs, *Constitutional History*, §371; Pike, *Constitutional History of the House of Lords*,

there was no need, as in impeachment, to bring in evidence or go through any other form of judicial procedure. Sometimes bills of attainder were a useful means of dealing with powerful misdoers, the nature of whose offences made it hard to furnish evidence at all satisfactory to any tribunal which regarded itself as a court of law. But punishing men by legislation has, for the most part, been an abuse, whether as in the Yorkist period, a means of wreaking factional vengeance, or when the Tudor sovereigns used their servile Parliaments to rid themselves by this means of their personal opponents.

Further administrative gains of Parliament in the Lancastrian period were its victory in the matter of auditing public expenditures, a function first claimed under Edward III., and its greatly extended counselling function in matters of national policy.[1] In 1406, the public accounts were demanded and, the king being ill at the time, it was replied in his name that "kings were not wont to render accounts." This, however, seems to have been but a feeble remonstrance, for Parliament continued to take measures to the desired end, and in 1407 the accounts were voluntarily produced by the king. From that time, this right of Parliament was never directly denied. In counselling the king, Parliament no longer showed the fear of assuming responsibility noticeable in the preceding century. So fully did it feel itself in control of the granting and expenditure of money that all crucial questions arising in the conduct of the war with France were entertained by it,

---

p. 229; Anson, *Law and Custom of the Constitution* i., 337; Medley, *English Constitutional History*, pp. 163, 164.

[1] See above, pp. 376, 378.

and there were few matters of national importance in
considering which the king did not take into his confidence the representatives of the nation.   In concluding this summary of Parliament's fifteenth-century
means of controlling the king, it should be stated that
in the right to audit public accounts and in impeachment and bills of attainder Parliament possessed a
much more permanent and real power than in its
more striking attempts to dictate the ministry.

An important evidence that Parliament was maturing
and growing more conscious of itself was the first formulation of what came to be technically known as the
privileges of Parliament.   It is, perhaps, in this that the
fifteenth century can base its most important claim to
creation.   Certain privileges and immunities had long
been more or less vaguely recognised, but here was
conscious insistence upon certain fundamental ones,
by statute and otherwise, until the term privilege was
becoming definable and technical.[1]   In 1554, at the

---

[1] "In the wide and loose application of the word 'privilege' the
privileges or peculiar functions and usages of the house of lords are
distinguished from those of the house of commons; the privileges
of individual members of the house of lords may be distinguished
from the privileges of individual members of the house of commons;
both again have common privileges as members of the parliament;
and the lords have special privileges as peers, distinct from those
which they have as members of a house co-ordinate with the house
of commons."   Stubbs, *Constitutional History of England*, § 448.
It is with the "common privileges as members of the parliament"
that we are concerned here, and it was in this connection that the
term took on its technical significance.   The important general
privileges or functions of the two Houses have been noted in the
consideration of parliamentary powers, and in Part III., § I., 3,
where the judicial functions of the House of Lords were mentioned.
For an exhaustive enumeration under the categories named in the
passage cited, see Stubbs, *Constitutional History*, §§ 448-453.

opening of Parliament, the Speaker of the House of
Commons first made the formal request of the sovereign
to recognise the three great privileges; and after 1571
such request at the opening of each Parliament became
regular.[1] The three privileges are these: freedom of
access to the sovereign, by the Lords individually and
by the Commons through their Speaker; freedom from
arrest or molestation during the time of Parliament;
freedom of speech.[2] Their origin and how they gained
recognition in the fifteenth century are now to be considered.

Freedom of access was almost always recognised
by the sovereign. Each peer had the right on the
ground that he was an hereditary counsellor of the
crown. This did not mean, of course, that he was a
member of the Council; the right went back to the
parent stem of both Council and House of Lords, the
Curia Regis, in which the king's vassals were in personal relation with their suzerain. The Speaker of
the House of Commons was the result of a growing
demand for a regular intermediary between that body

[1] Prothero, *Statutes and Constitutional Documents*, Introduction,
p. lxxxvii.

[2] For the first record of the exact words in which the request was
made, see *ibid.*, p. 117. The privilege numbered second in this request
was not usually reckoned one of the great privileges.   In the words
of the speaker, it was "that in repairing from the Nether House to
your Majesty or the Lords of the Upper House, to declare their
(the Commons') meanings, and I mistaking or uttering the same
contrary to their meaning, that then my fault or imbecility in de-
claring thereof be not prejudicial to the House, but that I may
again repair to them, the better to understand their meanings and
so they to reform the same."   This natural request was made in
perhaps clearer language in the very early days of the Speaker. See
the Speaker's request for the privileges of Parliament in 1401.   A.
and S., document 107.

and the king. Through him, the king spoke to the
Commons and the Commons to the king. To have at
all times the right to petition, counsel, or remonstrate
with their sovereign through their chosen representative was justly regarded by the Commons as a very
fundamental privilege.

In connection with most primitive assemblies that
were in any way identified with the king, is to be found
some idea of a royally sanctioned safe-conduct; the
king's peace was to abide in his assembly and was to
extend to the members in coming to it and returning
from it. Naturally, these royal sanctions applied to
Parliament as soon as it was in existence. But as
time went on, molestation of members was more likely
to be through some process of law than through direct
bodily injury or restraint.[1] Unless Parliament could
keep its membership intact, free from outside interference, whether or not the interference was with the
motive of embarrassing its action, it could never be
confident of any accomplishment. Early in Henry
IV.'s reign, a request was made that threefold damages
be exacted of any one assaulting members on their way
to Parliament. This request was not granted, but
what the king considered a substantial protection was
being enforced at that time. In 1429, Parliament asked
that the general principle be laid down "that no one of
your said lieges, that is to say, lords, knights from your
counties, citizens, burgesses, in your parliaments to
come, their servants or familiars, be at all arrested nor
detained in prison during the time of your parliament,

---

[1] But there may be a "modern importance of this point as a point
of privilege, rather in the threat of violence than in the actual
infliction."—Stubbs, *Constitutional History*, § 452.

except for treason, felony, or surety of the peace as was said before." But this the king was not ready to grant. [1] However, he allowed at the same time a specific instance of such immunity in the case of a member's servant who had been arrested in an action of trespass. In 1332, a statute was passed allowing double damages in case of assault upon a member on the way to Parliament. In 1453, came the famous case of Speaker Thorpe, the only exception to the privilege of freedom from arrest in the fifteenth century and manifestly the result of the bitter partisanship of the time. [2] There were many cases in the last half of the century which confirmed the privilege, one of the most prominent being that of Walter Clerk, who represented the borough of Chippenham in 1460. [3] By the end of Edward IV.'s reign, the privilege had become established, as also a method of procedure in case of its breach.

The privilege was in no case extended to imprisonment for treason, felony, or for security of the peace: it was loosely allowed to the servants in attendance on members, and it was claimed for a time preceding and following as well as during the session. The length of this period was variously stated, and has not been legally decided. The general

---

[1] A. and S., document 122.

[2] Thorpe was a Lancastrian and an enemy of the Duke of York; he was arrested at the latter's instigation for non-payment of a fine imposed for a trespass. The Lords consulted the judges, who somewhat grudgingly admitted that the privilege should be allowed, but carefully disclaimed any right to determine the matter, which, they said, lay wholly with the Lords. The Lords, under Yorkist influence decreed that Thorpe should remain in prison.

[3] The record of this case especially well illustrates how the matter was regarded and dealt with at this time. See A. and S., document 127.

belief or tradition has established the rule of forty days before and after each session.[1]

The third privilege named, freedom of speech, was by far the most important, though there could be no surety of its exercise until freedom from arrest had been established. When a king conceded freedom of speech, he was, consciously or unconsciously, conceding that Parliament was a higher power than he; conversely, there could be no assured government by the people unless their representatives had unquestioned possession of this privilege. Thus only the House of Commons was concerned in its vindication, and only in its connection with that House could it be a matter of constitutional importance.[2] As soon as the House of Commons can be spoken of as existing, it exercised this privilege.[3] Many matters concerning the king's powers were freely discussed and, until the very end of Edward III.'s reign, such freedom was absolutely unquestioned. In 1476, Peter de la Mare, who seems to have been acting in the capacity which was presently to be that of Speaker, was, after the dismissal of Parliament in that year, imprisoned at the instance of John of Gaunt. He had been very bold and pointed in presenting to the duke Parliament's opinion of the govern-

[1] Stubbs, *Constitutional History*, § 452.

[2] The Lords, of course, possess the right equally with the Commons, and thus it is considered one of the common privileges of Parliament. But it seems never to have been an issue with the Lords. As Stubbs says, "he would have been a bold king indeed who had attempted to stop discussion in the house of lords."—*Ibid.*, § 451.

[3] Parliament was so primitive a thing in 1301 that the imprisonment of the knight Keighley, because he presented for the barons a petition which exasperated the king, seems hardly a case in point. —*Ibid.*, §§ 181, 451.

ment's financial malversation. It was a time of faction, and the next Parliament was packed in the duke's favour; but some attempt looking to the release and fair trial of de la Mare was made, showing that there was a feeling that parliamentary right had been transgressed.

In 1397, a bill was introduced in the House of Commons containing one clause which particularly angered the king. It attacked the extravagance of the court, asserting that many bishops, lords, and ladies were living there at the king's expense. Richard felt that this was in special derogation of his prerogative and demanded the name of the man responsible for this clause. Acting for the Commons, the Speaker gave the name of Sir Thomas Haxey. Haxey was a clerical proctor, attending even at that late date under the *præmunientes* clause.[1] The king and Lords immediately enacted an ordinance making it treason to move in Parliament anything touching the king's royalty, and under this *ex post facto* law Haxey was, two days after, condemned to death. Perhaps the king had no real intention to execute him; at any rate, the archbishop claimed benefit of clergy for him and the claim was allowed by the king. Three months later, he was released. But the first Parliament of Henry IV., assembled in the Fall of 1399, was far from satisfied to let the matter rest in this negative condition. They claimed that "the said Thomas was adjudged a traitor, and forfeited all that he had, contrary to the right and

[1] See above, p. 331. The Commons assumed at this time a very humble attitude and raised no claim of privilege. Possibly they did not regard Haxey as a member of their House; but there is no doubt that they were intimidated by king and Lords, for they acknowledged an impropriety in entertaining the bill.

custom which had been used before in Parliament, in destruction of the customs of the commons." And a reversal of the former judgment in the case appears upon the roll of Parliament in these words:

The king wills, by the advice and assent of all the lords spiritual and temporal, that the judgment rendered against Thomas Haxey, clerk, in the parliament held at Westminster in the twentieth year of the late king Richard, be wholly annulled, reversed, repealed and made void and held of no force or effect; and that the said Thomas be reinstated in his name and reputation, and made and held an able person such as he was before the said judgment was rendered—as in the record made thereof and enrolled before in this roll of parliament as appears more at length.[1]

This notable vindication of the right of freedom of speech at the end of the fourteenth century was a most valuable asset for the Commons in the struggle for this vital privilege which was to last nearly three hundred years. It was the earliest clear indication on the rolls of Parliament of the recognition of a valuable parliamentary custom that must be preserved.

The second Parliament of Henry IV., assembling in January, 1401, was well placed to follow up this beginning. The needs of the king were very great, as shown by the opening speech of the Chief Justice. This gave the Commons a hold upon Henry which they were quick to see; they were a little nettled at the tone of the speech, which bade them give more than usual attention to the affairs of the nation and cautioned no one to go home until the business was over; and they were very fortunate in the temper of their Speaker, Sir Arnold Savage.

[1] A. and S., document 105.

The Speaker's first address to the king suggests those regular requests for privilege with which the Parliaments of Elizabeth were opened. He asked "that the said commons should have their liberty in parliament as they had had before this time and that this protestation should be recorded in the roll of parliament." This "seemed honest and reasonable to the king and he agreed to it." The Speaker further prayed that the Commons might have "good advice and deliberation" on the matters brought before them "without being suddenly called upon to reply to the most important matters at the end of parliament, as had been done before this time." The king replied that it was his intention "to follow this order of action and that he did not imagine any such subtlety, also that they should have good advice and deliberation from time to time as the need demanded."[1] Three days later, a further point was pressed, perhaps with the Haxey case in mind. The Speaker, in another address to the king, stated on behalf of the Commons "how on certain matters moved among them, it might happen in the future that certain of their companions, out of complaisance to the king, and for their own advancement, should recount to our said lord the king such matters before they had been determined and discussed or agreed upon among the commons, by reason of which the said lord our king might be grievously moved against the said commons or some of them." The reply of the king was "that it was his will that the said commons should have deliberation and advice, to discuss and treat of all matters among themselves, in order to bring them to a better end and conclusion, in

[1] A. and S., document 107.

so far as they know how, for the welfare and honour of himself and of all his realm. And that he would not hear any such person or give him credence, before such matters had been shown to the king, by the advice and with the assent of all the commons, according to the purport of their said prayer."[1] Thus explicitly was the right of free and ample deliberation guaranteed to the Commons at the very beginning of the Lancastrian period. In 1407, substantially the same promise was repeated.[2] The privilege seems to have remained unquestioned until the arrest of Speaker Thorpe in 1453.[3] Two privileges were invaded in this case: Thorpe was arrested while he was a member of Parliament and manifestly because of things he had done and said in Parliament. It has already been seen how unsatisfactorily the case resulted for the Commons, who practically acknowledged their defeat by allowing him to remain in prison and choosing another Speaker. Thomas Young, a burgess for Bristol, was imprisoned and suffered considerable loss of property for something which he said in the Parliament of 1451. Four years later, he presented a petition to the Commons, in which he told them that they "ought to have their freedom to speak and say in the house of their assembly as to them is thought convenient or reasonable without any manner challenge, charge, or punition therefore to be laid to them in anywise."[4] Compensation was procured him at the king's order. But "matter of privilege as it was, the prayer is for personal and private indemnity: the commons seem to have no remedy but petition,

---

[1] A. and S., document 108.   [2] *Ibid.*, pp. 176, 177.
[3] See above, p. 393.
[4] Cited in Stubbs, *Constitutional History*, § 451.

and no atonement is offered to their injured dignity. So the case stands in the last years of the Lancastrian rule."[1] Nothing can be added for the Yorkist period. This privilege, so clearly recognised at the beginning of the Lancastrian period was not to receive its final vindication until the long contest between king and Parliament resulted, nearly three centuries after, in the vindication of the Lancastrian constitution. The Bill of Rights says the last word upon the subject when it declares: "That the freedom of speech and debates or proceedings in parliament ought not to be impeached or questioned in any court or place out of parliament."[2]

The question naturally arises here, why the Lancastrian constitution had to wait so long for its vindication; whether there was anything about it or the conditions of the time which made it unfit for immediate use, or whether it simply suffered the untoward chance of falling a prey to a long line of powerful and despotically inclined sovereigns. The former alternative should probably be chosen. Parliament had gained power slowly and naturally in the fourteenth century. In the fifteenth, with the Lancastrian sovereigns having a parliamentary title and almost continually dependent upon it for money, it gained control over the executive very rapidly. But while the king was being thus limited, a very formidable amount of power was gathering in the hands of the higher nobility; in some respects, it was a veritable recrudescence of feudalism. It has been noticed how the Hundred Years' War brought forth generations of lawless nobles, whose misdeeds are usually summarised under the practices of livery and

[1] Stubbs, *Constitutional History*, § 451.
[2] A. and S., p. 465.

maintenance.[1] All the guarantees of liberty which lay in jury trial, in an uncorrupted bench, and genuinely popular elections to Parliament were weakened. Parliament was getting control over the king, but it was not getting, and was not of a character to get, control over the thing that was then more dangerous. The replacing of the constitutional Lancastrians by the legitimate Yorkists and the far more important and masterful Tudors has sometimes been regretted as constitutional retrogression. But at the end of the fifteenth century England's salvation lay in a powerful executive, for it alone could humble the nobility. The Wars of the Roses marked a period of constitutional atrophy. They were the nobles' own wars, and the other parts of the population were little concerned. There was nothing to do but wait until enough blood had been let to relax the vigour in that nexus of old family feuds and personal bitternesses that dated clear back to the reign of Edward II. All parts of the constitution fared badly enough during this time. If asked which suffered the least damage, one must probably say, the House of Commons. It was pretty openly and regularly packed, and reflected the sentiments now of the red and now of the white rose. But it is significant that it was packed; the party in power did not attempt directly to override it. And this was also true after the Yorkists had gained the throne. Legitimists as they were, they had to have Parliaments, and they did not think of the House of Commons as something to be ignored or browbeaten; rather as a part of the government to be carefully reckoned with and manipulated. And surely the House of Commons reached the date

[1] See above, pp. 203, 347–349.

1485 much less shaken than the House of Lords; it had stood for the most substantial element in England's population; the momentous union of knight and burgess had wonderfully vindicated itself. There was a refreshing and immediate clearing of the air when the first Tudor was on the throne. He seemed the embodiment of quiet and orderly strength. His coming was a prophecy that the unquiet local elements would be forever removed—elements that, for nearly two centuries, had threatened to destroy, by an inglorious process of erosion, England's new constitution before its creators had had time to learn to value it and strive for it. The field was cleared for the conflict between the great middle class, clad in the constitutional armour already forged, and the succession of incomparable Tudor and Stuart personalities.

26

INDEX

A

Abbots, grants of *bookland* to, 45; members of the witan, 58; attend ecclesiastical councils, 66; after the Conquest, 115, 117, 119; in House of Lords, 304–306, 331; in Convocation, 333

Access to sovereign, 381, 391, 392

Aids, 106, 328, 362, 363

Alfred, 18, 19, 54, 60

Angles, upon the continent, 9, 13

Annual Parliaments, 356 and note 2, 379, 380

Appeals, none from court to court in Anglo-Saxon system, 20, 60; lord's court not a court of, 182–184

Appropriation of supplies, 376, 378

Arrest, freedom from, 391–394

Assize, 135, note 2, 222

Assize, Grand, 135

Assize of Arms, 312, 324

Assize of Clarendon, 136, 137, 145, 158, 314

Assize of *darrein presentment*, 134, 135

Assize of *mort d'ancestor*, 134

Assize of Northampton, 134, 137, 158, 314

Assize of *novel disseisin*, 133, 134, 155

Assize *utrum*, 132, 133, 144

Attainder, bills of, 388–390

Audit of accounts, 376, 389, 390

B

Baron, Court, 181–184

Barons, meaning of, 299, note 2, 304; major and minor, 299–301; minor, as part of a middle class, 307

Barony, prelates holding by, 107, 117, 326, note 1, 335

Battle, trial by, *see* Wager of

Becket, Thomas, 240, 245–250

Bede, 65

Benefit of clergy, 249–252, 395

Benevolences, 384, 385, note 1

Bills replace petitions, 385

Bishops, in shire courts, 21, 67; grants of *bookland* to, 45; members of witan, 58; in primitive church, 64; peculiarities of, in Anglo-Saxon times, 65; attend ecclesiastical councils, 66; leave shire courts, 91; rights of excommunication limited, 113; displacement of, after Conquest, 115; as barons, 117, change in habits and character after Conquest, 117; courts of, 239, 240; relations to benefit of clergy, 249–251; in House of Lords, 304–306, 331; oppose an aid, 332; in Convocation, 333

Black Death, 185

Bookland, 42–46

Boors, 47

Borderers, 47

Boroughs, origin and early history of, Pt. I., § II., 3; their courts, 33–35; effect of Conquest upon, Pt. II., § II., 3; their courts in thirteenth century, 176, 177; general condition of, in thirteenth century, 322–324; representation of, in central assembly, 324–326; the electorate in, 350–354

Bot, 27, 28

Bracton, 183, 223–225, 268, 271, 284, 285, note 1

403

Britain, before Anglo–Saxon conquest, 7–9; effect of insular character of, upon Anglo-Saxon conquest, 9, 10, 15
Britons, effect of the Anglo-Saxon conquest upon, 10–12
Burgage tenure, 36, 86, note 1

C

Cabinet, 123, note 1, 294, 296, 297, 387
Canon law, 204, 211–213, 223, 227, 228, 244, 248, note 2
Canterbury, Archbishop of, 65; rivalry with Archbishop of York, 65, note 1; relations with king, 69; relations with Archbishop of York settled after Conquest, 114 and note 3
Carucage, 109, note 1, 315, 316
Ceawlin, 51
Celtic survival in England, 15
Ceorls, 17; value of their oaths, 25
Chancellor, 206, 210 (and note 2)–214, 218, 219, 292
Chancellor of the Exchequer, 163, 164, note 1
Chancery, makes writs, 139 and note 1; Court of, 211–219
Christianity, effect of, upon kingship, 52, 53; see Church
Church, grants of *bookland* to, 42–46, *passim;* Pt. I., § IV.; effects of the Conquest upon, Pt. II., § II., 6; courts, Pt. III., § I., 5; relation to Magna Carta, 261
City, a cathedral borough, 31; Roman cities in Britain, 32
Clergy, tried in communal courts, 21, 67; cease to deal with secular law, 228; criminous, 241–252; representation of, 327, 331–335; withdraw from Parliament, 337, 338
Clerk, case of, 393 and note 3
Cnute, 51, 54, note 1, 57, 60, 62, 104, 105, 147, note 2
Coke, Sir Edward, 232, note 2, 234, 275, note 1
Commendation, 39–42

Common law, limited, 206–209; relations to equity, 214; general account of, Pt. III., § I., 4
Common Pleas, Court of, 164–166
Commons, House of, a new source of law, 235; dictates to the Council, 292; origin and early form and composition of, Pt. III., § III., 2–6; gains its chief powers, Pt. III., § III., 7; develops powers in fifteenth century, Pt. III., § III., 8
Commutation of service, by vassals, 107, 108; by villeins, 184, 185
Compurgators, 24, 25, 141, 142, 150, 250 and note 2
Confirmatio Cartarum, 266, 274, 361
Conservators of the peace, 190–194
Constitutions of Clarendon, 132, 133, 136, 245–248
Convocation, 116, 327; origin of, 331–333; as a taxing body, 338
Copyhold tenure, 185 and notes 1, 2
Coroners, 147, 148; origin and early history of, 188–190, 313–315 and note 1
Cotars, 47
Council, king's, 102 and note 2, 166, note 2; jurisdiction of, 201–212; legislation of, 235, 236; origin and early history of, Pt. III., § II., 2; 328 and note 1, 387, 388
Counties palatine, 95, 96
County court, see Shire
Creation of peers, 300, 302–304
Curia Regis, 95, 102–104; Pt. III., § I., 1, *passim;* 200, 201, 222; as source of the Council, 285–287; as source of House of Lords, 298–302; new elements added to, 317–322; time of meeting, 379
Customary, Court, 182, 184–187
Customs duties, 360, 363

D

Danegeld, 56, 57, 97, 104, 105, 108, 109 and note 1
Danelaw, 18, 19, 52
Danes, effect of invasions of, 49; a cause of conquest of, 62; effect of, upon the church, 68, 69
De la Marl, case of, 394, 395
Despensers, 277, 356
Dioceses, creation of, by Archbishop Theodore, 64; number of, in early times, 65
Dispensing power of the King, 373, 374, 386
Dissolution of Parliament, 379, 380
Distraint of knighthood, 191, 192, 343, 363, note 1
Domesday survey, 101, 102 and note 1, 105, 140
Dunstan, 69, 117

E

Ealdorman, in the shire court, 21; becomes local noble, 29 and note 1; member of witan, 58, loses official character, 61, 62; attends ecclesiastical councils, 66
Earls, origin of, 29 and note 1; great families of, 59, 62; leave shire court and change in character, 91
Ecclesiastical councils, 66, 113; general character of, after Conquest, 116 and note 1
Ecclesiastical courts, 67; separated from lay courts, 116, 117; relations to lay courts, Pt. III., § I., 5
Edgar, 51, 61, 62
Edward the Confessor, 57, 60, 62, 92, 96, 100, 105
Edward the Elder, 33
Edward I., 160, 163, 164, 178–180, 192, 193, 208, 228–231, 235–237, 259, note 1, 266, 269–276, 289, note 1, 301, note 1, 321, 326–331, 334, 360, 361

Edward II., 192, 193, 203, 211, 259, note 1, 276–278, 302, 346, 355, 356, 400
Edward III., 161, 192, 212, 227, 251, 291, 292, 294, 301, 302, 305, 348, 356, 357, 364, 371–373, 378, 394
Edward IV., 194, 195, 219, 295, 384, 393
Egbert, 52
Election, of kings, 51, 52; of coroners, 193; of post-Conquest kings, 259 and note 1; of juries, 314–317; of members of Parliament, Pt. III., § III., 6
Elizabeth, 232, 296, 397
Enclosures, 185, note 2
Eorls, 17
Equity, 129 and note 2; criminal, 204; in Chancery, 213–219, 234
Ethelbert of Kent, 53, 60
Ethelred II., 56, 62, 145, note 1
Exchequer, 125 and note 2, 161–164, 166, 287

F

Feudal jurisdiction, in Normandy, 76, 77; origin of, 93, 94; in England after Conquest, 94, 95, 177–179, 271, 272
Feudalism, Anglo-Saxon, Pt. I., § II., 4; 62; continental, 74–75; continental brought into England, 85–90; as the source of constitutional government, Pt. III., § II., 1
Fines, in Anglo-Saxon courts, 27, 28
Firma burgi, 37, 97
Folkland, 43 and note 1
Franchise, see Election
Frankpledge, 168–170; view of, given to some boroughs, 177
Freedom of speech, 382–384, 391, 394–399
Freeholders, 83–85; as jurors, 156; part of a middle class, 307
Friars, as beneficiary holders of property, 215–217

G

Glanville, 223, 224
Grand Assize, *see* Assize
Grand jury, 136–138, 144–149

H

Hamlet, Anglo-Saxon settlement in west of England, 13 and note 2, 14; inclusion in parishes, 66
Harold, 62, 100, 114
Haxey, case of, 395, 396
Henry I., 78, 79, 92, 97, 103, note 1, 107, 116, note 1, 125, 127, 130, 131, 147, note 2, 163, 167–170, 188, 241, 256, 259, note 1, 263, 299
Henry II., 103, 107, 108 and note 2, 109, note 1, 131; Pt. III., § I., 1, 2, *passim;* 222–225; Pt. III., § I., 5, *passim;* 257 259, note 1, 266, 312, 313, 358, 359
Henry III., 109, note 1, 148, 160, 163, 165, 172, 174, 206, 228, 236, 259, note 1, 266–270, 286, 300, 319
Henry IV., 281, 291, 294, 296, 349, 387, 388, 392, 395
Henry V., 349
Henry VI., 292, 294, 296, 297, 304, 350
Henry VII., 251, 282, 296, 401
Henry VIII., 219, note 1, 232, 252, 296
Heptarchy, 52, 66
Hide, 87, 105 and note 1, 109, note 1
Hundred, 6; and hundred court, Pt. I., § II., 2; grants of *bookland* in, 44, 45; hundred court after Conquest, Pt. II., § II., 2; in Henry I.'s reign, 167–170; later history of, 174 –176; ecclesiastical cases removed from, 239; relations to boroughs, 352

I

Impeachment, 202, 279, 293, 376, 377 and note 1, 388–390

Incidents, feudal, 106 and note 2, 107
Ini, 51, 60
Inns of Court, 227–230
Inquest of Sheriffs, 187, 317
Inquisitio, 140–144, 312
Interpreter, Cowell's, 285, note 1
Investiture contest, 113, note 2, 115
Itinerant justices, 125–128, 158–161, 167, 168, 170, 195 and note 2

J

John, 108, 149, 259 (and note 1) –266, 270, 332–334
Judges, freemen as, 21, 141, 142; of common-law courts oppose new law, 206–209; hostile to Chancery, 214; limitations of, 226; intimidated by Richard II., 279, 280; members of Council, 288; royal control over, 374
Jury, judicial, 132, 136–138; origin and early history, 140–157; used by itinerant justices, 160; in manor courts, 181; used by justices of the peace, 196; corruption of, 203, 204; its service to law, 226, 227; non-judicial, 312–317; as origin of House of Commons, 317–322, 324, 340
Justices of the peace, 161, 175; origin and early history of, 194–199
Jutes, 9, note 2

K

Kin, 23; as compurgators, 25 and note 1; responsibility of, 41; leaders of, as primitive kings, 50 and note 2
King, Anglo-Saxon, 6; judicial matters carried before, 20, 21; relations to local courts, 27, 28; his *peace*, 30, 31, 392; his *peace* in the *burhs*, 33; boroughs on his domain, 35; revenue from boroughs, 36, 37; uses commendation, 41,

King (*Continued*)
42; grants *bookland*, 43, 44, 61; Pt. I., § III., 1; relations with witan, 59–61; attends ecclesiastical councils, 66; relations to post-Conquest feudalism, 85–90, *passim;* effect of Conquest upon, Pt. II., § II., 4; revenue of, after Conquest, Pt. II., § II., 5; relations to church after Conquest, Pt. II., § II., 6, *passim;* development of his courts, Pt. III., § I., 1, 2, *passim;* becomes a limited monarch, Pt. I., § II., 1; relations to Council and Parliament, 294–296; shares in forming the House of Lords, Pt. III., § III., 1; helps to make a middle class, 308–310; Parliament gains powers at expense of, Pt. III., § III., 7; relations with Parliament defined and adjusted, Pt. III., § III., 8

King's Bench, Court of, 164–166, 288

Knights, in post-Conquest feudalism, 86–88, 107; commissions entrusted to, 159; general local importance of, 188–192, 198; as forming a middle class 310–311; local activities of, 312–317; elected to central assembly, 320, 322; in primitive Parliament 335–337 and note 1; join the burgesses in Parliament, 339, 340; how elected to Parliament, 343–350

L

Lanfranc, 111, 114–116, 118
Langton, Stephen, 114, note 3
Law, Anglo-Saxon, 22, 23, 28, 60; administered in king's court, 129 and note 2; made by Henry II., 131, 132; limitations set to growth of, 206; *see* Common law and Statute law; relation of kings to, 268
Lawyers, 206, 223, 228, 343

Lay patronage, 118, 119
Leet, Court, 180
Legislation, of the witan, 60; of the Curia Regis, 103, 365, 366; of church councils, 116; of Edward I., 179, 180, 271–273; slight in early Parliament, 208 and note 2; of Henry II., 222, 223; a new form of, 236, 366, 367; of the Council, 288; origin of, in Parliament, 365–374
Letters patent, creation of peers by, 303, 304
Livery and maintenance, 203, 347, 348, note 1, 399, 400
Loans, forced, 384
London, Roman, 8; Henry I.'s charter to, 97, 98
Lords, House of, jurisdiction of, 201–203; origin of, Pt. III., § III., 1; 309, 331; attempts to control Commons, 348, 349; its share in impeachment, 377
Lords Ordainers, 276, 277

M

Magna Carta, art. seventeen, 165; of 1217 contains regulation touching shire court, 172; art. twenty-four, 188; heads the statute book, 235 and note 2; its character, 236; causes of, 260–263; fundamental principles of, 263–266; later editions and confirmations, 266–275, article fourteen, 300, 301; articles eighteen and forty-eight, 315; relation to Confirmatio, 362, to "articles of the barons," 368
Maltote, 360, 364, 365 and note 2
Manor, 38; *see* Feudalism, Anglo-Saxon; 82, 83; as tithing, 169, 175
Manorial jurisdiction, 38; in Normandy, 76; origin of, 93; in England after Conquest, 94; jury in, 156, 175, 179
Marriage, a feudal incident, 106 and note 2

Mercenaries, hired by scutage, 107, 108
Merchet, 82, 83
Militia, 87, 88
Ministerial responsibility, 371, 376, 377, 387, 388, 390
Model Parliament, 326, 329–331, 357
Monasticism, Anglo-Saxon, 67–69; after the Conquest, 118, 119
Mortmain, Statute of, 216, 217
Movables, tax on, 313, 359

N

Nationality, initiated by early church, 66, 67; consciousness of, in thirteenth century, 266, 267
Normandy, institutions of, in 11th century, Pt. II., § I., relations to papacy in 11th century, 110–112

O

Oath, fore-oath and in rebuttal, 23; of compurgators and witnesses, 24, 25; of Anglo-Saxon kings upon accession, 55 and note 2, 100; the councillor's, 287, 288
Oath-helpers, see Compurgators
Offa, 60
Ordainers, Lords, 276, 277
Ordeal, in Anglo-Saxon procedure, 26, 27 and note 1; superseded by jury, 146–149, 153

P

Palatinates, 95, 96
Papacy, in 11th century, 109–111
Pardoning power, 373, 374, 386
Parishes, origin of, 65, 66
Parliament, attempts to limit jurisdiction of the Council, 204; limited legislation of, in early times, 208 and note 2, 235, 237; controls group in the Council, 279; attacked by

Richard II., 280; relations to early Council, 289 (and note 1)–294; the making of, Pt. III., § III.; origin of the name, 320, 321, 335, note 1
Peasant revolt, 347
Peers, 302–306, 309
Peine forte et dure, 150, 151
Penitential system, 67
Peter's Pence, 112
Petitions, received by the Council, 288, 290; as origin of Parliament's initiative in legislation, 368 (and note 1)–370, 374
Petty Sessions, 196, 197
Pleas of the crown, 147, note 2, 165, 188, 191
Pope, slight relation of, to Anglo-Saxon church, 66; his relations with William I., 111–113; prohibits the ordeal, 149; relations with Edward I., 274, 275
Præmunientes clause, 331, and note 1, 395
Prerogative, royal, 283–285, 395
Priests, effect of Conquest upon, 117–119
Primogeniture, 218, note 2, 259, note 1, 281, 304, 309, 310
Privileges of Parliament, 390 (and note 1)–399
Privy Council, 296, 297
Provisions of Oxford, 191, 207, 269, 368
Purveyance, 56, 363, note 1

Q

Quarter Sessions, 196–198

R

Ranulf Flambard, 124, 255
Redress of grievances, 369 and note 1, 381
Relief, feudal, 106 and note 2
Representation, in local juries, 312–317; of counties in a central assembly, Pt. III., § III., 3; of boroughs, 324–326; of counties and boroughs in primitive Parliament, 326–331; of clergy, 331–335

Revenue of the crown, from local courts, 27, 54, note 1; from boroughs, 36, 37; in general in Anglo-Saxon period, 56, 57; after the Conquest, Pt. II., § II., 5; from sale of writs, 139
Richard I., 163, 179, 188, 257–259, note 1, 359
Richard II., 198, 227, 278–281, 290, 292, 293, 296, 302, 347, 348, 357, 373, 380, 381, 384, 387, 388, 395
Richard III., 282, 295, 385, note 1
Roger of Salisbury, 125
Roman, influence upon early Britain, 7–9; cities in Britain, 32; influence upon Anglo-Saxon central government, 53, 54; influence upon post-Conquest kingship, 101; law, influence of, 211–213, 223–225, 227, 229, 230

S.

St. Albans, Council of, 317, 318
Saladin Tithe, 313, 359
Salisbury oath, 89, 90, 253
Saxons, relations with Angles in conquest of Britain, 9 and note 2
Scutage, 107, 108, 258, 260, 263, 363
Sheriff, 6; in shire court, 21; origin and importance in Anglo-Saxon period, 29, 30; becomes chief official in shire court, 91, 168; his abuses in local courts, 92; limited by itinerant justice, 127; his *tourn*, 137; corrupts juries, 157, note 1; accounts to exchequer, 162; origin of his *tourn*, 170, 171; distrust of, 187; later judicial powers, 188, 189; decreasing powers of, 192–196; choice of non-judicial juries taken from, 314–317; his abuses as cause of early representation in Parliament, 341 and note 1; excluded from Parliament,

343; his share in elections to Parliament, 346 and note 1, 350–354; Commons report shortcomings of, 377
Ship-money 385
Shire, 6; and shire court, Pt. I., § II., 2; maintains fighters in *burhs*, 33; shire court held in boroughs, 33; shire court after Conquest, Pt. II., § II., 2; itinerant justices in, 128; in Henry I.'s reign, 167–170; later history of, 171–174; elects juries, 315, 316; represented in a central assembly, Pt. III., § III., 3; composition of full shire court in thirteenth century, 324 and note 2; elects representatives to Parliament, 345, 346, 348
Simon de Montfort, 269, 322, 324–326, 334
Slaves, 10, 13, 14, 16, 17, 38, 46, 47; after the Conquest, 80–82
Socage, free, 36, 83 and note 1, 84–86
Sokemen, 48, 80
Speaker of House of Commons, 380, 381, 391, 392, 394
Star Chamber, Court of, 204, note 2; 219, note 2
Statute law, 221, 234, 236, 237, 370–372
Statute of De Mercatoribus (1283), 328, 367; Gloucester (1278), 173, 175, 182, 271; Maintenance and Liveries (1390), 348, note 1; Marlborough (1268), 192, 236; Merton (1236), 173, 236; Mortmain (1279), 216, 217, 236, 272; Quia Emptores (1290), 237, 272, 273, 328, 367; Uses (1535), 219, note 1; Westminster II. (1285), 160, 207, 236, 237, 272; Winchester (1285), 192
Stephen, 188, 242–244, 256, 259, note 1, 303
Stuarts, 283, 285, note 1, 295, 384–386, 401
Succession to the crown, 51, 52, 259, note 1

Suitors of local courts, in Anglo-Saxon times, 21, 22; after the Conquest, 90, 91; decrease in numbers in later times, 173, 345

Suspending power of the king, 373, 374, 386

T

Tallage, 97, 108 and note 2, 329, 363

Taxation, Anglo-Saxon, 56, 57; in feudal period, Pt. II., § II., 5; 259, 260, 264, 287, 313, 315, 316; of clergy, 331–333, 337, 338; consent to, by early representatives in Parliament, 340, 341, note 1; national, origin of, 358–360; resistance to, 361; Parliament gains control of, 361–365; relation to parliamentary legislation, 369 and note 1; unlawful methods of, 384, 385

Tenth and fifteenth, 329, 360

Thegns, value of their oath, 25; origin of, 45, 46

Theodore, Archbishop of Canterbury, 64, 65

Thorpe's case, 393 and note 2, 398

Tithing, 168, 169

Tolls, 97

Tourn, sheriff's 137; origin of, 170, 171; inadequacy of, 187; decline of, 192–196

Township, early Anglo-Saxon, 12, 13 and note 2, 14, 17, note 3. as parish, 65; as tithing, 169

Treason, 251, 284, note 2, 377, note 1, 393, 395

Treasurer, 163, 164, 292

Tudors, 204, 233, 237, 282, 283, 296, 297, 381, 384, 389, 400, 401

Tunnage and poundage, 360

U

Universities, 227, 229

Uses, 215–219; Statute of, 219, note 1

V

Veto power, 372

Villa, Roman, 8, 14

Villeins, 47 and note 2, 48; after the Conquest, 80–85; in the manor courts, 181; emancipation of, 184–186, 347, 348

W

Wager of battle, lacking in Anglo-Saxon system, 27 and notes 1, 2; continuance of, 149, note 1, 150 and note 2, 153

Wagers, of justices of the peace, 198; of councillors, 290, 291; paid to representatives in Parliament, 346

Wapentake, 17, 18

Wardship, 106 and note 2

Wer, 27

William I., 57, Pt. II., § II., passim; 140, 142, 143, 239–241, 253–255, 259, note 1, 299

William II., 78, 79, 89, 92, 106, 107, 124, 255, 256, 259, note 1, 263

Witan, 6, 55; general account of, Pt. I., § III., 2

Wite, 27, 44

Witnesses, in Anglo-Saxon procedure, 25, 26, 141, 142; modern, origin of, 155, 156

Writs, 128–130; of right, 135; præcipe, 135, 136; in general, 138–140; creation of limited, 206

Y

Year Books, 230, 231

York, becomes seat of archbishop, 65; effect of Danish invasions upon, 68, 114; relations of archbishop of, with archbishop of Canterbury settled after Conquest, 114, and note 3; House of, on the throne, 282, 295, 380, 400

Young's case, 398

*A Selection from the
Catalogue of*

G. P. PUTNAM'S SONS

**Complete Catalogues sent
on application**